Latin American Monographs

Second Series

The Afro-Asian Dimension of Brazilian Foreign Policy 1956-1972

13

Center for Latin American Studies
University of Florida

The Afro-Asian Dimension of Brazilian Foreign Policy 1956-1972

Wayne A. Selcher

A University of Florida Book

The University Presses of Florida

Gainesville-1974

Latin American Monographs—Second Series

Committee on Publications

W. W. McPherson, *Chairman*
 Graduate Research Professor
 of Agricultural Economics

R. W. Bradbury
 Professor of Economics

Raymond E. Crist
 Graduate Research Professor
 of Geography

Lyle N. McAlister
 Professor of History

Felicity Trueblood
 Assistant Professor
 of Comprehensive English

Library of Congress Cataloging in Publication Data

Selcher, Wayne A. 1942–
 The Afro-Asian dimension of Brazilian foreign policy, 1956–1972.

 (Latin American monographs, 2d ser., no. 13)
 "A University of Florida book."
 Bibliography: p.
 1. Brazil—Relations (general) with Asia. 2. Asia—Relations (general) with Brazil. 3. Brazil—Relations (general) with Africa. 4. Africa—Relations (general) with Brazil. I. Title. II. Series: Florida. University, Gainesville. Center for Latin American Studies. Latin American monographs, 2d ser., no. 13.
 F2523.S44   301.29'81'05   73-19968
 ISBN 0-8130-0384-9

A University of Florida Book

SPONSORED BY THE
CENTER FOR LATIN AMERICAN STUDIES

COPYRIGHT © 1974 BY THE STATE OF FLORIDA
BOARD OF TRUSTEES OF THE INTERNAL IMPROVEMENT TRUST FUND

MANUFACTURED IN THE UNITED STATES OF AMERICA

Acknowledgments

RESEARCH for this monograph was made possible by a Fulbright-Hayes grant from the United States Office of Education and a faculty grant from Elizabethtown College. Among those Brazilians who helped me in the preparation of the study, my special appreciation must go to Cândido Mendes de Almeida and José Garrido Torres, who gave freely of their experiences and knowledge to orient and inform me. I must also thank Antonio Olinto, Antonio Houaiss, and Jayme Azevedo Rodigues, who graciously allowed me to benefit by their experiences in the diplomatic service. Professors José Honório Rodrigues, Cleantho de Paiva Leite, and Manuel Diégues Júnior granted generous use of the libraries of the Brazilian Institute for International Relations and the Latin American Center for Social Science Research. I am also grateful for suggestions and criticisms lent by Rudolph Rummel (University of Hawaii), Robert Keohane (Swarthmore College), Steven Brams (New York University), Roger Bastide (The Sorbonne), and H. Jon Rosenbaum (CCNY). My gratitude is extended as well to Professors Ruth McQuown and Thomas Page, who suggested corrections in the manuscript.

Finally, a special, unique vote of thanks is due my wife, who gave valuable assistance in collating statistics, typing, and proofreading and who lent me the encouragement to bring my research and writing to a successful conclusion. It is to her that this study is dedicated.

To each of the above I owe an intellectual and personal debt, but all debts accruing from deficiencies and errors in this undertaking must be attributed to my account alone.

WAYNE A. SELCHER

Contents

1. Introduction / 1

2. Features and Trends of Brazilian Foreign Policy since 1945 / 9

3. Afro-Asia in Brazilian Political Thought and Policy / 48

4. Dimensions of Brazilian Relations with Afro-Asia / 97

5. Decolonization, Human Rights, and Brazilian Policy in Southern Africa / 143

6. Economic Conflict and Cooperation with Afro-Asia / 197

7. Afro-Asia in the Global Context of Brazilian Foreign Relations / 223

Bibliography / 235

A nation such as ours, which has all the attributes to become a power, has the essential obligation to study and explore all the alternatives.

Adolpho Justo Bezerra de Menezes
Subdesenvolvimento e política internacional

1. Introduction

THE ANALYSIS of relations among developing nations is a field only recently attracting interest, as evidenced by research trends in professional journals and dissertations. Students of international politics have traditionally dwelt on the centers of power, with relatively little concern for areas other than Europe, the United States, the Soviet Union, China, and Japan. They have customarily studied lesser powers only when the lines of regional tension overlapped those of major power tension, as in the contemporary Middle East. Correspondingly, these studies, by authors from the metropolitan areas enmeshed in the larger conflicts, emphasized the relationships of the developing states with the major powers rather than their relationships with one another. The focus on power has led almost inexorably to an allocation of research efforts which relegates developing or "non-Western" states to peripheral status and attention. Even in the well-documented area of inter-American relations, the dominant framework has been erected by studies inspired by and concentrating on the foreign policy reactions of Latin American nations to American political and economic intervention, the

World Wars, or Communist subversion rather than on interrelationships among the Latin states. While not denying the importance or relevancy of such a great power-centered approach (especially to the great powers), I contend that this methodological bias has retarded the development of a general theory of international behavior by restricting most analysis to the sample of a few powerful states which may not be representative of the universe of states.

Within the last decade the horizons of international politics, like those of comparative politics, have expanded to include non-Western states. Enrichment and growth of the data base, the size of which had limited formulation of valid generalizations about nation-state behavior, has followed. The initial shedding of cultural and academic ethnocentrism resulted from the convergence of at least two currents of thought. The first trend was occasioned by the independence of those Afro-Asian states which champion a policy of nonalignment and seek to forge a Third Force as a vehicle for their interests vis-à-vis the developed states or the Western powers. Just as the birth of these Afro-Asian states has stimulated a lively academic dialogue on their place within comparative politics, under the rubric of political development, so has it also inspired international relations specialists to expound upon the determinants of a neutralist foreign policy, the viability of the Third Force concept, and the effects which the introduction of so many change-oriented new actors will work on the international system.[1] The number of the less-powerful states and the vote power they wield in the United Nations makes them a force which both the great powers and international relations analysts find hard to ignore.[2]

The second trend to bring the developing states of Afro-Asia and Latin America within the purview of general international relations theory was an intellectual one: the adaptation of the terminology of systems analysis to the study of

1. As an example of the neutralist nation studies, see, inter alia, Laurence W. Martin, ed., *Neutralism and Nonalignment: The New States in World Affairs.*
2. A useful assessment of the small (weaker) powers, both developed and developing, in international relations is Amry Vandenbosch, "Small States in International Politics and Organization." A more theoretical treatment with a model is found in Gustavo Lagos, *International Stratification and Underdeveloped Countries.*

international relations, by such scholars as Kaplan, Deutsch, Russett, and Rosecrance. Conceptualization of the complex network of interactions of all states as forming a patterned regularity—a global system—implicitly has set off inquiries about the existence of subsystems. Since the global system is said to be Europe-centered, the set of subsystems includes those operating in a more restricted fashion in other political, economic, or geographic regions. Impetus for the subsystem approach to developing areas has been added by attempts at regional integration in the Central American Common Market, the Latin American Free Trade Association (LAFTA), the Organization of African Unity (OAU), the Arab League, and others, not to mention the much more successful European Economic Community (EEC), against each of which the developing areas' progress can be measured. The subsystem problem has become the identification of various types of regional subsystems through empirical verification of transaction flows and their intensities, in much the same way as the problem in Rummel's Dimensionality of Nations (DON) Project defined quantitatively the form and content of the global system by identifying and measuring the basic dimensions of the foreign behavior of nations through computer analysis of statistical data. With the research problem thus stated, the methodological path has been made clear for the meaningful integration of the relations among developing states into the larger body of international relations theory. In contrast is the developing states' formerly isolated treatment merely as sui generis sets of relationships, archetypical of the course of the study of inter-American relations.[3]

Since terms like "subordinate system," "subsystem," and "regional system," along with diverse criteria for their identification, have been introduced, the analysis of relations among developing states within the same region has been furthered, and several subordinate systems have been delineated in the Middle East, Africa, West Africa, southern Africa, southern Asia, and Southeast Asia.[4] Curiously, little systemic interest

3. Analogously, the concepts of political development have begun to appear as a bridge to span the persistent chasm between Latin American political studies and the field of comparative politics as it developed during the 1960s.
4. The most significant subsystem essays on developing areas include the following: Leonard Binder, "The Middle-East as a Subordi-

in the Western Hemisphere has been forthcoming to date, perhaps because of the inertia of decades of more traditionally oriented research. The next step in theory would seem to be in the direction of examining interactions between regional systems; literature of this type is beginning to appear in both systemic and transaction flow models.[5]

Within the boundaries of this interregional research is set my investigation of the relations between Brazil, a member of one regional system, and the states of Afro-Asia, representing other regional systems. The central problem is the determination of Brazil's reactions to the emerging states of Africa, Asia, and the Middle East and the quantification of its reactions in transaction flow terminology. Such quantification furthers the analysis and evaluation of Brazil's newer relations with Afro-Asian states in comparison with the country's older, more strongly established ties to Western Europe, the United States, and Latin America. Although I single out bilateral relations with certain countries as being especially significant, my primary unit of interaction analysis (see Chap. 3) is the region.

A fundamental preoccupation in regional theory is resolving the problem of operationally defining "region" in order to classify and group nations. As Russett has demonstrated, several criteria have commonly been employed as differentiating variables: geographical contiguity, social and cultural similarity, similar foreign political behavior, institutional membership, and economic interdependence.[6] Because of possible ambiguities arising from this variety of usages, and the difficulty of placing precise boundaries on any region, however defined, I have chosen in the present study to define regions

---

nate International System"; Larry W. Bowman, "The Subordinate State System of Southern Africa"; Michael Brecher, "International Relations and Asian Studies: The Subordinate State System of Southern Asia"; Thomas Hodgkin, "The New West Africa State System"; George Modelski, "International Relations and Area Studies: The Case of Southeast Asia"; I. William Zartmann, "Africa as a Subordinate State System in International Relations," and Zartmann, *International Relations in the New Africa*.

5. See, for example, Steven J. Brams, "A Note on the Cosmopolitanism of World Regions," and Karl Kaiser, "The Interaction of Regional Subsystems."

6. Bruce M. Russett, *International Regions and the International System: A Study in Political Ecology*, p. 11.

along geographical lines, following the practice of most subsystem theorists. This definition plan is feasible because the usefulness here of a geographic determination of Africa, Asia, and the Middle East lies neither with the precision of the regions' boundary delineations nor with their amenability to rigorous intraregional systemic treatment, but rather in the ability of these general expressions to represent continents which have traditionally received little attention in Brazilian diplomacy and which, when taken together, make up nearly the totality of the world's developing nations outside the Western Hemisphere. "Africa," unless otherwise stated, denotes only sub-Saharan Africa, including the Republic of South Africa. The "Middle East" contains not only the Levant but also Turkey, Iran, and the Maghreb. "Asia" refers to non-Communist Asia, including the Philippines, Indonesia, Japan, Australia, and New Zealand; Brazil neither maintains relations nor has significant dealings with Peking, Hanoi, Pyongyang, or Ulan Bator, as of the present date.

In addition to these three regions, four more are postulated: Western Europe, Eastern Europe, the United States, and all other Western Hemisphere countries. The United States, while not a region in normal usage of the term, looms so large in Brazilian foreign relations that it deserves separate treatment. An aggregate of all Western Hemispheric countries (an alternative grouping) would not adequately reflect political, economic, or cultural reality for the purposes of this study, even though a hemispheric political subsystem may be said to exist, formally embodied in the Organization of American States (OAS).

By following a regional methodology, it is possible to extract higher-level generalizations from the data than those afforded by the conventional bilateral approach, which has characterized the majority of prior studies of Brazilian foreign policy (i.e., policy vis-à-vis the United States, Cuba, the Soviet Union, etc.). Then, within the global context of Brazilian relations with the seven postulated regions, the course of relations with Afro-Asia can be measured and charted to establish the nature, relative strength, and duration of any trends. These trends are explicated in terms of changes in regime, conflicting images of Brazil's role in the global system, and the cross-pressures arising from Brazil's multiple memberships in several political, economic, and cultural clusters.

The question of the relevancy of such research can be legitimately raised, for the research departs from the norm set by most studies of the foreign policy of Latin American nations, in both method and focus. Why should time be expended scrutinizing relations between Brazil and Afro-Asia? An initial motivation was the above-mentioned scarcity of substantive studies on relations among developing nations of different subsystems, sufficient reason in itself to demand such a case study. Brazil is well suited for inquiry because, among all Latin American states, it is in an advantageous position to carry on significant political, economic, and cultural relations with Afro-Asia and has in fact been in the forefront among the South American nations in this undertaking. Brazil stands as one of the significant powers among developing nations—when ranked by size, population, resources, and potential—so the course of its relations, both cooperative and conflictual, with other developing nations outside the Western Hemisphere is of special interest, especially because of the stated importance placed on these relations by several Brazilian administrations and also because of Brazil's ambitions of leadership and prestige among developing nations within and outside of Latin America.

The period since 1956 was chosen as a focus because almost all formerly colonized Afro-Asian nations received their independence after that year, while simultaneously Brazil was gradually embarking upon a more active diplomatic style, redefining in many ways the substance and range of its interests. The foundations of Brazil's Afro-Asian policy are now being set, exposing domestic disagreements, conflicting solidarities, and shifting priorities which are likely to persist in Brazil's future relations with these regions.

Through this dimension of Brazilian foreign policy some facets of the country's self-identification as a future power may be illuminated, a more comprehensive matter than bilateral relations with any single Afro-Asian state. In a world where the gap between developed and developing economies is widening, Brazil, with its regional diversity, maintains features of both developing and developed economies. Brazil is marked by an impressive national growth rate. At the same time, however, its expanding insular areas of industrialization are surrounded by a sea of poverty. The extent to which the foreign policy decision makers perceive the nation either as developed with some areas of backwardness or as underdeveloped with a few developed zones will heavily condition Brazil's relations not only with the developing Afro-Asian states but also with the developed members of the Western community. Should Brazil hope to benefit in the long run by retaining its position among the "proletariat of the free world" or should it seek the leadership of a Third Force to demand concessions from the industrialized states? What set of interests links it to the West? What set of interests favors greater multilateral cooperation with the Afro-Asian bloc? To what extent can relations with Afro-Asia be formulated separately from policy toward Latin America, the United States, and Western Europe—particularly Portugal? What levels of priorities are to be assigned? These are a few of the more weighty normative considerations surrounding the Afro-Asian dimension of Brazilian foreign policy, making this study a useful contribution to the body of knowledge about how emerging and potentially great powers elect to make their influence felt on a world scale, and thus to achieve greater international recognition and a broader range of diplomatic activity.

To delve into some of these questions and to assess the state of Brazilian relations with Afro-Asia, I undertook field research in Brazil under a Fulbright-Hays grant from the United States Department of Health, Education, and Welfare. My prime sources of written material were the Library of the Foreign Ministry, the Brazilian Institute for International Relations (IBRI), the Superior War College, the Latin American Center for Social Science Research (CLAPCS), and the National Library. I also used the facilities of the Getúlio Vargas Foundation and the Brazilian Institute for Bibliography and Documentation. To supplement and interpret statistics, accounts, and other written data, I conducted over thirty nonstandardized personal interviews with officials or former officials, Brazilian and foreign, who have had firsthand experience in Brazil's relations with the countries of Afro-Asia in both private and public spheres. Through such procedure I have ascertained what these officials consider relevant in the total context of those relations and how they interpret the events which they helped to create or in which they were involved. Numerous important insights have been gained in this way. Because of personal wishes of the interviewee, several of these sources have been kept anonymous.

2. Features and Trends of Brazilian Foreign Policy since 1945

THE PARTICIPATION of republican Brazil in the international system can be divided into three periods according to dominant interests and scope.[1] The phase of territorial diplomacy (1889–1917) fixed boundaries, while the country's extrahemispheric concerns were relegated to decidedly inferior status. In settling these boundary disputes, looking for a counterweight to rival Spanish America, and hoping to stabilize coffee markets, the Baron of Rio Branco, foreign minister from 1902 to 1912 and patron saint of national diplomacy, set the course for decades by establishing close ties with Washington to replace Brazil's former dependence on Great Britain. Seldom marred by significant frictions, this relationship came to represent an anomaly in the interAmerican system, in which the major feature has long been Latin antagonism toward and distrust of the United States. For about half a century Brazil adhered closely to American interpretation of international events, often acting as an advocate of the American position vis-à-vis the remainder of Latin America.

1. Nelson de Sousa Sampaio, "The Foreign Policy of Brazil," p. 626.

The second stage of foreign policy took the form of modest extracontinental initiation and limited participation in world events (1917–1945), marked by Brazil's participation in the League of Nations and the Second World War. The major portion of national attention still remained on the Western Hemisphere, as evidenced by disillusionment with the league and mediation in Spanish American border conflicts.

Since 1945 Brazil has undertaken a great-power apprenticeship; its globally active nationalistic policy is used both as a stimulus to economic development and as a means to more independence and prestige, in anticipation of the day when a more powerful Brazil will take on worldwide interests. The self-extension represented by the Afro-Asian dimension of Brazilian foreign policy is part of this present expansive period, closely related at any given time to the course of general foreign relations and the domestic debate concerning alternative courses of action. This matrix must therefore be described before the position of Afro-Asia in Brazil's national priorities and goals can be charted.

It was only after the experience of World War II, with the sending of an expeditionary force of over 25,000 to Italy, that the national political parties began to conceive of Brazil as an integral part of the world and to show greater concern for international problems outside the hemisphere. Some of the foreign policy issues previously reserved exclusively to the Ministry of Foreign Relations were thus brought before Congress and the public view.[2] In the decade immediately following World War II, under the presidencies of Dutra and Vargas, the topic of foreign policy played a minor role in domestic politics, but after 1955 greater challenges to the traditional foreign policy were posed by industrialization and the rise of nationalism. Under Vargas' direction, Brazilian nationalism, after a late start, became imbued with economic and welfare overtones and evolved from a purely intellectual phenomenon to a government-supported creed with foreign capital as its principal target. The most concrete nationalistic accomplishment was the 1953 establishment of Petrobrás as the state monopoly for petroleum deposit exploration and development. From 1956 to 1964, nationalism gained converts

2. José Honório Rodrigues, "The Foundations of Brazil's Foreign Policy," p. 337.

and influence in policy formation. The movement was soon taken over by activists of the political left who condemned foreign economic control (especially that of the United States) as imperialistic and who proclaimed that greater attention should be given to economic development, regulation of foreign investment, government intervention in the economy, and trade diversification.[3]

Rational, intellectually oriented "developmental nationalism" was fostered with the official creation in mid-1955 of the Superior Institute of Brazilian Studies (ISEB), a group of former Vargas advisers and nationalists of a wide spectrum of political views. The group functioned as a graduate-level research council to study problems of development and modernization. Short courses, lectures, and a year-long graduate seminar for military and government officials set an intellectual standard for future theorizing about nationalism. For the first time, departing from the usual academic legal-historical idealistic approach, institute participants attempted to apply social science to the definition and solution of Brazilian problems.[4] Publications and studies of ISEB stimulated a swelling flow of nationalistic writings as well as severe criticism from the conservative press for its increasing emphasis on Marxist terminology, national planning, and socialism. ISEB's policy recommendations for wide reforms were most strongly opposed when they threatened the domestic status quo. Although abolished as subversive by the revolutionary government in 1964, ISEB in its nine years provided the foundation for a high degree of consensus on foreign policy aims among large sectors of the attentive public. ISEB's studies centered on Brazil's aspirations for modernization, independence in international politics, broadening of foreign relations, and future great-power status.[5]

This *tomada de consciência* (national self-awareness), the greater popular interest in foreign policy, the establishment of Petrobrás, and the demands of industrialization and an expanded internal market during the Kubitschek years all moved Brazilian foreign policy into a transitional phase and marked the decline of the traditional style, which Itamaraty

3. E. Bradford Burns, *Nationalism in Brazil*, pp. 89–92.
4. Frank Bonilla, "A National Ideology for Development: Brazil."
5. "Brazil: Modernization, Independence, and Great-Power Status."

(the Ministry of Foreign Relations) had been following since the death of Rio Branco. The traditional approach has been characterized by one critic as inaction stemming from uncertainty: "All actions have consequences; these are unforeseeable, so we should not act; that is the general principle which governed our Ministry [of Foreign Relations] from 1913 to 1956."[6] This traditional, affective style was invoked as late as 1956. President Kubitschek stated then, in his annual message to Congress, that Brazil's foreign policy was expressed principally through the United Nations and the OAS and reflected primarily Brazil's position as an "American country, member of the Western Christian Community, defender of the judicial equality of states and the peaceful solution of disputes, supporter of friendly coexistence, and of all active forms of cooperation."[7] Foreign policy was framed in terms of values supposedly worth pursuing for their own sake, broad, permanent "principled objectives" faithfully sought because of a belief in their unconditional validity: obedience to international law, peace, justice, dignity, equality, adherence to treaties, and continuous consultation with the United States on policy questions.[8] All of these guidelines were alleged to have been distilled from the traditions of the Empire and the practices of Rio Branco, to be rooted in the Brazilian people's Latin-Christian origins, and to be sanctified by at least a century of experience.[9]

Despite differences in policy recommendations, the critics of the old orientation agreed on at least three serious flaws in the former conduct of Brazilian diplomacy and questioned whether the routine application of immutable principles derived from a different era could adequately represent the realities and enlarge the range of options of a rapidly changing nation in the present, multipolar international situation.

6. Rodrigues, "Uma política externa, própria e independente," p. 24.
7. Juscelino Kubitschek de Oliveira, *Mensagem ao Congresso Nacional* (1956), p. 131. Developmental overtones are much more prevalent in foreign policy comments toward the end of the Kubitschek administration. See, for example, Kubitschek de Oliveira, *Mensagem ao Congresso Nacional* (1959), pp. 54–55.
8. The term "principled objectives" is from George Modelski, *A Theory of Foreign Policy*, p. 96.
9. For an antirevisionist statement of the traditional position by a diplomat with long experience, see A. Camilo de Oliveira, "Linhas mestras de política exterior do Brasil."

First, the critics accused the older diplomatic caste and cultural elite of being unconditional admirers and imitators of Europe and the United States, of lacking a critical sense of historical perspective, and of striving to be as different as possible from the typical Brazilian. In its cosmopolitanism and search for a foreign model, this group had become so attracted to its European self-image and so dependent on foreign patterns that it had fallen into a state of alienation and utterly failed to represent Brazilian interest. Instead, it had concentrated on projecting a flattering but false image of Brazil, "for the English to see," as the Brazilian expression for pretentiousness so appropriately phrases it.[10] This cultural sentimentality for things European or American had led almost directly to support for colonialism and to a decided lack of fervor in anticolonialist statements.

Second, Brazilian diplomacy suffered from a strong legal-historical bias rather unrelated to the current demands of international relations and stemming from the fact that in Brazil academic social studies have been comprised largely of law and history, with very little evidence of the modern disciplines of political science and international relations. As recently as 1968, little had been done to remedy this deficiency at the Rio Branco Institute, where diplomats receive their training.[11] Historian José Honório Rodrigues notes that from 1889 to 1964, of 62 full and interim foreign ministers, 48 had earned law degrees. To this fact he attributes much of the juridical stagnation, unimaginative conformity, and lack of initiative evident from the days of Rio Branco to Kubitschek.[12] The abstract, legalistic encyclopedism fostered by this type of education had produced professionals who could recite the provisions of the Treaty of Westphalia but were unable to frame a concrete program of Brazilian interests in a given situation.

Finally, the critics decried what they felt was an automatic pro-Americanism exhibited by Itamaraty. They believed that Itamaraty had disregarded important conflicts between Amer-

---

10. J. O. de Meira Penna, *Política externa: Segurança e desenvolvimento*, pp. 167–72.
11. An excellent and unique study of the Brazilian diplomatic corps is H. Jon Rosenbaum, "A Critique of the Brazilian Foreign Service."
12. Rodrigues, *Interêsse nacional e política externa*, pp. 58–59.

ican and Brazilian interests and that its pro-American policy had resulted from a misinterpretation of Rio Branco's original intentions. According to a former foreign minister, representatives to international conferences and organizations on occasion had been merely given instructions to vote in agreement with the United States delegation.[13] Defenders of the necessity to support American positions argued unequivocally that the alliance with the United States had no alternative because national security ultimately rested on American deterrent power. For them the primary dimension of international conflict was East versus West. The pro-Americanists felt that, since the United States was the only Western nation capable of containing communism, other Western nations (including Brazil) would often have to sacrifice their narrow national interests for the common good and support American policy. Since all developing nations were to a great extent forced to depend economically on developed nations, and given the fact that the United States had been Brazil's best trade partner and source of aid, the alliance represented to those defending support of America the best of all possible dependencies and an infinitely better arrangement than a doubtful search for new economic ties and an ephemeral solidarity with Third World nations. According to the pro-Americanists, this dependency was especially worth retention in view of Brazilian treaty commitments to Washington, through the inter-American system, and in view of the geographical imperative of Brazil's proximity to the United States.

Nationalists countered that international politics is by definition the clashing of national interests of separate states, in which each tries to maximize its gains and minimize its losses.[14] They insisted that the primary conflict was not between two opposing civilizations or Christianity and atheism, but rather between the developed and the underdeveloped nations. In its personal struggle with the Soviet Union, the United States had been admirably successful in convert-

13. Afonso Arinos de Melo Franco, *Planalto*, p. 53.
14. One of the most logically constructed and informed defenses of a nationalist or neutralist foreign policy was written by the founder of ISEB and published by the institute: Hélio Jaguaribe, *O nacionalismo na atualidade brasileira*, pt. 2.

ing the defense of the American way of life into the ideology of the "free world," thus identifying the safeguarding of its interests and values with the preservation of Christianity and Western civilization. Although Brazil had formed part of this entity, to the nationalists, Brazil's policy options were neither described nor exhausted solely by classifying it as Western and Christian, nor by fatalistically assigning it a permanent position within Washington's sphere of influence. Since the common interests of Brazil and the United States were only partially overlapping, not completely congruent, the nationalists argued that discretion and autonomy rather than unconditional adherence would be imperative, lest Brazil be transformed into a mere instrument of American defense policy to the detriment of its own economic interests as a much less developed, industrializing producer of raw materials, in need of wider markets and higher, more stable prices.

Pointing to the examples of Yugoslavia, India, and the United Arab Republic, the nationalists warned that faithful allies are all too often taken for granted while a strategically important nation following a neutralist foreign policy might have a much greater opportunity for favorable negotiation and for achieving international prestige through arbitration. This type of appeal was particularly successful against the background of scant American concern with Latin American development during the Eisenhower "banker mentality" years, the subsequent disaster of Vice-President Nixon's 1958 trip, and the 1959 advent of Fidel Castro, as well as the decided contrast between Washington's flat refusal of Latin American requests for a "Latin Marshall Plan" in the 1950s and the large sums of American aid granted Yugoslavia in the same period.[15]

The essential change which these professors, journalists, and diplomats urged was for the nation to leave the former static policy of narrow horizons and real or imagined subordination to American interests and begin a diplomatic offensive in which Brazil's international conduct would be determined by internal events (i.e., development) rather than imposed by outside interests or pressures. Brazil's time had come to forge its own destiny, to move from being a *país grande* to

15. See also Adolpho Justo Bezerra de Menezes, *Subdesenvolvimento e política internacional*.

being a *grande país*, from being a *comparsa* to becoming a *protagonista* on the international scene, that is, to become a continental nation beginning to think in global terms. The increasing space dedicated after 1956 in newspapers, magazines, and books to polemics on foreign policy reached its highest intensity from 1960 to 1964. Representative of the optimistic nationalist aspirations was, the volume *O Brasil entre as cinco maiores potências no fim dêste século*.[16] Brazilians had begun to take seriously the potentialities of future greatness often ascribed to their nation by foreign observers.[17]

The Kubitschek Years

In a 1958 speech to students at Rio's Catholic University, President Juscelino Kubitschek exemplified the new mood, speaking for Brazil and of Latin America, when he cautioned, "We wish to align ourselves with the West, but we do not want to constitute its proletariat."[18] Nevertheless, he was careful to prescribe full cooperation with American hemispheric policy, to avoid references to foreign imperialism, and to justify the features of a more dynamic orientation as necessary, logical, and creative extensions of the time-tested, traditional lines of conduct. Although Kubitschek did take some of the first steps toward making foreign policy serve internal growth, only under the aegis of Quadros did the full thrust of the developmental nationalists' theses make itself felt. Kubitschek's programs were more characteristically mid-range, with an innocuous, culturally based, good-will approach which always stopped short of causing the clashes that would inevitably occur as Brazil defended its interests against those of developed states. Rather than engineer a complete readjustment of foreign relations, he insisted on only slight modifications.

The idealization of the Pan American Operation (PAO) was one of Kubitschek's most imaginative and timely foreign

16. Pimentel Gomes, *O Brasil entre as cinco maiores potências no fim dêste século*.
17. It should be noted that Gomes' predictions of great power status by the year 2000 are based on similar observations by a former American ambassador to Brazil. See Adolf A. Berle, Jr., *Tides of Crisis*, pp. 39–42.
18. *Revista brasileira de política internacional*, 2, No. 5 (March 1959): 139.

policy initiatives. Two weeks after Vice-President Nixon received hostile receptions at the hands of mobs in Caracas and Lima during his 1958 Latin America tour, the Brazilian president sent to Eisenhower an expression of continental solidarity. Kubitschek observed that misunderstandings in American-Latin relations had become evident, necessitating action to recompose the continental united front. Shortly thereafter, he proposed the PAO as a completely multilateral developmental effort. Its objectives would have been to reaffirm the principles of continental solidarity, define underdevelopment as a problem of common interest and collective responsibility in the Americas, stabilize the prices of primary products, increase available foreign financial and technical assistance, and reaffirm the role of private enterprise in development. The PAO was designed and strongly advocated as an adjunct of Western defense strategy, to strengthen and stabilize Latin America economically, lessen the probability of internal subversion, and thus make possible an increase in Latin contributions to global alliance defense.[19]

Although Kubitschek's PAO proposal stagnated in an OAS committee, under the pressure of circumstances and the change in American leadership, the kernel of his idea went on to become the Alliance for Progress. The alliance would be under American sponsorship and more unilateral than Kubitschek had originally envisioned. Nevertheless, those Brazilians interested in foreign affairs received vicarious satisfaction from the knowledge that this alliance had first been framed and presented by Brazil. Through this diplomacy, Brazil moved into a more prestigious political position in the Americas, restarted the hemispheric dialogue with Washington, brought about a long-sought economic reorientation of the previously legally oriented spirit of Pan-Americanism, and helped Latin American leaders to think in continental terms.

The effect of the new international economic development also became apparent in Brazil's foreign policy. Brazil pursued new export markets, most notably through its commercial mission which visited the Soviet Union in late 1959 and led to the completion in that year of an agreement regulating trade, disrupted since the breaking of relations between Rio

19. Brazilian government aide-memoir reproduced in *Revista brasileira de política internacional*, 1, No. 4 (December 1958): 119–23.

de Janeiro and Moscow in 1947. Itamaraty was reorganized to function more efficiently along commercial lines, collecting data, studying the world economic and political situation, and anticipating the creation of new diplomatic missions in Afro-Asia. These activities stemmed from a growing conviction that, in the following words of Foreign Minister Láfer: "It is our duty not to remain prisoners of a limited circle which we ourselves have drawn and which impedes us from expanding our exports and gathering the aid which would be most useful to Brazil's development. Without forgetting a single problem of a cultural or political nature, this Ministry will place itself increasingly at the service of the conquest of new markets for Brazilian exports."[20]

Política Externa Independente

The issue of nationalism played an important role in the 1960 presidential elections, turning on the questions of agrarian reform, foreign capital, and an "independent" foreign policy. Campaigning on an administrative-reform platform vague enough to draw support from all sectors of the electorate, Jânio Quadros won the presidency with 48 percent of the total vote compared to his chief opponent Marechal Lott's 32 percent. This was the greatest absolute number of votes ever gained by a presidential candidate in Brazil and the election of the first opposition candidate since the end of the First Republic. Interest in Quadros' foreign policy plans was immediately voiced, as he had been portrayed by the opposition as too lenient toward American capital, in spite of his advocacy of a "national interest" policy of independence and broader relations to end the country's obscurity. During the campaign he had visited Cuba at the invitation of the Cuban ambassador to Brazil; Lott had declined a similar invitation. Several weeks after his election he undertook a world tour of nearly three months' duration, including in his itinerary the USSR, the United Arab Republic, Yugoslavia, India, and Japan. He interviewed neutralist leaders such as Nasser, Tito, Nehru, and Bourguiba. Conspicuously absent was a visit to Washington, although both Eisenhower and Kennedy had invited him. This trip contrasted sharply with the route President-elect

20. Brasil, Ministério das Relações Exteriores, *Gestão do Ministro Láfer na pasta das relações exteriores*, p. 83.

Kubitschek had taken—to the United States, the Netherlands, the United Kingdom, Belgium, Luxembourg, France, Germany, Italy, Spain, and Portugal.

During his seven-month term, with the close collaboration of his foreign minister, Afonso Arinos, and presidential advisers (many of the "ISEB generation"), Quadros shaped a new activist "international point of view" for Brazil, to gain full advantage of the position the nation had achieved by virtue of its size, population, and level of industrialization, as well as to ease a critical balance of payments deficit and foreign debt problem. In his message to Congress, Quadros made clear the outlines which his administration would follow, including fidelity to the inter-American system; respect for the traditional position of Brazil in the Free World; collaboration with the United States for social and democratic progress in the Americas; anti-colonialism, anti-racism, and support for self-determination of peoples; recognition of and the attribution of the proper importance to interests and aspirations common to Brazil and Afro-Asia, such as economic development, defense of raw material prices, industrialization, and desires for peace; establishing and broadening of relations with the nations of Africa, Asia, the Middle East, and Eastern Europe; and foreign policy positions fully geared to meet the needs of internal growth.[21]

Quadros reaffirmed his dedication to Brazil's Western ideology and continued his cooperation with Washington. On the other hand, he maintained that Brazil's only defense treaty obligations committed it to a continental security pact (Treaty of Rio de Janeiro, 1947) which had implications in the eventuality of aggression against any member of the OAS, but did not require Brazil to align itself automatically with one side or another in the global context of the Cold War, nor even to consider itself a part of that conflict. "Not being members of any bloc, not even of the Neutralist bloc, we preserve our absolute freedom to make our own decisions in specific cases and in the light of peaceful suggestions at one with our nature and history. A group of nations, notably of Asia, is also careful to remain on the sidelines in any clash of interests which are invariably those of the great powers and not necessarily

21. Jânio Quadros, *Mensagem ao Congresso Nacional*, 1961, pp. 91–101.

those of our country, let alone of world peace."[22] With this philosophy and its mixed economic and population characteristics, Brazil, he reasoned, would be an autonomous force to lessen world tensions and mediate superpower disputes.

Elsewhere Quadros affirmed, "No less important today than the traditional bonds tying us to Europe are the interests, aspirations, and points of contact between Brazil and the peoples of Africa and Asia."[23] To the conservative elites, this often-reiterated identification of Brazil as a "sister nation" with Afro-Asian states of completely foreign culture and traditions rang of heresy or, at best, a woefully misplaced emphasis resulting from malicious ideological bias. The "Americanists" feared that this sudden elevation of Afro-Asia and the Eastern bloc in diplomatic attention would relegate relations with Washington to second place and ally Brazil in the United Nations with the groups that many of them saw as opponents and detractors of the West, with which they identified completely. Some of the conservative groups already viewed nationalism as nearly synonymous with communism; such plans for disengagement from the Cold War and a break from the tranquil diplomacy of the past led them to decry the imminent "neutralization" and "Africanization" of Brazil, and to further condemn nationalism. Supporters of Quadros' ideas countered with the examples of Canada and Great Britain, countries much more closely tied to the United States than Brazil, yet willing to follow what they judged to be their own interests in Cuba, Vietnam, and China. As time went by, the clash between these two schools of thought became increasingly acute, aggravated by the deterioration of the domestic political and economic situation.

To implement Quadros' principles, diplomatic and trade relations were opened with the Soviet Union, Eastern Europe (Bulgaria, Hungary, Albania, and Rumania), Ghana, and several other previously taboo or neutralist nations. Trade missions from Eastern Europe, Afro-Asia, North Korea, and Communist China were received and similar missions sent. These ambitious designs engendered some frustrations in two of Brazil's closest partners. West Germany, an important customer, protested so vigorously a planned trade agreement

22. Quadros, "Brazil's New Foreign Policy," p. 26.
23. Quadros, *Mensagem ao Congresso Nacional*, 1961, p. 96.

between Brazil and East Germany that the effort was almost abandoned. Washington was apprehensive not only of Vice-President Goulart's trade mission to Peking and Brazilian willingness to discuss Communist Chinese membership in the United Nations; the United States also found objectionable Brasília's persistent defense of "non-intervention and self-determination" for Cuba and its resistance to American-sponsored collective action against the Castro regime's attempts to foment insurrections in Latin America. Quadros' foreign minister would later argue that this Brazilian position, maintained until the revolution of 1964, was a natural outgrowth of Brazil's long-established role as mediator between the United States and Latin America, coupled with the long-accepted precepts of nonintervention and self-determination consecrated by OAS treaties.[24]

Unsuccessful in its first efforts to re-integrate Cuba into the Western Hemisphere system in the face of what it interpreted as the intransigence of both parties, Brazil under Quadros found itself pressured by a United States desirous of both isolating the Castro government through the OAS and recouping prestige lost in the failure of the Bay of Pigs invasion. Even then, Brazil reasoned that an isolation strategy would most likely be counterproductive and force Havana further under the influence of Moscow. On the basis of the right and necessity of all states to maintain communication with each other, especially in time of crisis or disagreement, Quadros also argued against the break up of inter-American relations. He felt that the best way to protect the hemisphere from Communist subversion was through social and economic reform rather than through police action.

In a March 1961 visit, Adolf Berle, Jr., of the United States Department of State expressed concern over this policy and spoke of American investments in Brazil. In April, Secretary of the Treasury Dillon discussed Brazilian foreign relations in the light of financial ties with the United States, but Quadros indignantly refused to regard his policy as negotiable in such a manner.[25] American Ambassador Cabot criticized the Cuban policy on several occasions, stressing Brazil's treaty commitments with the West. Quadros, sensitive to all apparent im-

24. Arinos, *Planalto*, pp. 75–103.
25. Castilho Cabral, *Tempos de Jânio e outros tempos*, pp. 303–4.

pugnation of his actions, expressed his displeasure at these remarks. The State Department assured all parties that the subsequent replacement of Cabot by Lincoln Gordon was a routine change, but Cabot's denunciations reached a peak just before he left Brazil in mid-August. Clearly the United States was disturbed by the new international behavior of its previously habitually compliant ally, which after fifty years the United States had begun to take for granted.

Important segments of the population and press, led most vocally by journalist-politician Carlos Lacerda, saw in Quadros' attitude a softness toward communism. Lacerda stridently criticized the whole new foreign policy orientation. When the impetuous Quadros decorated Ernesto "Ché" Guevara with the Grã Cruz da Ordem Nacional do Cruzeiro do Sul as he returned to Cuba from denouncing the United States at the Punta del Este Conference, where sanctions on Cuba had been discussed, the denunciations were magnified many times.[26] The high honor was awarded to "manifest our appreciation" for Guevara's "desire to broaden economic and cultural relations with the Brazilian people."[27] This act not only demonstrated Quadros' opposition to "archaic" sanctions, but sources at the presidential palace cited it as additional proof that, despite American aid granted Brazil at Punta del Este through the Alliance for Progress, Brazil's independent foreign policy remained nonnegotiable.[28] Soon after the Guevara incident, Quadros invited Khrushchev to visit Brazil.

In assessing the decisive role of the Cuban problem in the growing campaign of public and military opposition to Quadros and to certain aspects of Quadros' independent foreign policy, Arinos wrote: "The transition was very brusque, from Juscelino to Jânio; from Láfer to me. There was no preparation, not even sufficient explanation. The Cuban question, disastrously dealt with by the inexperienced Kennedy government in the United States, dominated the national panorama, provoking a chain of reactions which ran from the religious devotee and the fearful with good faith to the

26. Arinos contends that the award served principally as a pretext to communicate to the Cuban government, at the request of the Vatican, a Brazilian letter requesting an end to persecution of the Catholic Church. See Arinos, *Planalto*, pp. 102–3.
27. *Manchete*, 2 September 1961, p. 12.
28. José Leal da Silva, "Por qué renunció Jânio Quadros," p. 66.

self-seeking without it (self-seeking for political or economic motives), all uniting together in a sort of torrent of panic which shortly placed the new government under the greatest and most unfounded suspicions."[29]

Quadros considered himself the embodiment of the popular will expressed at the polls; he contended that any opposition, compromise, or attempt to deny him support would be a dilution of the electorate's desires. This was especially the case with his foreign policy, since he was following the policy he had pledged in the campaign. His lack of tact, pre-emptory approach, fitful personality, and insufficient efforts to reconcile estranged groups all contributed heavily to his downfall. His enigmatic resignation on 25 August 1961, precipitated in large part by military opposition to the Cuban policy and particularly to the Guevara award, was apparently intended to elicit a popular reaction returning him to office with greater powers and prestige.

Quadros' successor, João Goulart, pursued basically the same independent policy lines until his overthrow by the military on 31 March 1964. Goulart, however, was beset by severe domestic political and economic difficulties such as rampant inflation, suspension of American aid, declining support, and military as well as public distrust of extreme leftist and populist infiltration in the government, the distrust becoming clearer as the fateful crisis progressed through 1963 and early 1964. For these reasons and because of Goulart's personal preference, foreign policy was not the great point of attention that it had become in his predecessor's administration.

Friction with Washington reached new heights. Goulart's failure to establish responsible, austere fiscal policies resulted in the withdrawal of American credit and assistance. Brazil continued to oppose all sanctions against Cuba and maintained relations with Havana until the 1964 coup; this obstinate stance became a test case or point of honor in the minds of many nationalists determined to remove every last vestige of Brazilian subservience to American guidance. In 1962 a profit remittance law was enacted, limiting to 10 percent of its registered invested capital the amount of profits a foreign company could yearly return to its homeland. In the last

29. Arinos, *Planalto*, p. 76.

three months of his regime, Goulart threatened a unilateral moratorium on all of Brazil's foreign debts.

Although it did not neglect Latin America, Brazil's Afro-Asian and Eastern European diplomatic initiatives were expanded and official visits exchanged. The most significant arena of diplomacy for Itamaraty, however, swung to the United Nations, where Brazil often strove to enlist the support of other developing countries or to act as their spokesman in the solution of common problems. In the opening speech of General Assembly debate on 19 September 1963, Foreign Minister Araújo Castro set forth the three fundamental themes of Brazilian foreign policy, the so-called 3D's: development, disarmament, and decolonization.[30] This triad of objectives would make possible ample cooperation between Brazil and Afro-Asia, since these were the general objectives of almost all the neutralist and former colonial states and formed the core issues of the North-South international conflict between developed and developing nations.

Public statements defined Itamaraty's more aggressive posture as, in the words of one foreign minister, "an internal self-awareness of the Brazilian community, relating to its own identity, its interests, and its purposes, as a conscious national grouping which will not relinquish the command of its own destiny."[31] No longer would Brazil be content merely to increase exports to all possible markets; nothing less than a complete revision of the conditions and structure of international commerce was indicated, to eliminate unfavorable trade terms for producers of raw materials and to make commerce a positive force contributing to development. In addition, the efforts of each developing nation were to be added to the efforts of the whole international community to facilitate industrialization and the mobilization of capital. No less than a form of economic collective security was being advocated to stave off the economic disasters facing the Third World.

Disarmament, besides being connected with the customary, ostensible purpose of reducing tensions and decreasing the probability of nuclear war, was advanced by Brazil, in the

30. João Augusto de Araújo Castro, *Desarmamento, desenvolvimento, descolonização*, p. 4.
31. *Revista brasileira de política internacional* 6 (June 1963): 273.

country's mediating capacity as a neutral member of the Eighteen-Nation Disarmament Commission, as a means to divert huge arms expenses to the work of economic development. In combating colonialism, Brazil emphasized that it was opposed as well to all forms of neocolonialism—political, economic, or police (military)—and urged United Nations action to defeat these more subtle forms of subjugation to foreign interests which might stand in the way of the autonomous growth and true independence of the United Nations' weaker members.

Under Goulart, Brazil also defended the necessity of strengthening the United Nations to reflect more precisely the desires of mankind and allow implementation of the worthy but unrealized ideals propounded in its charter.[32] Such provisions as would have enabled the specialized agencies to serve as dynamic, successful promoters of development, disarmament, and decolonization were blocked by the fact that the charter represented a victorious great-power interpretation of the results of World War II. The solution of the 3D questions was hindered by an "invisible veto" of the great powers working to defeat passage and execution of resolutions prejudicial to their interest. Laying the blame completely on the supremacy of large, established, developed states in the world organization, Brazil charged that "The effective implementation of the Charter has collided with the effective Directorate exercised by the Great Powers," and warned of the possible future *immobilisme* of the United Nations resulting from this obstructionism.[33]

Of course Brazil did not originate the 3D issues. What is significant about this Brazilian position is that it represents a general summation and acceptance of the Third World image of international relations by a nation which scarcely six years earlier had officially subscribed almost wholly to the image of international conflict on an East-West Cold War axis. Why did Itamaraty decide to frame its policy in terms of these slogans and use the United Nations as the principal forum in which to accomplish its goals? A statement by the chief ambassador to the United Nations Specialized Agencies at Geneva is very instructive in this regard. In a speech to the

32. Araújo Castro, pp. 27–33.
33. Ibid., p. 28.

National Economic Council, a presidential advisory body, Josué de Castro pointed out that in a case such as policies of the European Economic Community contrary to Brazil's interests, Brazil could hope to accomplish little bilaterally, standing alone against much stronger forces. However, he continued: "If our position should be in defense of our universal interests, then it will be easy to make ourselves heard. It is not a dichotomizing, isolating action we should have in mind, neither for the great powers nor much less for a dependent power such as Brazil. In that perspective, Brazil established a tripod which, coincidentally, is also a trouvaille, having three words beginning with the letter 'd': development, decolonization, and disarmament. These are the interests of Brazil, which makes them coincide with those of the majority of humanity, which is valid. That trilogy constitutes the territory on which are designed perspectives for aggressive action."[34]

By universalizing these broad goals through the multilateral semiparliamentary procedure of the United Nations and with the cooperation of Afro-Asians, Brazil planned to mobilize the developing states and present disarmament, development, and decolonization as of utmost importance to the international community and the only alternatives to death, hunger, and slavery. In the belief that sufficient consensus for agreement on these issues existed among the new nations and in Latin America and with the further conviction that enough pressure could be exerted on the developed states to extract concessions, Brazil's Ministry of Foreign Relations began to prepare itself for a role of leadership in restructuring the framework of international politics and economics. The possibility of effective reforms accomplished through the OAS was discounted because of American preponderance in that body and the hemisphere, making the OAS an unfit body in which to resolve problems where American interests were really threatened. Thus in two important cases, the Haitian-Dominican dispute (1963) and the Panama–United States conflict (1964), Brazil defended the thesis that any hemispheric problem could be taken directly to the United Nations without passing through the OAS.

34. Josué de Castro, "Contribuição da ONU e seus organismos à economia brasileira," p. 570.

According to Keohane, several prerequisites reinforce and aid a nation's exercise of leadership in the General Assembly: a drive to upset the international status quo, a broad interpretation of national interests, a high evaluation of the importance of the United Nations for the state's foreign policy, desire for prestige and publicity, and a foreign policy independent of the great powers.[35] These characteristics were precisely those of Brazil under Goulart. Brazil thus found itself in an excellent position to use the General Assembly to achieve its purposes. That Brazil in fact gave high priority to United Nations diplomacy is shown by the fact that, within the group of one hundred states continuously represented in the United Nations from 1961 to 1966, it ranked seventeenth in total number of diplomats sent abroad in 1963–1964, but ranked seventh in mean United Nations delegation size from the sixteenth through the twentieth sessions (1961–1966).[36] If we assume that relative allocation and absolute number of diplomats sent to a post represent an accurate measure of a nation's interest and activity in that post, we must conclude that Brazil exhibited a higher interest and activity in the United Nations during these sessions than would be statistically normal or expected compared with other states.[37]

35. Robert Owen Keohane, "Political Influence in the General Assembly," p. 17.
36. Keohane, "Who Cares about the General Assembly?" p. 143.
37. By "predicting that the nth state on the diplomatic rank list [of total diplomats sent abroad] should have as large a UN delegation as the nth state on the UN delegation list, and so on for all other states," Keohane finds a nearly normal distribution of difference scores in which 80 percent of the delegation sizes can be predicted within ±6, and over half to within a margin of ±2.4. Within this configuration, Brazil represents a deviant case, with a delegation 10.6 larger than predicted and a rank order 10 positions higher than expected. Of the eleven "oversize" delegations, Brazil ranks fifth in magnitude of size difference from the predicted value. This finding is more relevant in comparative perspective with the distribution of difference scores of the various continents of the developing areas:

DIFFERENCE FROM EXPECTED DELEGATION SIZE (NUMBER OF STATES)

Continent	Positive	Negative	Zero
Sub-Saharan Africa (excluding S. Africa)	20	2	1
Latin America (excluding Cuba)	8	10	1
Asia (non-Arab only)	6	9	0
Arab states	0	10	1

Only seven other Latin American states had delegations larger than predicted, none of them as much as +6. Ibid., pp. 145–47.

The Conservative Reaction

These imaginative and grandiose plans, partially illustrated by Brazilian leadership in preparations for the First UNCTAD (United Nations Conference on Trade and Development), were frustrated in the early stages by the strong reaction of the revolutionary government of Castello Branco to what the military considered the Jacobin excesses of the independent foreign policy of Quadros and Goulart. Immediate moves were taken after the 31 March 1964 coup to return to old alignments and allies. A purge of the Foreign Ministry led to the dismissal of three top diplomats for "subversion" and one for "corruption," while many proponents of "independence" were demoted to lesser posts. Relations with Cuba were broken, Castroite subversion condemned, and Guevara's award retroactively rescinded as part of an all-out effort to repair the strained relations with Washington. Obsessed by anti-communism and a drive for national security, spokesmen of the Castello Branco government applauded the United States in glowing terms, as did Foreign Minister and former Ambassador to Washington Juracy Magalhães in his first speech as head of Itamaraty in which he referred to the United States as "the leader of the Free World and the principal guardian of the fundamental values of our civilization."[38]

Returning to the East-West image of world politics, Castello Branco emphasized the need for "interdependence" rather than "independence" within the Western democratic system, while at the same time he made distinctions between interests of the West as a whole and those of a specific Western power.[39] According to the policy of the revolution, the principle of sovereignty was to be based on a common political-social system and not on political or geographical frontiers (now considered obsolete).[40] The most criticized remark of the postrevolutionary period was made by a newly named ambassador to Washington in a speech to the American Chamber of Commerce in São Paulo: "What is good for the

---

38. Brasil, Ministério das Relações Exteriores, *A política exterior da revolução brasileira.*
39. This attitude provoked cartoons changing Dom Pedro I's famous "Grito de Ipiranga" cry for independence or death to "Interdependência ou morte!" *Correio da Manhã*, 25 May 1965, p. 1.
40. *Correio da Manhã*, 23 May 1965, p. 1.

United States is good for Brazil." Nationalists fastened upon this phrase as a synopsis of what they considered Castello Branco's *entreguista* (sellout) policy toward the United States.[41]

After sending a contingent of troops to the Dominican Republic to take part in 1965 OAS peacekeeping operations, with a Brazilian general as head of the multilateral force, Brazil strongly supported Washington's idea of a permanent Inter-American Peace Force for collective security operations. Juracy Magalhães tried to find additional support in South America, but met with such fierce opposition in all countries but military-ruled Argentina that the Foreign Ministry decided instead to try to institutionalize the Inter-American Defense Board as a Consultative Defense Committee to advise the Executive Council on defense questions.[42]

Brazil's plans of being a bridge between Africa and the West or a leader in the Third World were heard no more. Latin America was again regarded as the proper and natural ambit for diplomatic action, and at first few warm references were made to Afro-Asia above normal diplomatic courtesies. Neutralism, in the view of Castello Branco, necessarily implied passivity, indetermination, immature emotionalism, extortion, and a flight from reality, as well as positions which tended to be anti-Western.[43] Brazil again gave Portugal full backing in its struggles in the United Nations over Angola, Mozambique, and Guinea. Although economic cooperation and trade with Afro-Asia were deemed mutually desirable, perhaps more indicative of Brazil's political attitudes was Itamaraty's announced intention to assist the United States in strengthening the OAS so that organization could serve as a regional counterweight to offset "domination of the UN by the Afro-Asian countries."[44]

The Diplomacy of Prosperity and Its Aftermath

After the March 1967 inauguration of President Marechal

---

41. Confidential interview with a former cabinet member, 22 October 1968.
42. *O Globo*, 4 November 1966, p. 9.
43. Brasil, Ministério das Relações Exteriores, Departamento Cultural e de Informações, *Textos e declarações sôbre política externa (de abril de 1964 a abril de 1965)*, p. 10.
44. *Correio da Manhã*, 23 May 1965, p. 1.

Arthur da Costa e Silva, a gradual change in orientation could be detected as Itamaraty came under the direction of José de Magalhães Pinto, who, as governor of Minas Gerais, had defended the ideals of Quadros' independence policy.[45] In his first major foreign policy address, Costa e Silva proclaimed, "Development is the new name of peace." He introduced the slogan "diplomacy of prosperity": "We shall therefore give priority to the problems of development. The diplomatic action of my government visualizes at all levels, bilateral and multilateral, the expansion of foreign markets, just and stable prices for our products, the attraction of capital and technical aid and, of particular importance, the necessary cooperation for the nation's rapid nuclearization for peaceful purposes. By virtue of geographic conditions, coherent with cultural traditions, and faithful to its Christian formation, Brazil is integrated into the Western world and adopts democratic models of development. We are, however, attentive to the new perspectives of cooperation and commerce resulting from the dynamics of the international situation itself, which has evolved from a rigidity of positions characteristic of the 'Cold War' to a situation of relaxation of tensions. Faced with the slackening of the East-West controversy, it makes no sense to speak of neutralism nor of automatic coincidences and oppositions. The only thing that can guide us is the national interest, permanent foundation of a sovereign foreign policy."[46]

That the new administration accepted frameworks other than the older stereotyped democracy-versus-communism image was further exemplified by Magalhães Pinto's statements to the press club a year later, when he affirmed a belief that the splits in the Communist bloc demonstrated the low importance of ideology in today's scientific-technological revolution. The watershed among nations had become the degree of development, as shown in the Second UNCTAD when the Soviet Union and the United States often joined votes to resist proposals of the developing states. For Brazil, the

45. Mário Victor, *Cinco anos que abalaram o Brasil (de Jânio Quadros ao Marechal Castelo Branco)*, pp. 270, 296.
46. Brasil, Ministério das Relações Exteriores, Secretaria Geral Adjunta para o Planejamento Político, *Documentos de política externa (de 15 de março a 15 de outubro de 1967)*, p. 12.

foreign minister concluded, the greatest threat is not the danger of communism but rather the problem of how to accommodate a probable population of 200 million within thirty years.[47]

As part of its more nationalistic stance, the new administration immediately de-emphasized the viability and necessity of the Inter-American Peace Force, taking a cautious, typically Spanish-American view of the matter in reiterating the values of nonintervention and sovereignty. Great stress was placed on possibilities of full use of nuclear power for peaceful development, including the right to fabricate nuclear explosives for nonmilitary purposes. This emphasis culminated in adamant Brazilian refusal to sign the Nuclear Non-Proliferation Treaty.

Projects for tripling of export value and for product diversification led to intensified exchange of trade missions, not only with traditional partners but also with Eastern Europe and Afro-Asia. New offices were created to foment increased exports to new markets. Most notable were the Export Promotion Center of the Bank of Brazil, and Itamaraty's Associate Secretariat-General for Commercial Promotion. The Commission of Commerce with Eastern Europe, also in the Foreign Ministry, was reorganized. Manufactures and semi-manufactures were regarded as the most promising products, given their higher and more stable prices on the world market, so various tax reduction and finance incentives were adopted to encourage entrepreneurs to export their latent capacity and eventually produce a larger share of their output expressly for sale abroad. This strategy is proving especially favorable since Brazil has advanced well beyond the import-substitution phase of its industrialization but does not yet have a large domestic market. In conjunction with rapid expansion of exports, Brazil has continued pressing for reorganization of international commerce to benefit developing states, through both UNCTAD and the General Agreement on Tariffs and Trade (GATT).

The foreign minister also indicated a security motivation for this heightened effort to mobilize the nation for a diplomacy of prosperity. Speaking to the National War College, a

47. *Jornal do Commércio*, 26 March 1968, p. 1.

high-level course on national problems offered to civilian officials and military officers, he underlined the positive correlation between low national income levels and political violence, as well as the high cost and inadequacy of purely military solutions to guerrilla warfare problems: *"In other words, the distribution of national wealth should, whenever possible, rise to a higher income level, to avoid impasse and social rigidity surmountable only by violence.* Only the tranquility coming from possession of a roof over one's head, employment stability, just wages, and equality of opportunity can produce the climate of security in which the rules of democratic order become viable. In the last analysis, *the only secure societies are those whose individual citizens feel secure.* This is the reason for the emphasis that I have been giving in the Ministry of Foreign Relations to the problems of development, in obedience to firm directives drawn from the beginning by the President of the Republic."[48] This type of philosophy grew out of the "Security and Development" motto of the National War College and formed the rationale for what was to become a more closed and repressive conservative political system, which, nevertheless, vigorously attacked the international status quo with a reformist foreign policy allowing more cooperation with Afro-Asia than a superficial assessment of domestic political conditions would suggest to the ideology-conscious.

Costa e Silva's two and one-half year administration was transitional in several other respects. Economically, with successful lowering of inflation rates, encouragement of industrial and agricultural production, and expansion of exports, the country was for the first time building a sound domestic power base for more efficacy in foreign relations, for realizations rather than rhetoric. Political stability and continuity were enforced upon the nation, creating an unfavorable image abroad but at the same time allowing for important planning, coordination, efficiency, and central direction. Programs of national integration were emphasized in the colonization of the Amazon, economic development of the North-

48. Brasil, Ministério das Relações Exteriores, Secretaria Geral Adjunta para o Planejamento Político, *Documentos de política externa (de 15 de março a 15 outubro de 1967)*, pp. 81–82. Italics in the original.

east, education, health, communications, transportation, ship-building, science, and technology. The next government would continue and expand these programs. A sense of nationalism and purpose began to emerge. Through pragmatic, objective realism, diplomats learned to capitalize on and maximize these assets and their negotiating skill to become recognized as quite capable bargainers and aggressive opponents to be reckoned with in commercial issues. Greater experience and more sophisticated knowledge of the international system led to appreciation of how economic and political multipolarity could flexibly be used to national advantage as new and more widely ranging interests were acquired and competition became more difficult.

These favorable trends have accelerated during the presidency of Emílio Garrastazú Médici, inaugurated in October 1969 with a term of office extending to March 1974. Several important themes now dominate national diplomacy, all with the goal of accomplishing the dream of major power international status by facilitating in all possible ways the rapid development of economic and political potential. Any obstructions are to be eliminated by either bilateral or multilateral action, the latter commonly used for the strength of its collective pressures. The most delicate issues have been those involving untapped resources or revenues which could be used to speed growth if more beneficial international practices could be arranged. To initiate such beneficial changes, Brazil sponsored in late 1969 a United Nations resolution to freeze all seabed exploration until ratification of a control treaty which would protect the rights of developing states. Brazil declared ownership of two hundred miles of territorial seas (including the air and seabed) in March 1970 in order to protect its fishing and oil industries and achieved tacit United States recognition via a fishing treaty on licensing. The Nuclear Non-Proliferation Treaty is still resisted as a technological monopoly in disguise. International efforts at population control are staunchly criticized as inapplicable to Brazil, where leaders wish rather to allow the space and resource relationship to stabilize naturally, with a much larger population, than to stunt the nation's future power by aiming at artificially low levels of balance. At the United Nations Conference on the Human Environment (1972) Brazil took the position that pollution control and its cost should be the responsibility of the industrialized nations rather than those in which the evil of poverty overwhelms that of pollution. Commercially and technologically, Brazil has attacked protectionism, patent rights, reciprocal concessions, prevailing freight arrangements, and most-favored-nation clauses as wedges impeding transfer of technology and resources and widening the gap between rich and poor. Although willing to use international organizations to defend these and other interests, Brazil has been jealous of its sovereignty and leery of supranationalism in any form.

Significantly, in his first foreign policy statement, to the graduating class of the Rio Branco Institute in April 1970, Médici was the first president since 1964 to stress an "independent" foreign policy. In fact, Brazil has not consulted with the United States, as it formerly did on many important issues before setting policy. An impressive economic standing (the "Brazilian miracle"), with a growth rate of 10.4 percent in 1972 and a 1969–1971 average of 10.4 percent, has allowed a freedom of action and hard-line policy implementation not experienced before. Plans are to double by 1980 the 1972 per capita income of $420. With 1972 exports a little over $3.9 billion (with nearly 31 percent manufactured commodities), a record inflow of foreign investment, IMF-approved fiscal and monetary measures, and an international reserve of $5.4 billion in mid-1973, Brazil has assured itself an important role in negotiations for the reform of the international monetary system. National spirit was boosted by the results of Médici's December 1971 visit to Washington, during which Brazil was accorded "equal" status, recognition was made of its economic progress, and its pivotal and leadership role in Latin America was commented upon by President Nixon. This visit, however, led to Spanish-American uneasiness over what the contents of this Washington-Brasília understanding or partnership could have been and what the rightist Brazilian challenge and antisubversion stance might mean to them, especially in light of recent leftist movements in Bolivia, Uruguay, and Chile. As further evidence of change, Western Europe has surpassed the United States in importance as Brazil's trading partner by a factor of almost 2. Within Latin America Brazil has begun its own foreign aid program, with $70 million in import credits made available to Paraguay, Bolivia, Ecuador, Chile, Guyana, and several Central American republics. Trade and general relations with Eastern Europe have quickened, and Afro-Asia has received at least as much attention as given by Brazil's previous government. In other words, a worldwide political and economic outreach is being built.

At the same time, as an aspirant to more wealth and influence, Brazil has been preoccupied with a phenomenon it terms the "freezing of the structure of world power," or "containment," the attempt by the established states to prevent the growth of new contenders by using political, economic, and military means to permanently institutionalize inequality through instruments such as the Nuclear Non-Proliferation Treaty, frozen permanent membership in the United Nations Security Council, spheres of influence, United States–Soviet détente and collaboration, "technical" status for certain political matters in the United Nations General Assembly, and stress on international interdependence. This fear of being blocked, reflected even at the bumper-sticker level with *Ninguém segura êste Brasil* (No one's going to hold back this Brazil), derives from a feeling that Brazil, because of its superior potential, has more to lose than any other developing country from resistances to international mobility or internal development. Much of its foreign policy in this decade is likely to be aimed at preventing that from happening. In the succinct words of one of its most important diplomats, "The international policy of Brazil has as its basic objective the neutralization of all external factors which can contribute to limiting its national power."[49]

Patterns of Growth and Nationalism

During the period from 1956 to the present, a time of rapid and sometimes seemingly contradictory transformations in foreign policy, certain regularities or patterns have emerged, ranging from the slow-paced legalism of the early Kubitschek administration to the hopes for Third World leadership exhibited by Quadros and Goulart, the return to anti-communism and solidarity with the West under Castello Branco, the

49. Araújo Castro, "O congelamento do poder mundial," p. 29.

"diplomacy of prosperity," and finally the self-confident nationalism of the Médici government. Perhaps a knowledge of these recent patterns as well as historical trends will allow a more accurate gauging of the probable future directions of Brazilian diplomacy.

The first noticeable tendency is an increase in the size, complexity, and range of activity of the Foreign Ministry, as measured through time by number of personnel, budget allo-

TABLE 1. Total Personnel Employed by the Brazilian Ministry of Foreign Relations, 1956–68

Year	Home office	Diplomatic posts	Career consulates	International organizations	Total
1956	633	408	385	43	1469
1957	624	426	379	41	1470
1958	605	453	403	40	1501
1959	615	492	405	51	1563
1960	572	529	423	56	1580
1961	804	510	439	65	1818
1962	827	533	419	69	1848
1963	918	758	408	81	2165
1964	1076	924	440	97	2537
1965	973	802	450	97	2322
1966	1026	834	501	102	2463
1967	1227	920	509	117	2773
1968	1319	982	539	115	2955

SOURCE: Compiled from the following mimeographed series lists: Brasil, Ministério das Relações Exteriores, "Lista do pessoal" (1956–1961); Brasil, Ministério das Relações Exteriores, "Lista de endereços" (1962–1968); and Brasil, Ministério das Relações Exteriores, "Lista do pessoal no exterior" (1962–1968). Figures for each year are taken as close to mid-year as possible, given the intermittent publication of the "Listas." Honorary consuls, vice-consuls, and special consuls are not included in the statistics on consulates.

cations, and number of diplomatic and consular posts abroad. The broadening of relations and activity from 1961 to 1964 was largely responsible for the rapid increase in total personnel during those years (see Table 1). This period stands in marked contrast to the very slow growth from 1956 to 1959 and even into 1960, as well as the abrupt cutback occasioned in 1965 by the conservative military government. With the Costa e Silva regime, the figures again show a sharp rise, accompanying the Foreign Ministry's more aggressive, vigorous posture and the opening of several new embassies and legations in Afro-Asia, along with staff increases in other posts and the creation of new departments. Clearly the Foreign Ministry's tendency is toward expansion of personnel; although progressing at various rates in different years, this trend resulted in a 1968 total personnel strength over twice that of 1956.[50] If we are correct in assuming that additional staff was hired to meet an additional workload, we have a rough measure of the growth in Itamaraty's activity.[51]

To compare the importance attributed to or the emphasis placed upon foreign relations at different times, budget figures were compiled for 1956 through 1968 and are presented in Table 2. Both the percentage of executive expenditures and the absolute sums yearly assigned to Itamaraty have shown a gradual overall increase, even though this rising level has fluctuated from year to year. The most rapid increases occurred in 1960 and from 1966 through 1968, at which times the greatest allocation of funds to the Foreign Ministry relative to other ministries is noted (see Table 2).

Attributing levels of relative or absolute budget expenditures to specific governments is somewhat hazardous, since the 1961, 1964, and 1967 budgets were prepared by outgoing administrations. In addition, the only figures available are those for allotments rather than actual expenditures, and year-end budget reductions are common in all ministries. Two important observations can be made, however. In terms of dollar value, total federal budget expenditures allocated grew 435 percent from 1956 to 1968, while allocations for the Foreign Ministry in the same period grew 700 percent, or 1.6

50. The number of career diplomats rose much more slowly and linearly, from 435 in 1956 to 473 in 1962 and 582 in 1968.

51. Ironically, considering the great public exposure given to the supposed advances of the 1961–1964 independent foreign policy in making Brazil known to the world, Brazil in 1962, compared to 1960, was represented abroad in more diplomatic posts but by only 4 more individuals, while at the same time there was actually a staff decline of 4 in the principal consulates. Almost all of the early staff increases of 1961–1964 were in the Foreign Ministry itself. Only in 1963 and 1964 did the number of personnel stationed or employed abroad rise appreciably. One factor which decidedly led to an increase in embassy staff abroad from 1963 to 1965 was the existence in those three years of "Expansion and Commercial Advertising Services" in from 15 to 22 embassies, mostly in Western Europe and the Western Hemisphere, with the exceptions of Beirut, Tokyo, Moscow, and Warsaw.

TABLE 2. Selected Features of Foreign Ministry Budget Allocations, 1956–1968

Fiscal year[a]	Foreign ministry as per cent of total allocations of executive branch[b]	Dollar value of foreign ministry allocation (in millions)	Diplomatic and consular missions as per cent of total foreign ministry allocations[c]
1956	0.63	6.03	13.6
1957	0.56	8.47	12.6
1958	0.48	5.11	12.7
1959	0.47	4.56	12.8
1960	1.19	12.04	12.3
1961	0.58	9.10	11.0
1962	0.88	12.80	17.5
1963	0.62	10.89	18.4
1964	0.51	7.69	17.1
1965	0.49	9.47	14.3
1966	2.04	42.76	30.4
1967	1.48	37.11	31.5
1968	1.24	42.04	27.3

SOURCE: Compiled from budget figures given yearly in 1955–1967 editions of Brasil, *Diário oficial*. Dollar conversion rates were based on the yearly averages of daily free market exchange rates given in Banco do Brasil, *Relatório*. The exchange rate for 1968 was that in effect on 1 June 1968.
a. The Brazilian fiscal year is coterminous with the calendar year.
b. Executive expenditures average 98–99 percent of total federal expenditures.
c. Does not include amounts earmarked as contributions to international organizations or for participation in international conferences.

times as rapidly as overall federal spending. This indicates a greater degree of relative attention paid to this ministry and, consequently, we may assume, to foreign policy. Second, the percentage of Itamaraty's budget set aside for use in embassies and consulates abroad, very low and stable from 1956 to 1961, more than doubled by 1966. Large increases are again evident from 1966 through 1968, denoting a greater growth rate in activity carried on abroad as opposed to within the Home Office (*Secretaria de Estado*).

Concomitant with increases in personnel and budget came the opening of new embassies, legations, and consulates to make possible the program of increased relations with the rest of the world. As indicated by Table 3, the greatest ex-

TABLE 3. Total Number of Brazilian Diplomatic and Consular Posts, Selected Years

Year	Embassies	Legations	Cumulative embassies and legations[a]	Consulates-general	Other consulates[b]
1956	41	12	3	24	141
1962	63	4	12	30	157
1968	65	4	19	37	146

SOURCE: The following diplomatic lists: Brasil, Ministério das Relações Exteriores, "Lista do pessoal" (July 1956); Brasil, Ministério das Relações Exteriores, "Lista do pessoal no exterior" (April 1962 and August 1968).
a. A cumulative embassy or legation is one installed in a country with which formal relations have been initiated, but to which no permanent diplomatic personnel have been assigned. Rather, this post is made subordinate to a permanently staffed Brazilian mission in a neighboring capital.
b. Includes consulates, special consulates, honorary consulates, and honorary vice-consulates.

pansion in diplomatic missions and consulates occurred during the first half of the twelve-year period (1956–1968), most of them being installed between 1960 and 1962. Almost all of the several additions during 1962–1968 took place between June 1966 and June 1968. To be more precise, the opening of new representations, far from being a uniform, gradual process, was carried out largely in two roughly year-long spurts or peaks, 1961 and mid-1967 to mid-1968, accompanied in both cases by public pronouncements of the undertaking of a dynamic new style of diplomacy.[52]

52. Even greater increases of diplomatic representation abroad, in old and new posts, were originally projected for 1968, but the plans suffered from a lack of funds, especially those required to employ more third secretaries. Itamaraty received authorization for about 100 more third secretaries than in fact were covered by the funds later received. The personnel regulations authorized the following number of career diplomats (Decree No. 2, 21 September 1961):

Third secretaries	190
Second secretaries	175
First secretaries	165
Ministers, second-class	96
Ministers, first-class	60
Total	686

Comparing the authorized figure of 686 with the actual 1971 total of

The second major tendency from 1956 to the present related to this increase in diplomatic activity has been the economic development orientation, which has pervaded and dominated policy formulation under all regimes. Even the Castello Branco government, composed of and backed by strong conservative and anti-Communist elements, made clear immediately upon assuming power that Brazil would continue to diversify its trade without ideological distinctions. In actual practice, commerce with Eastern Europe and Communist China was continued and in some cases intensified. It can be expected that additional trade, aid, and capital may be sought in Eastern Europe in the future, judging from events since 1967. In September 1968, to cite one example, the Bank of Commerce of Czechoslovakia made available, through the Brazilian National Bank of Economic Development, over seven million dollars in credit to be used to purchase Czech industrial equipment.[53] At the same time, the Industrial Bituminous Ore Company was conducting field studies with the Soviet firm Neftechimpromoexport for equipment financing and technical assistance to exploit large deposits of bituminous shale in the state of São Paulo and to build a huge industrial complex to produce cement, fertilizers, sulphur, and other products, all under terms specified by an earlier Brazilian-Soviet treaty.[54] Exchanges of this type find a mutual

---

639, we see that the foreign service had not yet reached the full strength prescribed a decade earlier. (See Brasil, Ministério das Relações Exteriores, Departamento de Administração, Divisão de Organização, *Servico exterior brasileiro*, p. 38.) Regarding the level of Brazil's diplomatic activity, it should be noted that in 1963–1964 Brazil ranked twentieth among 119 nations in number of diplomats sent abroad (300), surpassed among non-Communist developed nations only by the United Arab Republic (550), India (467), Turkey (392), Indonesia (348), and Argentina (301). In the same biennium, in number of diplomats received, Brazil ranked eleventh with 431, exceeded only by the United Arab Republic (559) and India (530) among the developing nations for which data were available. It shared memberships in intergovernmental organizations with 108 nations, a total surpassed by only four states. Additionally, in 1963–1964 Brazil held a seat on the United Nations Security Council, being the only nonpermanent member elected to that post more than three times in the first two decades of the history of the world organization. See Chadwick F. Alger and Steven J. Brams, "Patterns of Representation in National Capitals and Intergovernmental Organizations."
53. *O Globo*, 12 October 1968, p. 7.
54. *O Jornal*, 11 October 1968, p. 7.

interest, and Brazilian missions to Eastern Europe and Brazil's participation in trade fairs there are becoming more common. They are resulting in exchanges such as that with Czechoslovakia in 1972 in which Brazil supplied the Czechs with $100 million in iron ore and in turn imported two thermal electric generating plants. Nor can the People's Republic of China be left out of consideration, for by late 1968 the Foreign Ministry was beginning plans to reactivate the lagging trade with that nation, carried on via Hong Kong, an effort made more politically acceptable three years later by American rapprochement policies. After a 1971 visit of a private sector group to the People's Republic, an official of the Finance Ministry visited Peking for trade negotiations, at which time the Chinese requested a trade mission from the Association of Brazilian Exporters. These commercial meetings were the first held between the two countries in eight years.

A final trend, apparently gaining adherents in most areas of the politically attentive public, is the demand for an "independent" foreign policy based on Brazilian national interests in each specific case rather than on submissive alignment with or systematic deference to American wishes. This idea is expressed in many ways, with different connotations, but usually can be summarized as the desire for *uma política externa própria*—a flexible foreign policy suited to and tailored for Brazil alone, appropriate to its internal dynamics and able to take maximum advantage from rapidly changing international conditions. The roots of this feeling can be traced to a rising nationalistic spirit and national pride which manifests itself externally through self-assertion and claims the international status befitting an industrializing resource-endowed nation covering nearly half a continent and embracing 100 million individuals, ranking fourth in the world in contiguous territorial extension and seventh in population.

This widespread attitude in favor of greater Brazilian autonomy and prestige in world politics was verified by the first comprehensive national public opinion survey conducted in Brazil, sponsored by the Institute for International Social Research in late 1960 and early 1961. Although both the sample public and the interviewed legislators exhibited very high admiration for the United States and regarded Brazilian-

American relations at that time as at least moderately satisfactory, strong sentiment favoring cooperation with all countries or all those which wished advantageous relations with Brazil was present among the urban sample and the legislators. A majority of legislators and those of the urban sample holding opinions opposed following the orientation of the United States. Sixty-three percent of the congressmen felt that Brazil should be "as neutral as possible" in the Cold War.[55] With the observation that large percentages of the legislators (42 percent) and the urban public (36 percent) favored siding with neither the United States nor the Soviet Union, while slightly smaller percentages favored siding with the United States (39 percent and 30 percent, respectively), the study concludes, "Considering the fact that Brazil is a traditional ally of the U.S., the Brazilians, both congressmen and general public, exhibit only weak 'alliance-mindedness' when it comes to functional relationships with America in the cold war context."[56]

Unfortunately, later samples to increase the value of this pioneering survey were not forthcoming, and valid comparison or generalization is made difficult by the near-absence of scientifically sound political opinion polls and by the high proportion of the uninformed public which registers "no opinion." However, in 1967, a prominent analytical magazine conducted an in-depth, extensive series of interviews with 246 federal senators and deputies (out of a total of 409 deputies and 66 senators in the National Congress). Of those questioned, 149 were of the government-sponsored ARENA party and 97 from the opposition MDB. When asked, "What international policy would you adopt for Brazil?" the congressmen responded as follows:

    58.5% independence in relation to any blocs
    13.4% strengthening of a bloc without ties to the United States or Russia
    3.7% strengthening of such a bloc plus independence
    2.8% neutrality
    4.9% neutrality and independence

---

55. Lloyd A. Free, *Some International Implications of the Political Psychology of Brazilians*, pp. 1–16.
56. Ibid., pp. 18–19. Negligible opinion favored siding with the Soviet Union.

5.7% unconditional support of American foreign policy
0.4% support of the United States plus independence
7.7% other answers
2.9% no answer

Clearly an impressive majority (83.3 percent) favored an "independent" or "neutral" position, while over an eighth supported, in addition, the formation of a "Third Force," over twice as many as advocated unquestioning obedience to Washington leadership. To the question "Do you see as correct the present American policy toward underdeveloped countries, especially those of Latin America?" 64.6 percent answered "No" and only 19.1 percent "Yes."[57]

Among the military, evidence appears of growing nationalistic convictions, originating in its self-image as the national conscience and fueled by the success of Médici's foreign policy, but the extent of this feeling is difficult to gauge. Nationalist sentiments are said to be strongest among the rightist *linha dura* (hard-line) group, whose highest-placed and most visible leader, General Alfonso Albuquerque Lima, was among the possible successors of Costa e Silva in the presidency at the time of the latter's stroke. He was passed over for Médici, who was more moderate, and was forced to retire in March 1971 because of his criticism of the government's authoritarian practices.[58] The idea of Brazil as a great power, possibly with a nuclear capability, intrigues those who think in terms of national security and the future role of the military, as exemplified by "Project Brazil." This is a plan begun in late 1969 under the auspices of middle-rank officers advising Médici on how to transform Brazil into an industrialized major international actor by the year 2000 via a "technological leap" comparable to those taken over several decades by the Soviet Union and Japan. Despite the undeniable optimism behind the plan, the scheme seems more

57. Carlos Castello Branco, "Como pensa o Congresso (e como votaria se pudesse)," p. 41.
58. Information on the military and its nationalism as well as the security and development ideology of the influential Superior War College is found in Ronald M. Schneider, *The Political System of Brazil: Emergence of a "Modernizing" Authoritarian Regime, 1964–1970*; and Alfred Stepan, *The Military in Politics: Changing Patterns in Brazil*. Articles on foreign policy are often found in the military journals *Segurança e desenvolvimento* and *Nação armada*.

plausible given the political stability and record economic growth experienced under the Médici government. Brazilians, as well as foreigners, are beginning to take their nation more seriously, and the great power modernization concept could provide both a generally accepted goal and a mobilizing and legitimizing device for the government, as civilian rule is pushed into the indefinite future.

Continuity and Change

The ascendant desire for freedom of action is certainly not likely to be translated into a form of neutralism as professed in the first years of their independence by various Afro-Asian states. Some ideologues have used the term "neutralism" to describe the 1961–1964 foreign policy, but government spokesmen even then judiciously refused to label the policy as "neutralist." They preferred, instead, to call it "independent," determined only by Brazil's interests as opposed to a doctrinaire philosophy seeking a theoretical, symmetric midpoint in the Cold War. Foreign Minister San Tiago Dantas defined this independence as "that position which does not bow to the interests of one bloc or another, which does not wish to see its international conduct predetermined by an alliance or predecided by certain political affinities systematically considered irremediable."[59]

In evaluating the employment of the word "neutralism" in politics of the 1961 to 1964 period, we must keep in mind that neutralism very prominently came to symbolize nationalism and independence in certain developing nations precisely at a time when Brazil, after many years of unusually close association with the United States, was beginning to reappraise the effects of this partnership on its future economic development and political autonomy. In a sense, both Brazil and Afro-Asia were opening to the world at the same time. Influenced by the political philosophies of the time and common economic conditions, they rapidly perceived that world politics resembles more of a multi-sided than a two-sided contest, in which many different values are at stake and each nation is forced to protect those which it deems important. In Brazil's case, the previously overwhelming influence of the United

59. *Revista brasileira de política internacional*, 7 (September 1964): 432–33.

States, especially of the American image of international relations, was rejected in part as new international contacts were established. The extreme closeness of Brazil to the American position in world affairs until 1961 perhaps made the initial exploratory efforts seem to Washington much more of a desertion of the camp than they actually were in the long run. Brazil's exploratory efforts should be interpreted in the light of the proposition that a nation gathering enough power and influence to enter international relations in its own right will attempt, in degrees that vary with each case, to free itself from the hegemony of the alliance's senior partner.

Quadros may have hoped for too much too soon. Although he could have taken advantage of his popularity and the propitious moment to build gradually but firmly from the foundations set in the last years of the Kubitschek government, Quadros, with his taste for the flamboyant and the dramatic, set out publicly at breakneck speed to use his executive direction to alter Brazil's international outlook. He did so despite the strong resistance to change exhibited by some congressmen, the military, and many diplomats in Itamaraty itself. Seizing on the Cuban issue at a point when Washington's Latin American policy was obsessed by fears of Castro communism, and opposing Portuguese colonialism in Africa, Quadros managed to touch two domestically explosive subjects and lose the support of important conservative elites who had worked for his election. In addition, he antagonized many military and foreign service officers. His personal eccentricities and resignation succeeded in discrediting what may otherwise have been lauded in his foreign policy program. The ensuing spiraling chaos, demagoguery, and threatening instability of the Goulart years further cast doubts, by association, on his brand of independent foreign policy. As the pendulum swung to one extreme in 1963 and early 1964, so with the revolution of 31 March it swung heavily in the opposite direction, as if in compensation. Under Castello Branco and Juracy Magalhães, few diplomats spoke up to defend the previous nationalistic stands so heavily denounced under the energetic return to the old ways. Yet within several years and still under military rule, nationalism reasserted itself, even more effectively, in the foreign policies of Presidents Costa e Silva and Médici.

Like many other developing nations, Brazil has been hampered by various internal weaknesses from attaining a more powerful, effective foreign policy. The most serious are a low per capita income and a level of industrialization which still engenders economic dependence upon foreign capital and markets and limits the capabilities and instrumentalities at the disposal of the foreign policy decision makers. These problems have been relieved somewhat by recent rapid economic growth. Domestic ideological and political pressures can exert crucial influence on the foreign policy of a given administration. Quadros' case demonstrates how idiosyncracies of a single personality can mold foreign policy. His downfall as well as Goulart's are illustrations of the tacit veto used by the military commands to impose parameters upon foreign policy options. Severe disagreement over ends and means still marks general discussion of Brazil's role in world affairs. Such discussion is complicated by a central question: what attitude toward its traditional ally to the north should Brazil take, given the United States' clear predominance in the Western Hemisphere? Administratively, imperfect interministerial coordination and occasional broad latitude granted to individual diplomats have also contributed to preventing the course of foreign policy planning and execution from being completely coherent, calculated, or linear.[60]

Examined superficially, Brazil's recent foreign policy might seem to vary from legalistic hesitancy to ideological impulsiveness and to fluctuate indecisively from pro-Western to neutralist to pro-Western, making generalizations or a definitive assessment rather risky. The continuities of nationalism, diplomatic expansion, trade diversification, and preoccupation with industrialization, common to all governments since about 1960, lend credence to an opposite conclusion: that the 1961 to 1964 experimentation in foreign policy, despite what

60. The problem of rationalization and coordination of the activities of all ministries whose operations impinge on foreign affairs was a key concern of Magalhães Pinto. He wished to impart a uniform, coherent orientation to Brazilian positions in functional organizations and bilateral negotiations under the central direction of the Foreign Ministry. Similarly, wide areas of discretion previously accorded delegates to international organizations constituted a problem attacked by Itamaraty in the 1961–64 period, along with extensive internal reorganizations aimed at greater efficiency and bureaucratic rationalization.

may be regarded by some as its excesses, hit a responsive chord in many sectors of the populace and elite groups and was not merely an exploratory, unproductive aberration, completely rejected by more level-headed leaders after 1964. Although eclipsed by the immediate postrevolutionary government, some of the premises of the Quadros-Goulart years have been generally accepted and were quietly resurrected by Costa e Silva and Magalhães Pinto under the guise of technical and diplomatic questions. The Médici regime has boldly made national points of honor of them, going even further in areas such as the 200-mile territorial waters declaration. Quadros and Goulart, in pushing rather similar points of view, had clothed their programs as ideological crusades tied to internal reforms, thus startling the conservative groups into forceful reaction.

National interest concepts, stripped of ostentation and the emotional connotations of such expressions as "Third World" or "neutrality" and applied aggressively by a government with the confidence of the military and internal economic and political support, will likely guide Brazil in the future. The days of passive acceptance of a role dictated by political or economic relationships with developed countries have passed. In the last several years Brazil has shown that it not only knows how to adapt skillfully to political and economic multipolarity but also that it is likely to be one of the countries to benefit most from this multipolarity.

3. Afro-Asia in Brazilian Political Thought and Policy

IN 1955, Ambassador Adolpho Justo Bezerra de Menezes, surveying the state of Brazilian knowledge about "Darkest Africa," concluded that with the rare exceptions of coffee and cocoa planters and scholars, "Africa, for us, is more remote than the lunar craters."[1] Popular ideas about the neighboring continent were reduced to stereotypes engendered by safari films produced in the metropolitan areas to which Brazilian attention was directed. Notions about Asia were extremely sketchy and vague. Thus, almost no diplomatic or commercial intercourse was carried on with Afro-Asia. Between 1945 and 1955, no Brazilian head of state, vice-president, minister or influential senator or deputy visited these continents, although Brazil received official visits from the president of Lebanon, the vice-president of India, and the first lady of Nationalist China. In the same period, the only Afro-Asian dignitary awarded a Brazilian honorary decoration was Farouk of Egypt, not exactly a popular figure in the Third World as it emerged after 1956.[2]

1. Adolpho Justo Bezerra de Menezes, *O Brasil e o mundo ásio-africano*, p. 50.
2. Ibid., pp. 354 55.

Brazil had clearly done nothing to make itself known in Afro-Asia, much less to elaborate a coherent policy concerning its interests in that area. Yet, only five years after the publication of Ambassador Bezerra de Menezes' book *Brazil and the Afro-Asian World* (the first to give attention to the topic), Afro-Asia was rather suddenly a point of great contention and controversy as a symbol of Quadros' independent policy and a new front of diplomatic activity. A flurry of discussion about Afro-Asia ensued among diplomats, businessmen, and professors, stimulated by worldwide interest in the end of colonialism and the sudden independence of many new nations. In spite of the relatively high degree of attention various elite groups accorded Afro-Asia from 1961 to 1964, interest in the area has been quite low in the populace as a whole, deriving from both the low status of foreign affairs in the popular mind and the fact that most Brazilians attentive to events abroad concentrate on the United States and Europe. Most Brazilians tend as well to acquire from the United States and Europe any information or interpretations they may have about Afro-Asia. Before 1960, the dearth of Portuguese language studies on Africa and Asia (excepting pro-colonialist material from Lisbon) was especially a problem. Thus we have the paradox, confirmed by initial contacts in 1961 and 1962, that Brazilians and Afro-Asians view each other primarily through European and American eyes or news dispatches.

Public Opinion and Afro-Asia

Few public opinion polls are available to give an accurate indication of the degree of Brazilian knowledge about or opinions of Afro-Asia, but several of the more reliable polls can be cited as illustrative of opinion in urban areas. One of the most prominent African problems in recent years was the conflict between Nigeria and Biafra, which was given wide coverage and comment in Brazilian newspapers and news magazines. On 7–9 September 1968, sixteen months after the outbreak of the civil war, a public opinion survey was taken in Rio de Janeiro by the *Jornal do Brasil* and Marplan. To the question, "Do you know of the existence of a war between Nigeria and the province of Biafra?" 70 percent of the total sample answered, "No," although among the upper-income group only 35 percent were unaware of the war. Among the 30 percent cognizant of the conflict, 51 percent had no opinion about which side (if either) was correct in its stand.[3] The same sample was asked, "Do you accept or not the existence of the Third World, that is, a world formed by neutral and united countries at the same level of economic development?" Of the total sample, 53 percent affirmed belief in the existence of a Third World, 30 percent did not, and 17 percent had no opinion. Among the men, 60 percent replied affirmatively and 29 percent negatively, showing majority male acceptance of the thesis, although only 39 percent of the males were aware of the Nigerian-Biafran war. This war probably represented one of the concrete facts about the Third World most likely to be known at that time.[4]

At the time of Indira Ghandi's 1968 visit to Brazil, during which the position of India as an independent, neutral power was emphasized, the *Jornal do Brasil* and Marplan again conducted a poll in Rio de Janeiro. The following question was asked: "As you know, Indira Gandhi, Prime Minister of India, visited Brazil. In your opinion, India has played on the international scene, a role which is . . . ?" To this question, 30 percent of the sample chose the answer "Independent," 24 percent "Favorable to the United States," 7 percent "Favorable to the USSR," and 39 percent "No opinion." Among the upper-income group, 43 percent answered in favor of independence, 35 percent had no opinion, and 22 percent ascribed to India a role favorable to either of the superpowers.[5]

In 1963, a sample of 116 social science, law, geography, and history students at the University of Recife was selected to measure student acquaintance with newly independent African countries and to ascertain student opinions on possibilities of Brazilian cooperation with Africa.[6] Sixty-one percent of the group was classified as holding a "quite precarious" knowledge about Africa: they had categorized Laos and/or Angola as independent African nations. A mere 9 percent of

3. *Jornal do Brasil*, 15 September 1968, p. 32. The sample size was 302.
4. Ibid.
5. Ibid., 29 September 1968, p. 36. The options were listed; the sample size was 305.
6. René Ribeiro, "Opiniões de uma 'elite' estudantil sôbre o diálogo Nova África-Brasil," pp. 1–13.

the students were classed as well informed. Only Algeria, the Congo, Nigeria, and Ghana were widely recognized; 23 percent named Angola as independent. The study concludes that among the students, "There is very limited knowledge . . . about Africa in general and the new countries of Africa in particular," despite the fact that their curriculum and majors should have given these students greater exposure to foreign affairs than that received by students of other disciplines.[7]

African conceptions of Brazil proved to be equally vague and erroneous. During a visit to Brazil, Joseph Medupe Johnson, Nigerian labor minister, declared that Brazil was almost completely unknown in Nigeria until the institution of Quadros' open door to Africa policy.[8] Raymundo Souza Dantas, the first ambassador to Ghana, in describing the state of mutual knowledge between Brazil and Africa, confirmed, "The ignorance is almost absolute."[9] Another early emissary found West Africans to show "ignorance or contempt" of Brazil, but he noted their disposition to learn.[10] On a later occasion, the African division of Itamaraty reported that "Brazil, although considered favorably, is almost totally unknown in the African countries."[11]

It was against this type of adverse, nearly virgin background that Brazil began expanding its relations with Afro-Asia, and the domestic discussion was carried on among concerned sectors of the elites as part of the over-all polemical, theoretical, and analytical debate concerning various components of the new foreign policy orientation. The role of Afro-Asia in foreign policy was seldom considered in isolation or as a problem which could be judged solely on its intrinsic merits. The central international issue at stake, almost always raised by both advocates and opponents of increased contacts, was the effects it would work on Brazil's relationships with the Communist bloc, the industrialized nations, and traditional allies (especially the United States and Portugal).

7. Ibid., p. 8.
8. *O Globo*, 18 July 1961, p. 3.
9. Raymundo Souza Dantas, *África difícil*, p. 31.
10. Confidential interview.
11. Ministério das Relações Exteriores, Divisão da África, "Intercâmbio comercial Brasil-África subsaárica," p. 52.

By virtue of its size, geographical location, historical antecedents, economic potential, and population characteristics, a case can be made that Brazil has the prerequisites to play a larger role in Africa than any other Latin American nation. Of all the regions of the developing world outside the Western Hemisphere, Africa has stirred the greatest interest and debate in Brazilian foreign relations discussion, both in the popular press and among intellectuals. Many statements concerning the Third World were in large measure extrapolations from the literature about Africa; Brazilian thinkers applied the same generalities to the Middle East and Asia and assumed a general uniformity in African, Middle Eastern, and Asian problems and perspectives. Rather little published material has appeared on the Middle East and Asia specifically; they are farther from Brazil geographically and in terms of actual experience. Although there is some overlap, six contending approaches to the problem of Brazilian relations with Afro-Asia may be isolated and identified: cultural, Luso-Brazilian, economic, nationalist-neutralist, the "Western World"–oriented, and the military.

The Culturalists.—In their study of Afro-Brazilian culture, anthropologists and ethnologists have documented the extensive influence exerted on Brazil by the vast numbers of slaves which were brought from West Africa, the Congo, and Angola until the traffic was prohibited in the late 1850s.[12] In the fields of religion, arts, music, folklore, language, literature, and family life, Negroes in Brazil and especially in the Northeast and Minas Gerais have imparted to the general culture much which serves to distinguish it sharply from the traditions of the rest of South America or Portugal.[13] Yoruba and Ewe peoples brought to Bahia introduced their system of deities and rites, which are still worshipped and practiced in the cults of *candomblé, umbanda,* and *macumba.* The mystique of these cults is apparently gaining in popularity throughout Brazil and is being interwoven with the reverence of Catholic

12. For a guide to a good bibliography on the subject, see Manuel Diégues Júnior, "The Negro in Brazil: A Bibliographic Essay," pp. 97–109.

13. A summary of these contributions was published by Itamaraty for distribution at the 1966 Negro Arts Festival in Dakar. See Brazil, Ministry of Foreign Relations, *The African Contribution to Brazil,* pp. 1–109.

saints to the point of popular confusion. Yemanjá, Ogun, Shangô, Nanã Buku, Oyá, and other deities blend with the Christian figures of Santa Barbara, Santo Antonio, and the Virgin Mary. In music, the famous samba, the *maracatú*, and the *baião* are of African origin, as are such instruments as the *cuica* and *reco-reco*. The latter is particularly in evidence at carnival time, and the *berimbau*'s twanging notes signal the start of the *capoeira* fight-dance imported from Angola.

Bahian recipes based on coconut, dende palm oil, shrimp, rice, pepper, spices, and other typically West African ingredients have come to symbolize the Brazilian culinary art. African expressions have become an integral part of Brazilian Portuguese. At the same time, the African languages have changed the accents of Brazil to make its language quite distinct in pronunciation and terminology from that of Lisbon. Many African words have slipped into the speech of the Brazilian without his awareness, common terms such as *bengala*, *cachaça*, *caçula*, *canjica*, *carimbo*, *careca*, *dengoso*, *fubá*, *marimbondo*, *moleque*, *quitanda*, *xingar*, and countless others.[14] These folklore studies, carried on for many years without political implications, provide proof of important African contributions to Brazilian civilization far too numerous to cite here, but which were heavily instrumental in conditioning initial Brazilian images of Africa and which were invoked by scholars, writers, and humanists after 1960 to justify reactivation of what they believed to be cultural and historical ties unjustly relegated to inferior status. Commenting on such Brazilian views of Africa, a West African ambassador noted that Brazilians are attracted to Africa by a search for the exotic because they seem to look at that continent as a "wellspring of folklore."[15]

One of the less-familiar aspects of the Afro-Brazil association is its reciprocity, that of Brazilian influence in Africa, particularly along the coast of the Gulf of Guinea. Former slaves returned there during the 1800s after winning their independence in Brazil and brought back with them some of the language, skills, and religion which they had acquired

14. Renato Mendonça, *A influência africana no português do Brasil*, pp. 166–247.
15. Interview with Ambassador Henri Senghor of Senegal, 24 September 1968.

during their stay in the Western Hemisphere. Brazilian diplomats and visitors in Nigeria, Ghana, Dahomey, Togo, the Ivory Coast, Sierra Leone, and Cameroon have found prominent Catholic families with names like Silva, Almeida, Borges, Gonçalves, da Rocha, and Souza. The Brazilian quarter of Lagos, with architectural styles reminiscent of Bahian *sobrados*, the existence of a small Union of Brazilian Descendants (founded 1919), the survival of Brazilian customs, dances, and festivals among these descendants, and the important role assumed by some of the descendants (such as Sylvanius Olympio, Joseph Modupe Johnson, Adetokunboh Ademola, Jacinto Freitas, and Domingos Coco) in the creation and governance of their republics suggest that these nearly forgotten historical ties could be expanded upon for the growth of future political and economic relations.[16]

For this purpose, a cultural program was begun, centered in Lagos. It concentrated on eventually diffusing Brazilian culture throughout West Africa through the medium of these descendants, estimated by a cultural attaché to number 15,000 in Lagos and 10,000 in the rest of Nigeria.[17] Through contacts between the embassy and interested Nigerian organizations, a growing cultural interchange has proceeded up to this time, resulting in 1963 in the formation of a Brazilian Descendants Association. The greatest publicity was attained by a visit to Lagos of the Vasco da Gama soccer team and the 1963 visit to Brazil of Portuguese-speaking Romana da Conceição, originally from Recife and living in Nigeria for sixty-three years. Under the joint sponsorship of a Brazilian industrialist with investments in Nigeria and the Ministry of Foreign Relations, she spent three months in the country of her birth, receiving great recognition from news media, writers, and politicians. Despite some nativist reaction, stemming from the clannishness of the descendants and fears that Brazilian activities may tend to retard even further their assimilation, the Brazilian government regards this venture favorably. A former ambassador to Nigeria, openly dubious about the efficacy of his country's diplomacy in many Third World nations, especially between 1961 and 1964, enthusiastically praised efforts aimed at these descendants: "This is the precious nucleus

16. Antonio Olinto, *Brasileiros na Africa*, pp. 113–279.
17. Ibid., p. 215.

thanks to which our cultural influence can eventually find a point of support for later expansion. This is the historic and ethnocultural base upon which we may dare to conceive a long-range Brazilian policy on the African continent. This is what justifies our political interest, the opening of diplomatic missions, the granting of some modest scholarships, the sending of professors and the creation of cultural centers."[18]

A second strand of cultural arguments maintains that Brazil is uniquely suited to approach nonwhite Afro-Asia because it has achieved a racial democracy through lack of racial discrimination and a natural process of miscegenation, which represents the ultimate solution to the dangerous racial problem. Sociologist T. Lynn Smith observes that this characteristic of Brazilian society has been elevated to the status of a national creed: "There has arisen in Brazil what amounts to a veritable cult of racial equality. It numbers among its adherents most of the nation's leading scholars and many of its outstanding political figures. Although not formally organized and possessed of no written creed, two fundamental tenets, both designed to secure racial equality, seem to have general acceptance: (1) under no circumstances should it be admitted that racial discrimination exists in Brazil and (2) any expression of racial discrimination that may appear should be attacked as un-Brazilian."[19]

The first systematic treatment of Brazilian–Afro-Asian relations in the postcolonial years predicted that the main future world conflict would be that of racial differences and would take place in the uncommitted Afro-Asian states while they were being courted by the superpowers. Condemned to failure by their colonialist past and racist ideas, white Europeans and Americans would have little chance of avoiding a racial conflict more intense than the ideological Cold War. Brazil could step in to solve the psychological dilemma, "not as an acolyte but as an orchestra conductor," conciliating the antagonistic races by means of a moral example of conduct, made possible by the privileged position endowed by its ethnic composition. In the process Brazil would accumulate prestige and perhaps even become a candidate for world

18. J. O. de Meira Penna, *Política externa: Segurança e desenvolvimento*, p. 148.
19. T. Lynn Smith, *Brazil: People and Institutions*, p. 66.

leadership after the eventual decline of American power, if its rulers would know how to capitalize proudly on the reality that theirs is a nation of mixed races. Without antagonism, inferiority feelings, or presumptions, the most desirable course of action for Brazil, according to Bezerra de Menezes, would be "practice and example," to publicize throughout the world Brazil's existing social situation and to base foreign policy plans upon it.[20]

This idealistic theme, heavily conditioned by Bezerra de Menezes' observations at the 1955 Bandung Conference, was echoed frequently by spokesmen convinced of (1) the urgency of the problem in areas like South Africa, Algeria, Cyprus, and the Middle East; (2) the uniqueness of Brazil's ethnic system; and (3) the probability of Brazilian success in mediation and negotiations to eradicate racism as a threat to international peace and security. Citing Brazil's prestige in areas of race conflict, derived from its domestic racial harmony, Foreign Minister Arinos suggested, "Truly, if Brazil has a concrete contribution to offer at the moment in the field of international relations and human solidarity, it is probably in the racial problem."[21] Historian José Honório Rodrigues, author of many works on Brazil and Africa, called social and racial equality "our principal political-diplomatic weapon" with which an effective Afro-Asian policy can be waged.[22] Envoys from Afro-Asia find some of these boasts and goals a bit pretentious and occasionally irritating, but are reluctant to offer candid comments on the Brazilian racial situation because of the tenacity with which Brazil's national myth of racial democracy is held. It may be readily observed, however, that no career foreign service officers are Negroes nor are many Negroes found in high government positions of any type. A Negro writer was sent as ambassador to Ghana, but was subject to criticism that he was selected primarily on the criterion of race. It is reported that Nkrumah, Ghana's ruler, although pleased with the choice of this talented individual, curtly remarked to a Quadros special envoy that if Brazil

20. Bezerra de Menezes, *O Brasil e o mundo ásio-africano*, pp. 307–22.
21. Afonso Arinos de Melo Franco, "Racismo e nacionalismo," *Digesto econômico*, p. 29.
22. José Honório Rodrigues, "Nueva actitud en la política exterior del Brasil," p. 408.

really wished to give proof of its racial harmony it would do well to send Negro representatives to important white countries as well.[23]

Whites almost completely dominate exclusive clubs, prestigious occupations, and higher education, while Negroes are most likely to be found in menial tasks and the lower social classes. Mixed-bloods occupy various intermediate levels depending, among other things, on the lightness of their skin and their economic position.[24] Interpretations of the 1950 national census show that whites enjoyed a higher literacy rate of 59.2 percent in contrast to 31.0 percent for mixed-bloods and 26.7 percent for Negroes. Among the literate Negroes, only 3.1 percent had in 1950 completed either middle- or upper-level courses of study, in contrast to 8 percent of the literate mixed-bloods and 19 percent of the literate whites. Negroes and mulattoes were also less than proportionately represented among the ranks of employers and public service employees.[25] A Negro federal deputy from São Paulo asserted that in the 1968 National Congress, of 63 senators none were Negroes and only 3 were of mixed race by "self-identification and admission." Among 409 deputies, only 2 were Negroes and 46 of mixed blood. Of the hundreds of deputies in the state assemblies a mere 3 were Negroes, in a country which boasts of a population consisting of over 40 percent Negroes and mulattoes.[26] These statistics do not negate or deny the existence of a high degree of racial tolerance; they demonstrate rather that the lauded racial democracy is still in development rather than existing as an accomplished fact. Reluctance to admit this and maintenance of myths in dealing with Afro-Asia impede frankness and introduce an uneasiness into personal relations.

Some of the predominantly Negro elite groups, such as the Soberano (Sovereign) Clube and the Quênia (Kenya) Clube in Rio de Janeiro, have taken the initiative in contacts with

23. Confidential interview.
24. One of the most comprehensive studies on the contemporary racial situation in Brazil is Florestan Fernandes, *The Negro in Brazilian Society.*
25. "Os negros na sociedade brasileira." Since the 1951 Afonso Arinos law against racial discrimination, questions pertaining to race are not included in the census.
26. Interview with Adalberto Camargo, 23 June 1968.

African embassies in order to advance Brazilian-African relations. Also concerned with furthering racial integration within Brazil, these clubs speak freely of their nation's African heritage and try to obtain scholarships for Brazilian students interested in studying in Africa.[27] Beyond the activities of these clubs, however, ambassadors looking for pro-African feelings among Brazilian Negroes, based on color or cultural affinities, have found little to fulfill their expectations. Not only do most Negroes orient themselves as Brazilians rather than as Afro-Brazilians or transplanted Africans, but also the mulattoes with aspirations for social ascension conform to the mores of the whites, which include disparagement and rejection of African contributions to Brazilian culture and acquisition of the outward manifestations of Western culture. The greatest proponents of Africa-awareness in Brazil, perhaps not surprisingly, were white intellectuals, with ideologues predominant.

In spite of much that is admirable in the "Brazilian solution" to the racial problem, such an example is exceedingly difficult to impart to other more troubled cultures because of the particular historical circumstances which have led to peaceful Brazilian miscegenation as opposed to, say, South African apartheid or violence between Arabs and Negroes in the Sudan. Brazilians, acknowledging this obstacle, aver that the Brazilian example still stands both as evidence that racial tensions need not be the universal rule and as a working relationship which belies both white and black myths of racial superiority. Nevertheless, the central question remains, to what extent will miscegenation be acclaimed by an Africa enthralled with négritude and racial pride, and faced with the intransigence of whites in Rhodesia, South Africa, Angola, and Mozambique?

Another component of the Brazilian melting pot which enters into consideration in Afro-Asian relations is the presence of a Japanese colony numbering 138,637 immigrants and 291,332 descendants in 1958, concentrated in the states of São Paulo and Paraná.[28] By 1968, the size of this ethnic group

27. "Brasil: A escalada do negro," *Manchete*, No. 763 (3 December 1966): 63–76.
28. Commissão de Recenseamento da Colônia Japonêsa, *The Japanese Immigrant in Brazil*, pp. 6–19.

was estimated at about 632,000, creating within this Brazilian region the greatest agglomeration of Japanese natives and their descendants outside Japan. First arriving in 1908, the immigrants chose Brazil once emigration to previously popular countries (especially the United States) was curtailed. Initially the stream of immigration, reaching its heights from 1929 to 1934, was aimed at furnishing labor for São Paulo's coffee plantations. With intensive agricultural techniques brought from their homeland, the Japanese soon dominated the market supplying vegetables to São Paulo; they became prosperous farmers. Although many continue to live in separate communities and in successful rural cooperatives, increasing migration to the cities and integration into national culture has been the rule. A few older immigrants have sentimental ties to Japan, but of the younger generations only about 10 percent speak Japanese and 5 percent read the language.[29] Since 1961 few immigrants have arrived, because of increased employment opportunities offered by the industrial development of Japan, coupled with solution of Japan's overpopulation problem, which represented the principal stimulus for officially sponsored emigration before World War II.

During their sixty-five years in Brazil, the immigrants have largely overcome the earlier strong objections raised to their presence—alleged militarism, completely alien customs, and community exclusiveness—and have won prestigious positions in society, commerce, and politics.[30] Their contribution to national life has been enthusiastically called "the Japanese example" by Brazil's largest newspaper chain.[31] In a speech on the occasion of celebrations commemorating the fiftieth anniversary of the arrival of the first ship bearing immigrant families, President Kubitschek explained in the presence of Crown Prince Takahito Mikasa how positive sentiment to-

29. Interview with Hiroshi Saito, 20 June 1968.
30. The most complete survey of the subject is Hiroshi Saito, *O Japonês no Brasil*. See also papers prepared for the symposium, "O Japonês em São Paulo e no Brasil," sponsored by the Faculdade de Filosofia, Ciências, e Letras of the University of São Paulo and the Fundação da Escola de Sociologia e Política de São Paulo, 18–21 June 1968, in São Paulo.
31. "O exemplo japonês," special supplement of *O Jornal* and other Diários Associados, 26 June 1968.

ward these immigrants had favorably affected relations between the two countries: "We do not become tired of proclaiming how much the sons of Japan integrated in our midst have grown in our esteem, spreading admirable nuclei of economic vitality. Winning with great difficulty the esteem they enjoy in national public opinion, these tireless creators of wealth multiplied in Brazil so many benefits and so many accomplishments in such a short time that Japanese-Brazilian friendship is today an exponential theme of our international relations. . . . Fifty years of an immigratory influx of a high degree of productivity have convinced us of the advantages that can come from a new type of immigration in which capital and industry themselves move from Japan to Brazil, as is now happening in the steel industry."[32]

In a 1961 opinion survey of Brazilian congressmen, Japan was ranked as highly as the United States on a scale preference rating system, thanks in large part to the favorable opinion generally accorded to the numerous Japanese immigrants.[33] The existence of the Japanese colony has made each country more salient to the other in spite of the intervening distance. It has also, since 1955, facilitated the development of economic relations and Japanese investment in Brazil; the Japanese businessman can count on the atmosphere of understanding already cultivated by the colony's historical experience and size.[34]

The culturalists' final defense of greater relations with Afro-Asia is that Brazil is the prima facie example of a successfully industrializing tropical civilization that has learned how to defeat some of the ecological problems faced by Afro-Asian nations and has smashed the myths concerning the alleged inferiority of tropical peoples. Besides transmitting these experiences accumulated over a longer period of independence, Brazil, according to the culturalists, could itself gain from any exchange of ideas with Afro-Asia. It could glean new ways to solve the technical problems it shares with other tropical nations. In this mutual aid program, Bra-

32. Reproduced in *Revista brasileira de política internacional*, 1, No. 3 (September 1958): 177.
33. Lloyd A. Free, *Some International Implications of the Political Psychology of Brazilians*, pp. 1–3.
34. Interview with Ikuzo Hirokawa, 20 June 1968.

zil, as the "Africanized West," as the "largest African nation outside Africa," would be able to give that continent sincere, effective collaboration without deforming its culture, because Brazil's culture is partly African and therefore less likely to "de-Africanize" the nations with which it cooperates. Nor would Brazilian assistance appear as another attempt to compromise Africa's jealously guarded neutrality in the Cold War.[35] This special aptitude to approach Afro-Asia would be enhanced by Brazil's status as a former colony which never practiced imperialism. It is thus free from guilt complexes and could lead a moral crusade in defense of these smaller, weaker nations of the world, as a way of repaying the moral debt it owes Africa.[36]

By interrelating its Western and African heritages, said Quadros, Brazil could become the bridge or link between Africa and the West with which to avoid a decisive political split between the two cultural areas. Brazil already presents evidence of a synthesis of the values of both.[37] Such hopes of assuming a crucial mediating role between former colonizers and colonial peoples is best understood as a transference to the global international system of Brazil's traditional intercessory role within the Western Hemisphere subsystem. Lacking in political and economic instruments of policy, Brazil elected to pursue a culturally based policy in order to establish increased prestige and channels of interaction in both bilateral and multilateral relations. Thus has Brazil laid the foundations for long-range accretion of political and economic cooperation and influence in Afro-Asia. If later conditions should warrant, the innocuous "bridge" imagery could rapidly be replaced by one of Third World leadership; but this was too radical to achieve important domestic support among conservative groups when Brazil was just beginning to reappraise its world position in 1961.

Lusotropicology.—The second major theoretical approach to Afro-Asia is the Luso-Brazilian, the view that Brazil can best relate to the Third World through Portugal in an Afro-Luso-Brazilian community erected on the phenomenon which

35. Eduardo Portella, "O dilema cultural da África e o Brasil."
36. Bezerra de Menezes, *Asia, Africa, e a política independente do Brasil*, p. 71.
37. Jânio Quadros, "Brazil's New Foreign Policy," p. 24.

sociologist Gilberto Freyre terms Lusotropicalism—the interpenetration of race, language, and culture which is supposedly peculiar to Portuguese colonization and finds its highest expression in Brazilian racial democracy. Freyre argues that Portugal has been the only nation able to adapt European values to tropical regions in a harmonious process of gradual fusion, rather than through destruction of either of the conflicting systems. Because of this creative interpenetration and experience in tropical areas dating from before 1500, Lusotropical societies should not be confused with the products of the more recent imperialism of racist white powers, which merely attempted to project copies of European states into the tropics while trampling underfoot the cultures of their exploited subjects.[38] Brazil, as the foremost member of "the world the Portuguese created," should take advantage of the common sociological situation it enjoys with places like Angola, Mozambique, Guinea, Macao, and Timor. These nations could together promote a union of Lusotropical peoples for the defense of their type of civilization and function as mediators between European civilization and the tropic peoples.

This frame of reference, which also finds exponents in official circles, asserts as a logical consequence that Brazil must therefore collaborate with Portugal in its "civilizing mission" in the tropics, to preclude the "absorption and disappearance of a Lusitanian world, *which is our world*, whose preservation also is our duty and concerns us, as a people, culturally, politically, and economically" (italics in original).[39] To so collaborate would be no more than to observe the natural solidarity which a firstborn son owes to his father. Through a new type of commonwealth, composed of Brazil, Portugal, and the "overseas provinces," Brazil would present itself to Black Africa as a product of the Portuguese to whom Angola and Mozambique, emerging new Brazils, look for guidance. Only in this way can Brazil defend the threatened common culture, help avert the racial extremism of Negro exclusivists

---

38. Gilberto Freyre, *Uma política transnacional de cultura para o Brasil de hoje*, pp. 45–60 passim.
39. José Garrido Torres, "Trópico e desenvolvimento," *Journal of Inter-American Studies*, p. 231.

and white segregationists in southern Africa, prevent the extinction of Portuguese culture in Africa, and avoid the complete de-Europeanization of the continent. Only in this way can Brazil forestall the absorption of the people of Angola, Mozambique, and Guinea by either communist or capitalist imperialism, whose onslaught would be precipitated by a premature granting of independence. For Brazil to join the anticolonialist chorus condemning Portugal would be equivalent to its rejection of the valuable Portuguese heritage it enjoys.

Most advocates of the Luso-Brazilian approach agree with Lisbon that the overseas territories are not colonies but integral parts of the Lusitanian world, part of a singular culture which transcends national boundaries. This world defines Brazil's first circle of loyalty; to ignore it and to try to appeal to Afro-Asia on any other basis would undermine Brazil's best opportunities for self-extension within its own language and culture. Brazilian opinion on the question of the future status of these colonies is in reality seriously divided, representing as it does a conflict between the established "special relationship" with Portugal and Brazil's aspirations as an independent spokesman for the developing world. It is impossible to completely separate Brazil's relations with Portugal from its objectives in sub-Saharan Africa. Because it is an important conditioning factor in Brazil's reaction to decolonization, we explore this quandary more fully in chapter 5.

Economic Conflict and Cooperation.—Economic preoccupations were the first stimuli that brought Africa to Brazilian attention in the postwar period. Agricultural producers feared greater competition in production and marketing of raw materials such as coffee, cocoa, cotton, and tropical woods and oils; these products suffered from limited elasticity of demand. At first, even official reports discounted the possibility of serious agricultural competition in the near future, as did a 1950 technical mission sent from the state of São Paulo to eleven colonies in western and central Africa to assess future economic potentials. The study concluded that Africa was not a "land of the future," but to the contrary was already nearly stripped of its resources and cursed with infertile land, deserts, disease, harsh climate, and other conditions which would greatly hinder its development into an imminent competitor or customer. The only exception hypothesized was its possible rivalry in production of robust varieties of coffee.[40] Within a few years this scepticism vanished as increasing African cocoa and coffee exports began cutting into Brazil's formerly privileged markets. Since Brazil was taken by surprise in this seeming turn of events, having failed to anticipate the new competition, it was slow to frame a policy adequate to meet the challenge.

For a while, many diplomats and economists were given to the erroneous theory that Africa was able to vie successfully for world markets only because colonialists were utilizing "slave labor" at very low pay rates to enable African coffee and cocoa to undersell the Brazilian products. With independence, so the argument reasoned, a freer work system would be introduced and the resultant higher wages would force African producers to compete on a fair basis. In addition, with African independence, the United States was expected to increase its trade with Brazil, while Europe, forced to pay fair prices for raw materials from former colonies, would likely also turn to Brazil. Not only did these premises prove false, but the newly independent nations' rapid voluntary association with the Commonwealth and the European Common Market confounded those who had predicted a split between Europe and the new Africa. The specter of a united Eurafrica, implying a lockout of Brazilian raw materials in Europe, provoked strong condemnatory remarks from Josué de Castro, ambassador to the United Nations Special Agencies: "Faced with the two monsters, Russia and the United States, Europe will survive only if it has a strong economy. At this point enters Africa, which was liberated only in appearance. Its countries are not political colonies but they are economic colonies, and they have no other choice. That is why they are now our enemies. When we want to shake up the European Common Market, the Africans are not in agreement. We, who talk so much about Afro-Asian policy, about common interests, should see that in that matter the interests are antagonistic. They have interests which they do not wish to yield and they say that it is the positive inheritance of colonialism, which had so many negative aspects. If they did

40. Rui Miller Paiva, *A agricultura na Africa*, pp. 224–32.

not have those preferences which they enjoy to export to Europe, they would not be able to compete."[41]

With the inclusion of Africa in the World Coffee Agreement and the Cocoa Producers Alliance, Brazil gained confidence in its ability to compete and lost its earlier apprehensions about being excluded from Western European markets. Industrialization began to reveal the possibility of penetration into the substantial Afro-Asian market, so opportunities for trade were explored by venturesome and imaginative economists and later by Itamaraty itself. The economic problem was the disposal of manufactured and semifinished goods produced in factories running at less than optimum capacity in the mid-1960s because of a slowly expanding internal market limited most stringently by a national per capita income of a little over $200. Afro-Asia, along with Latin America, was presented as a natural outlet for such goods, since it was believed that industrialized countries would not purchase large quantities of Brazilian manufactures. Industrialization would best be advanced by simultaneous extension of both domestic and international markets. Concurrent with this trend of thought occurred greater Brazilian–Afro-Asian cooperation through the United Nations to reform the terms of world trade. Gradually, without forgetting conflicts arising from continuing competition for economic markets and aid for development, Brazil saw Afro-Asian nations less from the perspective of competitors and more in the potential roles of customers and allies.

The Neutralist Viewpoint.—Since the idea of national interest as the guiding principle of foreign policy led to desires for independence in international politics, and since neutralism was the predominant philosophy of disengagement from the struggle between the superpowers at this turning point in Brazilian foreign policy, an ideological debate ensued about whether or not the Quadros-Goulart policy represented a variant of neutralism, and, if so, what consequences for relations with Afro-Asia would follow. Among the vocal defenders of nonalignment were those who spoke most favorably of (1) increasing contacts with the Third World; (2)

---

41. Josué de Castro, "Contribuição da ONU e seus organismos à economia brasileira," p. 572.

identifying Brazil's political and economic similarities with the Third World; (3) criticizing Brazil's position as a neglected ally trailing along in the wake of the industrialized West; and (4) urging recognition of each nation's economic development level as the watershed in international relations. For these individuals, Afro-Asia interests Brazil because of similar problems in nation-building and eliminating colonial structures.

With the underdeveloped Afro-Asian nations, Brazil and Latin America form part of the "periphery" of the world, that group of weak nations which could be described in neo-Marxist terms as the "historical proletariat" of the industrialized powers, especially of the superpowers. This periphery is characterized by having lacked, over the past four centuries, full decision-making power to solve its central political-economic problems; "it was organized as a pole which was either passive or dependent on a political-economic system which transcends its borders."[42] The peripheral countries are now simultaneously engaged in a common conflict to assert their independence vis-à-vis the center, end neocolonialist domination, secure world peace, and promote their economic development. In brief, they are faced with the tasks of correcting the distortions brought about by colonialism, solving the economic contradictions between themselves and their wealthy creditor states, and taking firm control of their own national destinies. To gain the initiative, the periphery must unite to present its complaints to the developed center; to accomplish this, it must use the principal weapon at its disposal—nationalism.

In comparison with Afro-Asia, Latin America finds itself in a slightly different situation. Although long independent in a political sense, Latin America still suffers from economic dependence. When interpreted as a form of neocolonialism and when taken in conjunction with its backward social and political structures, its economic dependence fully qualifies Latin America for membership in the periphery and for solidarity with Afro-Asia in the pursuit of their identical objectives despite different cultures, geographical distance, compe-

---

42. Cândido Mendes de Almeida, *Nacionalismo e desenvolvimento*, p. 4.

tition in the production of raw materials, and variations in degree of development attained.[43] Overlying economic rivalries between the regions one finds common problems of national integration, low income levels and high illiteracy levels, intranational regional inequalities, declining prices received for exports, and difficulties in public administration arising from commitment to a large role for the government in national life. According to the nationalist-developmentalist thesis, Brazil, as a key country of the developing world, has the urgent and essential obligation to serve as promoter of an identification between Latin America and Afro-Asia, regions with comparable problems in nation-building but which have been kept apart by adverse historical circumstances and machinations of the dominant powers. This identification could most readily be accomplished, on one side, by the marshalling of Brazil's prestige within South America and, on the other, by increased Brazilian communication with Afro-Asia in general. Special attention could be paid to "progressive" neutralist countries such as Ghana, Guinea, Mali, and the United Arab Republic, Third World leaders in advancing unity and class consciousness against the metropolitan areas.[44]

Anticolonialism would be a logical concomitant of such a posture, which was designed not only to confer a position of Third World leadership on Brazil but also and primarily to create an international climate favorable to broad economic and social reform within Brazil, including control of foreign capital, erasure of all vestiges of neocolonialism, and acceleration of the national self-awareness of which the ISEB generation spoke. Should Brazil fail to take this step as the core of

43. Mendes de Almeida, "Política externa e nação em processo," pp. 56–59.
44. These particular ideas came closest to fruition under Quadros, who was aware of Nkrumah's theory of "diastatic countries," i.e., those key countries of the developing world whose exemplary action would trigger a chain-reaction effect and forge unity in the developing world as a whole. These countries were Ghana, Brazil, the United Arab Republic, and India. Like plans to further Latin American–African cooperation through Brazilian diplomacy in the OAU, the diastatic idea was relegated to intellectual drawing boards and never was put into practice in the short months of Quadros' presidency, even though he unsuccessfully tried to start a dialogue with Nkrumah through a personal emissary.

an independent policy, argued the neutralists, Brazil would be condemned to being left even further behind the development levels reached by the industrialized North, which was controlling the flow of international economics in its own behalf. Vigorous defense of anticolonialism, nonintervention, and the self-determination of peoples, for a long time mere rhetoric of conservative spokesmen within Itamaraty, was now necessary to protect the central value of independence—greater national freedom of choice, which was inherent in the higher per capita income levels being sought and was now being defined in economic as well as political terms.

Thus, for the neutralists, the Afro-Asian policy was very much an extension of the domestic political contest. It provided a means of expanding the scope of the conflict in order to bring into play international pressure (judged beneficial to their interests and political philosophies) against the traditional, Western-oriented elites' resistance to reform. Once this internal opposition could be overcome, the ideologues felt they could continue to rely on the nationalistic support of the masses to continue the attack on the monopoly of international decision-making exercised by the two superblocs to the detriment of the periphery. Any increase in bargaining power obtained through an Afro-Asian type of positive neutralism would be welcome, but the final goal would always remain the construction of an international system to facilitate development, to be attained by negotiations with the North through the united front of all developing nations spanning the metaphorical Southern Hemisphere.

Interdependence with the West.—If the neutralists believed that the Afro-Asian policy should be constructed chiefly as an integral part of the campaign to sever all traces of dependence on foreign centers of political and economic decision, many of their conservative opponents not only rejected the desirability of closer relations with Afro-Asia but also depicted dependence on the West as a valuable asset which did not conflict with Brazil's best interests but rather preserved them. The conservative judgment, most in evidence in the Castello Branco government, betrays very markedly an acceptance of the American image of international relations prevalent during the mid-1950s, a view conditioned by belief in rigid bipolarity, moralizing, and a fear of Communist power expansion.⁴⁵ While the neutralists used economic and sociological reasoning to explain Brazil's great dependency on the United States and Western Europe and condemned it as prejudicial to rapid development, the Western world–oriented affirmed that such dependency on other Western civilizations was a moral obligation which could not be auctioned off. The pro-Americanists also believed close Western ties were a prerequisite for national security from Communist subversion. Any clashes of interests with Western nations were considered secondary to the benefit which would accrue from full cooperation on a bilateral or multilateral basis.

Not only did these conservatives warn that neutralism is deceitful, frivolous, and immoral; they also believed that both this phenomenon and Afro-Asian nationalism were inspired and manipulated by Communists as weapons in the war against the West. To them the case of Soviet control in Eastern Europe was much more imperative and poignant than conditions in any colony struggling to free itself from European control, most likely only to become a prime target for Communist imperialism. Any campaign to set Brazil on an anticolonialist path which would collide with the interests of the United States, Portugal, Great Britain, or France was, to the pro-Americanists, indeed ill-advised and against the interests of the West as a whole. They disagreed wholeheartedly with Quadros' profession that Brazil owed a cultural debt to Africa. They classified the Afro-Asian rapprochement as Quadros' "preposterous creation" which merely encouraged local Communists because it took on anti-American and anti-European features and threatened to transform Brazil from a staunch American ally into an adherent of the abhored Indian line, in defiance of solemn treaty commitments to the West.⁴⁶

Assis Chateaubriand, former ambassador to London and owner of Brazil's largest newspaper, radio, and television chain, in an editorial entitled "Our Kingdom is Not of This Hindu-Arabic World" decried the visit to Brazil by several

45. Such opinions were also affected by widespread admiration for Portugal in this group and their consequent acceptance of Portuguese interpretations of world affairs.
46. Glycon de Paiva, "Política exterior vista pelo homem da rua," p. 63.

neutralist leaders as a waste of time conducive to useless academic arguments over "Third" and "Fourth" Ideological Positions irrelevant to Brazilian reality. Chateaubriand wrote, "We should realize that for the recovery of Brazil we neither can nor should hope for anything from the United Arab Republic, India, or Yugoslavia. The projected visit of the heads of state of those countries will be a purely touristic excursion destitute of any practical significance. Our salvation depends on the Atlantic Community and Japan."[47]

In discussing Afro-Asia, conservatives emphasized competition in agricultural exports, the unwise inversion of priorities implied in the utopian courting of the Third World, and the alien (i.e., non-Western or nondemocratic) values which these other cultures possessed, not to mention the Communist propaganda which could only be encouraged by increased communication with the anti-Western states. To the pro-Americanist, it was even less justifiable for the ideologues to turn Brazil into an imaginary colony, much less a vanguard of the "historical international proletariat" supposedly composed of all underdeveloped nations. Economic, cultural, or political identity with the Third World was a demagogical distortion of the facts, since economic underdevelopment in Brazil, merely a temporary delay in an industrial revolution, could not be compared with the underdevelopment in Africa and Asia. There progress would require structural and attitudinal modifications on a large scale. Brazil, on the other hand, according to the definition of the Castello Branco regime, is a developed country with only pockets of underdevelopment. This perspective led to assessments like that of Ambassador J. O. de Meira Penna: "Our foreign policy should therefore be based on the expectation of an imminent entrance of Brazil into the society of the industrialized and developed nations of the West rather than remaining bound to economic judgments originating from feelings of inferiority."[48]

So strongly did such sentiments pervade the post-1964 reaction to the independent foreign policy and to the neo-Marxist terminology of the developmental nationalists that many of the prime movers of the opening to Afro-Asia now feel that an active political role for Brazil in those continents

47. *O Jornal*, 28 April 1963, p. 3.
48. Penna, *Política externa: Segurança e desenvolvimento*, p. 45.

is in the first instance foreclosed by domestic conservative elites (including sectors of the military) who would consider such action "leftist" and perhaps "subversive." In the opinion of a former foreign minister, this fear is presently the greatest single hindrance to penetration of Brazilian influence into Afro-Asia.[49] Perhaps, in retrospect, it is most valid to conclude that, although these ideological and Western-oriented global philosophies continue to clash in the contemporary formulation of Afro-Asian policy, elements of both were accepted by Itamaraty under Costa e Silva. With time and experience, the thesis and the antithesis have yielded a synthesis, a course of action more suited to Brazilian potentials and possibilities than either doctrine taken by itself would have produced.

Africa in Military Thought.—Brazilian military thought, based on a geopolitical approach imposed by the nation's limited conventional capabilities, underlines the fact that, while by virtue of its territorial mass Brazil is affected by whatever happens on the South American continent, its unusually long 4,000-mile coastline charges it with the mission of watching over the South Atlantic. This task is, of course, to be performed in conjunction with the United States and other friendly states, such as Argentina. Brazil's military mission grows naturally from popular recognition of Brazil as a nation which is not only fully facing the sea but geographically "leaning out over it" (*debruçado sôbre o mar*), with a population heavily concentrated along the ocean's shores. On the other side of this ocean lies Africa, making Brazil an interested neighboring observer of events on that continent.

High ranks of the military are not indifferent to the significance of Africa in national security, for western Africa falls within Brazil's first inner hemicircle of defense against conventional attack and possible subversion originating outside Latin America. Strategist Meira Mattos, in contemplating an enemy invasion of the Western Hemisphere from Western Africa, defines Brazil's geopolitical position as the largest power bordering on the South Atlantic and as controller of one end of the 1,600-mile Natal-Dakar strait, which proved crucial in Western strategy in World War II. Mattos insists: "Today we cannot escape the truism which places on the

49. Confidential interview.

Atlantic coast of Africa the line of immediate coverage of the Brazilian coast. The moment a military power hostile to Brazil occupies Africa's Atlantic coast, at any point from Morocco to the Republic of South Africa, we will begin to feel in our country a climate of intranquility and bellicose pressure without precedent in our history. . . . In the framework of continental defense and Western strategy today Africa concerns Brazil much more than any other area of the universe. It will be there that we will have to protect our own territory from the horrors of war."[50]

Of all the regions which form Brazil's extended lines of defense, Africa is considered by many the most vulnerable to Communist penetration and the most likely to become a center of Cold War tensions. The minimum, then, which Brazil must do to defend its eastern approaches is to contribute to South Atlantic military security and to promote conditions in Africa which would engender political and economic stability and prevent any state along the Atlantic coast from falling into hostile hands. This task is made more difficult by the weakness of African naval and air forces, requiring deterrence from attack provided in part by operation of extra-continental balance of power mechanisms and tacit agreements rather than by exclusive reliance on local forces. "We are, in other words," as one diplomat expressed it, "an interested party in an African Monroe Doctrine, which constitutes the strategic basis by which we can demand local respect of the principle of non-intervention and self-determination."[51]

General Golbery do Couto e Silva, head of the National War College and former chief of the National Intelligence Agency, assigned high priority to Africa in any Brazilian defense activities outside its borders, in view of Africa's susceptibility to political subversion by virtue of its social and economic weaknesses: "Combat underdevelopment in backward areas in Brazil and the rest of the continent, cooperate also in the immunization of the young African countries to the fatal infection of Communism, be vigilant and attentive to any Soviet advance toward the Atlantic coast of Africa where the advanced and decisive frontier of our own national security is situated, collaborate by all means to keep it totally

50. Carlos de Meira Mattos, *Projeção mundial do Brasil*, p. 25.
51. Penna, *Política externa: Segurança e desenvolvimento*, p. 149.

free of Communist domination—these are, more or less well-delineated, in a tentative order of decreasing priority, the principal directives which seem to us to be non-deferrable in a Brazilian geopolitics adequate to the present agitated and cataclysmic period, in a struggling world in the throes of a most brutal collision of antagonistic civilizations."[52]

To many military officers pondering the problem of effective action around the South Atlantic, the so-called overseas provinces of Portugal seem excellent bases of operation and points of support in Brazil's attempt to increase its radius of action throughout the world. This is one of the key advantages for Brazil in the Luso-Brazilian community which an important segment of Brazilian officialdom finds attractive and difficult to repudiate in spite of explicit unfavorable reaction from several African nations. Such a community, if fully realized, would embrace a land area greater than that of Communist China and a population of over 125 million located on four continents, representing, with its economic concessions, a substantial power increment for Brazil through its ally Portugal, with which it already has several military treaties. This community concept has stirred strong emotions pro and con and has become a major issue of Brazilian policy in Afro-Asia, acerbated by the uncertain state of the Portuguese occupation of Angola, Mozambique, Guinea, and Macao.

Afro-Asian Area Study Centers

The rather sudden concern for Afro-Asian affairs and the repercussions which events there were producing in world politics led to the creation of several Afro-Asian study institutes in major Brazilian cities. The oldest is the Center for Afro-Oriental Studies (CEAO), established at the Federal University of Bahia, at Salvador, in September 1959. It initially received assistance from both UNESCO and the Ministry of Foreign Relations. The location of this interdisciplinary center is due in large measure to the pronounced African cultural milieu found in the state of Bahia. The CEAO has maintained an ongoing program of association with African educational institutions since its foundation. It has specialized in undergraduate- and graduate-level historical, geographical, anthro-

52. Golbery do Couto e Silva, *Geopolítica do Brasil* (2d ed.; Rio de Janeiro: José Olympio, 1967), p. 137.

pological, sociological, and linguistic courses and research on Africa, African ethnographic patterns in Brazil, and Brazilian cultural traces in West Africa. It reached the apex of its activity between 1961 and 1963. Language courses offered on various occasions have included Yoruba, Arabic, Hebrew, Hindi, Russian, and Japanese, all of which have received very little consideration in other Brazilian universities. CEAO publications include several monographs on Africa, intermittent bulletins, and the semiannual journal *Afro-Ásia*. Many of the Afro-Brazil cultural exchange programs which came into being, including exchange of students and professors, have been handled and coordinated by the CEAO. Since crippling financial problems loomed in 1964, however, the CEAO's course offerings have not formed part of an integrated plan of study or research but have been administered on a sporadic, noncredit basis.

The most politically important study center was the Brazilian Institute for Afro-Asian Studies (IBEAA), created in April 1961 as a graduate-level institute to promote relations between Brazil and the Afro-Asian world. The IBEAA was the unusual product of Quadros' technical staff, the consequence of the fusion of two pro–Third World currents—the relatively apolitical cultural inclinations of the CEAO and the ideological bent of members of the ISEB generation. Directly subordinated to the presidency, the IBEAA, with its Consultative Committee of rectors and area specialists from important universities, was intended to be nothing less than a Kennedy-style advisory body of national intellectuals created to attack any given problem area from many disciplines, an innovation in Brazilian politics.[53]

Executive Decree 50,465 of 14 April 1961, which created the IBEAA, stated that the institute's objectives were fourfold: to stimulate, develop, and publish cultural, social, political, and economic studies concerning the Afro-Asian world; to facilitate and develop relations between Brazil and the countries of Africa and Asia; to promote the comparative study of the developmental process in Brazil and in African and Asian countries, for the exchange of techniques and solutions adopted, for mutual benefit; and to promote university stu-

53. Interview with Cândido Mendes de Almeida, 17 June 1968.

dent and professor exchanges between Brazil and the African and Asian countries.

From the very beginning the IBEAA's ideological predisposition was conspicuous and Africa was the favored continent. Similar organizations were set up to give regional cooperation to the central body, but these enjoyed only a short life at the Federal University of Pernambuco (Recife), the University of Ceará (Fortaleza), and in the state-sponsored Center for Afro-Asian Studies in Natal (Rio Grande do Norte). Only in November 1961, after the resignation of Quadros, did the IBEAA start to function. It offered an ambitious program of seminars, expositions, debates, and lectures, including participation by African ambassadors and representatives from two liberation movements, the National Liberation Front (FLN) of Algeria and the People's Movement for the Liberation of Angola (MPLA). The institute aided in the preliminary organization of the first economic mission to Africa and sent two delegates to the First Disarmament Assembly in Accra in June 1962.

The domestic political configuration, however, was unfavorable to the realization of the goals set for IBEAA by the Africanists. Originally designed to operate under Quadros and with collaboration from his circle of sympathetic advisors, it was transferred to the Ministry of Education and Culture in the parliamentary regime which accompanied Goulart's assumption of the presidency. In March 1962 it was made subordinate to the Foreign Ministry. Each of these distinct environments implied a different set of ideas, and lacking Goulart's personal support and interest, the IBEAA soon found itself cut off from the privileged access to policy formation which was its original raison d'etre. A bulletin was circulated and about ten books and a bibliography on the Third World published before the institute was thrown into a moribund state by the Castello Branco government, which questioned some of its activities and labeled one of its published works (*Axé opô afonjá*) as subversive. Antipathy toward the institute exhibited by high officials in Itamaraty, especially those incensed by anticolonial positions, almost led to IBEAA's extinction. Its demise was averted for a time only by the negative repercussions this would have produced in Afro-Asia at a time when the revolution was trying to improve its image abroad, but it was deprived of public funds in 1968 and later extinguished.

The third and final major Afro-Asian area study program is the Oriental Studies Department of the School of Philosophy, Sciences, and Letters of the University of São Paulo, offering undergraduate and graduate courses since 1963, leading to a degree in Oriental letters. This department specializes in Japanese studies, but also maintains courses in Russian, Hebrew, Arabic, Armenian, and Sanskrit languages and literature; some historical and cultural background is provided. Of the 117 students in the regularly offered Arabic, Armenian, Hebrew, and Japanese programs in 1966, 77 enrolled in the Japanese section (the vast majority of these were descendants of Japanese immigrants).[54] The response on the part of native Brazilians to this pioneering effort has been rather restrained, perhaps due to competition from courses in the traditionally more popular Western areas.[55]

Area study programs are still novel and not well developed in Brazil, but it is instructive to note that the above-mentioned Afro-Asian centers were the only such substantial Brazilian programs for any world regions, although the new State University of Londrína, Paraná, is organizing an Institute for Latin American Studies.[56] The origin of each of these three centers can be traced primarily to particular domestic factors rather than to generalized intellectual interest in Afro-Asia: to the nuclei of Japanese and African culture in the case of the University of São Paulo and the CEAO and to ideological inspiration in the instance of the IBEAA. The two centers presently active have an almost completely humanistic orien-

---

54. Eurípedes Simões de Paula, "Breve nota sôbre o curso de estudos orientais na Faculdade de Filosofia, Ciências e Letras da Universidade de São Paulo," p. 287.

55. A Japanese social scientist from the University of Kobe estimated that in 1966 there were only 50 students of the Portuguese language in Japanese universities, reflecting the disinterest of the Japanese in the study of developing regions. He remarked that this figure is surprisingly low in view of the number of Japanese descendants in Brazil and the concentration of Japanese investment in that country. See Yoshiaki Nishimukai, "Estudos brasileiros no Japão", p. 241.

56. Mention must be made of the valuable work done by the Centro de Estudos Nipo-Brasileiros (Japanese-Brazilian Studies Center) of São Paulo, which specializes in the sociology of the Japanese immigrant but serves to publicize Japanese culture as well.

tation while largely shunning political studies and involvement.

Delusions of Grandeur or an Efficacious Policy?

To many of the enthusiastic Afro-Asianists in the early 1960s, Brazil's obvious credentials as a South Atlantic power, a cultural bridge, a predestined leader of the developing nations, and a moral example of racial harmony qualified it to such a degree that they expected independent Africa and perhaps some of Asia to naturally and inexorably turn toward Brazil for cooperation and guidance as Western Europe withdrew from its former colonial domains. This supposedly logical non sequitur arose as a consequence of the fact that initially the controversy often took the form of emotional polemics. A more rational, objective examination of the potentials for conflict and cooperation in the light of Brazil's interests and capabilities within Afro-Asia itself was not conducted. Much of what was written in Brazil about Afro-Asia and particularly about Brazilian opportunities for leadership there was founded on meager factual knowledge and optimistic illusions. The realities of international politics and economics were ignored. Rather, a wishful projection of philosophical or cultural notions about Brazil, fabricated completely within Brazil and based almost solely on Brazilian problems and perspectives, emerged. In the words of a former ambassador to Ghana, Africa became Brazil's *capital de sonhos* (dream castle in the sky) in its search for greater influence and prestige. The dream led to many distortions and unjustified hopes.[57]

For example, the director of the CEAO asserted that after Kubitschek's Pan-American operation, Africa lay open to Brazil: "The Negro peoples are waiting for us, in a way. Free of European colonialism, fearful and mistrustful of the offers of assistance made to them, with the firm purpose of imposing Black culture on the world, with a refusal to assimilate the culture which European colonialist peoples tried in vain to impose on their populations, they wish union with us, they trust us . . . we are the natural ally of the Black peoples of Africa. . . ."[58] And Ambassador Josué de Castro believed that

57. Interview with Raymundo Souza Dantas, 14 September 1968.
58. Waldir Freitas Oliveira, *A importância atual do Atlântico Sul*, p. 14.

a latent diplomatic love affair existed between Brazil and Africa: ". . . Africa has until the present time been holding open a great window for our country, just waiting until someone should go by to begin the courtship which is necessary as a type of diplomatic introduction."[59]

Foreign Minister San Tiago Dantas also predicted great opportunities for Brazil among the new nations of the Third World: "These countries turn toward us, seeing in a nation with our demographic mold, with our political tradition, and with our cultural unity an eternal example of attention and often an example for imitation. For this reason, the position of a country such as ours may already be termed one of leadership, for leadership is nothing more than the capacity of expressing through one's own purpose and experience the solution of problems weighing upon others."[60]

Quadros himself felt that, "The great states being born in Africa and Asia must find in Brazil's international maturity the courage they lack to expedite their inevitable emancipation." He thus cast Brazil in the peculiar role of inspirational midwife in the difficult process of the birth of the progeny of decolonization.[61] His foreign minister, also impressed with Brazil's supposed power of attraction for Black Africa, declared, "It is not we who are searching for Africa; it is the young African nations which are searching for Brazil."[62] Such euphoric but common expectations were not, of course, borne out by subsequent events. And many of the early efforts of Itamaraty in Afro-Asia suffered from this romantic approach, grounded as it was in false images and lack of experience with local conditions. Thus, if Brazilian policy in Afro-Asia appears to lack aggressiveness or deep purpose, one reason could be that until recently it has been not only a developing policy, but also a cautious one of information, of "listening posts" represented by the new embassies and legations opened in Africa and Asia. On the basis of the observations and intelligence gathered over the last few years,

59. Castro, "O Brasil e o mundo afro-asiático," p. 14.
60. *Revista brasileira de política internacional*, 7, No. 27 (September 1964): 411.
61. *O Globo*, 31 May 1961, p. 7.
62. Quoted in Penna, *Política externa: Segurança e desenvolvimento*, p. 149.

and within the restrictions of economic and political priorities, a new, more realistic and modest Afro-Asian policy is being shaped along more pragmatic lines than those embraced during the Quadros-Goulart years and on a higher level of diplomatic and commercial interaction than previously exhibited.[63] In turn, a more propitious information atmosphere exists within Brazil for the limited sector of the public interested in the matter to form accurate opinions and informed value judgments about Brazil's relations with Afro-Asia. For a long time, however, for the mass of the populace, Afro-Asia will continue to symbolize an exotic or unknown world, "more remote than the lunar craters."

The Course of Bilateral Relations

Before 1956, Brazilian representation in Afro-Asia was scanty, a consequence of the modest size and budget of the diplomatic corps; the predominance of Western Europe, Latin America, and the United States in national planning; a politically and geographically narrow definition of Brazilian interests; and the prevalence of European colonial control in Africa. In July 1956, Brazil maintained diplomatic relations on the African continent only with the Union of South Africa and Egypt and with small consular posts in Casablanca, Algiers, Tangiers, Dakar, and Cape Town. Of the twenty-five major independent non-Communist states of Asia and the Levant, Brazilian diplomatic representation was present in eleven, with career consulates in Kobe, Hong Kong, Shanghai, Calcutta, Bombay, and Istanbul.[64] Around July 1956, however,

---

63. In November 1966, Presidential Decree No. 69 stipulated that service in Latin America, Africa, Asia, or Oceania was required for certain diplomatic merit promotions. Elevations in rank to first secretary require a minimum of two years, and promotions to minister second-class a minimum of four years of assignment to posts in the above-mentioned regions. This regulation reflects the importance now being placed on relations with the developing world and also the fact that capitals in these areas may not be as glamorous and attractive as those of Western Europe, to which Brazilian diplomats have traditionally been drawn. One consequence of this decree is that a greater number of career diplomats are gaining experience in Afro-Asia, a very rare commodity in Itamaraty at the time of Quadros' administration.
64. Brasil, Ministério das Relações Exteriores, *"Lista do pessoal"* (July 1956).

concerned officials within Itamaraty were beginning to address themselves to the problem, which was becoming clearer with the projected independence of many African nations and the energetic international role undertaken by the Middle East and Asia in the United Nations.

Although Quadros is generally credited with awakening Brazil to the Third World's existence and importance, some preliminary strides were quietly made during the Kubitschek administration under the rubric "Operação Brasil-Ásia." Brazil had routinely exchanged diplomats with major Asian powers for some time—China (since 1893), Japan (1897), Australia (1945), India (1948), Pakistan (1951), Indonesia (1953)—but a more dynamic response to rapidly moving Asian events seemed politically imperative and economically useful to alleviate the unfavorable balance of payments situation which appeared during Kubitschek's presidency. In July 1957, Brazil's ambassador in New Delhi paid official visits to South Vietnam, Laos, Cambodia, Thailand, and Burma with the intention of sounding out opportunities for increased Southeast Asian contacts. This mission grew out of a Foreign Ministry policy study on the reorganization and expansion of consular and diplomatic representation in Afro-Asia, the negotiation of treaties, and the dispatch of special delegations for ceremonial and observation purposes.[65] As revealed in the final report of a second official economic and political mission representing various governmental departments and visiting Iran, Thailand, Indonesia, Singapore, Malaysia, the Philippines, and Hong Kong in 1959, commercial considerations were paramount in this spate of activity which was replacing Brazilian neglect. Brazil's need for rubber and tin, for example, led directly to the installation by the 1959 mission of an embassy in Bangkok. This mission also provided Itamaraty with its first post on the Southeast Asian mainland as well as a new customer.[66]

As a direct consequence of Operação Brasil-Ásia, relations were begun in 1959 with Malaysia, Thailand, and South Viet-

65. Brasil, Ministério das Relações Exteriores, *Relatório* (1957), pp. 87–88.
66. Hugo Gouthier de Oliveira Gondim, *Missão especial ao Sudeste da Ásia—Relatório apresentado aos Ministros das Relações Exteriores e da Fazenda*, p. 39.

nam and in 1960 with Ceylon and South Korea. In 1959 the legation in Canberra was raised to embassy status. Even this measured attempt to extend diplomatic interchange provoked criticism from the domestic press, as some newspapers declared it utopian and diversionistic. Sukarno's 1959 visit to Brazil was the first by any Asian head of state; Emperor Haile Selassie's short stay in 1960, abbreviated by an abortive Ethiopian coup, represented the same for Africa. Rather little was modified in Middle Eastern representation, but a legation in Accra and a cumulative legation in Addis Ababa were added in sub-Saharan Africa. Brazil made plans to initiate relations with Senegal and Guinea. Engrossed in the Pan American operation, Brazil made few ventures into the Third World from 1956 to 1960. Those made were confined mainly to South Asia and remained decidedly subordinate to other foreign policy matters, meriting barely a mention in the Foreign Ministry's annual reports.

The year 1960 was the celebrated "Year of Africa," in which seventeen African states gained independence and applied for United Nations admission. Such a spectacular event as the birth of so many new nations across the South Atlantic could not but engender curiosity and apprehension in Latin America and particularly Brazil. No longer were these economic competitors mere colonies of Western Europe; they were now legally sovereign entities which would wield considerable vote-power in the General Assembly and specialized agencies and would most probably act in conjunction with the Afro-Asian caucusing group to bring to vote and approval questions which affected their interests. The proportional trend of regional strength within the General Assembly had already become quite apparent. Whereas in 1945 Latin America's share of the assembly seats was 39 percent, by 1 January 1964, it would be more than halved to 18 percent, while Afro-Asia's participation (excluding Commonwealth associates) would rise from 24 percent to 52 percent in the same period.[67] Such a relative gain in voting strength by a bloc which represented possibilities for both conflict and cooperation in international forums could scarcely go unnoticed by a Latin Amer-

---

67. Sydney D. Bailey, *The General Assembly of the United Nations: A Study of Procedure and Practice*, p. 36.

ica already affected by Africa's growing contribution to the world production of raw materials.

Both major candidates in the 1960 Brazilian presidential election defended the importance of rapprochement with Afro-Asia, not a surprising, radical, or undue development in the context of the international headlines, the nationalistic tenor of the campaign, the challenges presented to the nation by the "winds of change" sweeping Africa, and the circumspect extension into Afro-Asia already under way. Before his trip through the Third World, Quadros seemed to have no real interest in Brazilian–Afro-Asian relations, but his careful observations impressed him to such an extent that, when elected, he set out to make Afro-Asian relations a prime component of his independent foreign policy.[68] His foreign minister saw a dual motive in this decision: the first motive was the popular appeal of this expansion if heralded as a positive act of national independence, and the second stemmed from economic preoccupations which signaled the search for new markets in view of the inelasticity of traditional ones.[69]

Quadros' program for Afro-Asia gave highest priority to Africa, although Asia was not to be neglected. First, reciprocal cultural ties with West Africa were to be accented to overcome the usual Europeanization explanation of Brazil's cultural process and to present Brazil to the world as a nation which had partaken unashamedly of both African and European cultures and races and was therefore in a position to understand and benefit from both sources, as well as to act as mediator if necessary. Brazil was joined to Africa by common cultural and ethnic roots to such a degree, said Quadros, that no amount of approximation and cooperation could ever repay the immense national debt contracted through the Negroes' sufferings and labors in the evolution and enrichment of Brazil's distinctive civilization.[70] This official glorification of the Negro, however slight, had no substantial precedent in recent Brazilian history and disturbed the white cosmopolitans, who found it more profitable and prestigious to identify with Western Europe and the United States.

The second point involved the creation of a historical-

68. Interview with Cândido Mendes de Almeida, 15 March 1968.
69. Interview with Afonso Arinos, 22 May 1968.
70. Quadros, *Mensagem ao Congresso Nacional*, p. 97.

political-economic linkage to mitigate the competition in coffee and cocoa, which was detrimental to Brazil, to open African markets to Brazilian goods, and to build up a store of good will to make possible cooperation in defense of raw material prices. In the political sphere, an Itamaraty study group was charged with proposing concrete means to advance national goals in Africa. The study group enunciated a maxim which has in general governed Brazilian policy in Africa, Asia, and the Middle East—"The active presence of Brazil in the African political complex should be free of any interventionist tendencies or partisan attitudes in local matters or in questions not yet settled internationally."[71] This minimal political involvement decision flowed from a desire to avoid antagonizing parties in any heated dispute in which Brazil was not an interested party, as well as reinforcing the principle of nonintervention, which is designed to prevent large powers from using a conflict on the periphery to advance their own interests to the detriment of those of the local states. Also, if closely followed, this prudent admonition would place Brazil in a position of availability for mediation in cases such as Biafra or Portuguese Africa.[72]

71. Brasil, Ministério das Relações Exteriores, *Relatório* (1961), p. 40.

72. Such mediation is a role which Itamaraty has been preparing itself to assume—should favorable circumstances and an invitation present themselves—as a means to promote Brazil's prestige in Africa and strengthen the basis for medium- and long-range cooperation vis-à-vis developed economies. This availability is recognized in influential quarters, but whether it is ever drawn upon depends largely on the wishes of the parties in conflict. Upon the breakdown of Nigerian-Biafran talks in June 1968, *The Economist*'s Latin American edition suggested editorially that Brazil offer to mediate in the war, given its exceptional characteristics for such an effort and its disinterested political stance of nonintervention. Extraofficial Foreign Ministry sources expressed interest and readiness in the possibility, but reiterated as well the necessity for the initiative or request to come from either of the affected parties. Later, in a statement of official policy on the war, Magalhães Pinto affirmed, "Respect for Nigerian sovereignty keeps Brazil from taking any initiative not agreed to by the federal government of Nigeria in the Biafran conflict episode." Brazil was therefore also safeguarding its amicable relations with Lagos, obviously the most probable victor of the war and the controlling power of the greatest part of Nigerian territory and resources. See, in order: "Una oportunidad en busca de Brasil," p. 9; "Brasil pode mediar conflito sôbre Biafra," *Jornal do Brasil*, 13 June 1968, p. 2; and "Chanceler diz como Brasil julga Biafra," *Correio da Manhã*, 13 November 1968, p. 9.

The final phase of Quadros' plan was to forge ties with the OAU allowing Brazil to become the linkage between Latin America and Africa and thus push it into the forefront among developing nations. The realization of this bold aim was frustrated by the brevity of Quadros' term and the rather low degree of acceptance actually accorded Brazil by African nations. Expectations that African states would welcome Brazil with open arms as a fellow exploited nation had been misleading. On the contrary, Brazil always had to be content with the status of ordinary observer at OAU meetings and all-African political and economic conferences.

As recounted in Chapter 2 within the context of the independent foreign policy, Brazil established new Afro-Asian embassies and consulates, most notably, embassies in Accra, Dakar, Lagos, and Porto Novo, with cumulative embassies in Addis Ababa, Bamako, Niamey, Nouakchott, and Manila. Consulates were created in Nairobi and Salisbury, soon followed by increases in the number of consulates in Portuguese Africa. Many of these consulates and some embassies, however, never were actually installed, for lack of resources or because of political inexpediency.

This inauguration or intensification of bilateral relations was accompanied by other measures designed to appeal to the whole Third World. The naval officer candidates' training cruise on the *Custódio de Mello*, normally scheduled for Europe, was rerouted to Africa, featuring an on-board course in African affairs and carrying an industrial exposition to eighteen African and Middle Eastern ports, the first such Brazilian display in those areas. Afro-Asian cultural institutes were founded and a seminar on African affairs begun for diplomatic personnel stationed at the Foreign Ministry.

Scholarships for African students to receive training in Brazilian universities were sponsored by the Foreign Ministry, financed by deductions from diplomatic salaries over a certain level and in part administered through the CEAO. This program ultimately benefited twenty-two students from Nigeria, Ghana, Senegal, the Cape Verde Islands, Sierra Leone, Portuguese Guinea, and Cameroon. They arrived in 1961 and 1962 and specialized in such diverse fields as medicine, engineering, letters, architecture, economics, law, and geology. After 1962, the program was definitively suspended, ostensibly for lack of funds. If continued, it might have proven a valuable project, given the importance of education in leadership formation in Africa and possibilities for Brazilian exchange of information with Africa in such areas as tropical medicine, architecture, civilian aviation, and the arts. Since 1962, the Foreign Ministry has continued its scholarship program as before 1961, with almost all grants reserved for Latin Americans. Apparently a change in regional emphasis as well as financial difficulties were involved in the discontinuance of scholarships for Africans. However, to increase African exposure to Brazilian culture, Itamaraty has at various times maintained Brazilian professors at universities in Ghana, Nigeria, and Senegal.[73]

In international organizations and bilateral contacts, the bases were set for economic cooperation in common export products, typified by the 1962 formation of the Cocoa Producers Alliance with Nigeria, Ghana, the Ivory Coast, Togo, and Cameroon. These same states were, significantly, the first sub-Saharan nations with which Brazil opened relations after 1960. The alliance was framed to exchange technical data, promote discussion of mutual problems, maintain market price levels, and encourage expansion of cocoa consumption.

Political positions were modified to enhance Brazil's image in Afro-Asia, as Itamaraty began withdrawing its former assiduous support for Portuguese colonial policies in Africa and began to take a stronger stand against colonialism in general. Observers were sent to the Belgrade Conference of Non-Aligned Nations (1961), the Cairo Conference on Problems of Economic Development (1962), and the Second Conference of Non-Aligned Nations (1964), all of which were attended by few Latin American states.

Several political missions were sent to Africa, the foremost of which was a delegation headed by Foreign Minister Arinos to witness the independence ceremonies of Senegal. A later special mission headed by Federal Deputy J. P. Coelho de Sousa, and including three diplomats, attended the inde-

---

73. For purposes of comparison, in 1961, while Itamaraty furnished three professors through cooperative programs in Africa, it sent three to the United States, five to Germany, nine to France, and one each to Austria and Japan. Ministério das Relações Exteriores, *Relatório* (1961), p. 164.

pendence ceremonies of Sierra Leone. Afterwards it traveled through West Africa gathering political and economic data and delivering a personal message from Quadros to the president of Cameroon. Official visits were also received, including those of missions from Cameroon and Nigeria, the Minister of Labor of Nigeria, the Minister of Economics of Gabon, President Sukarno of Indonesia, the Minister of Food and Agriculture of India, a commercial delegation from the Republic of China, and one from New Zealand, a good-will mission from South Korea, and several Japanese commercial and political missions. Although the level of interaction with the Middle East rose more gradually from 1959 to 1961, the rapidly increased exchange of diplomats and missions with Africa and Asia contrasted sharply with the much lower levels of activity in preceding years. But the increased activity blended in quite well with the general 1961 upsurge in Brazilian foreign relations intensity.

On the administration level, an area desk for Africa (Divisão da África) was created in the Foreign Ministry, but subordinated to the Western European General Secretariat. It nevertheless constituted, in the words of Itamaraty, "one more demonstation of the special importance and attention which the Brazilian government dedicates to the strengthening of its relations with the peoples of Africa."[74]

Many of these efforts in Afro-Asia, however, suffered greatly from a lack of continuity of interest and attention during the Goulart years. Even with Quadros, many of the gestures proved to be ill-founded, uninformed, or sterile of further results. Such ventures as the inauguration by the Brazilian Lloyd Lines of regular bimonthly sea routes to West Africa and Djakarta to stimulate trade were dropped after a few voyages because of insufficient cargo. As expressed by José Honório Rodrigues, "There was an initial impulse, a passionate interest in Africa, but an African policy, properly speaking, was never formulated."[75]

The spurt of Brazilian attention to Afro-Asia soon revealed itself to have passed with the resignation of Quadros. The Goulart government, beset by domestic instability and inflation, struck upon the issues of decolonization, development,

74. Ibid., p. 39.
75. Rodrigues, *Brasil e África: Outro horizonte*, 2: 385.

and disarmament but neglected bilateral relations with the Third World. Goulart planned an African trip which never came about because of domestic preoccupations. In 1963, Brazil, at a meeting of African finance ministers in Khartoum, offered to place $20 million worth of credit in cruzeiros in a special trust fund of the African Development Bank for the purpose of encouraigng and financing African imports of Brazilian manufactures. This proposed contribution, although it would have represented 15 percent of the bank's total capital and caused a great repercussion among those present, was not in fact forthcoming because of Brazil's own financial difficulties. Means of implementing this or a similar proposal are presently under discussion between Brazilian and African officials.

The degree of reduction in interest and efficiency which Brazil lost in its Afro-Asian policy is depicted in the frustration and discouragement of an ambassador to Ghana who had hoped for a more aggressive posture in Africa: he concluded by mid-1963 that the embassy had become a mere bureaucratic listening-post to which little importance was attached by the government, since neither Goulart nor Itamaraty gave *cobertura* (support) to the African embassies.[76] Reflecting upon his African experience while still at his post and contemplating resignation, he wrote: "I intend to emphasize that nothing much was done, within the objective of increasing our commercial relations, in spite of innumerable requests for steps which, I recognize, doubtless could not have been taken without greater studies relating to problems of exchange, payments, tariffs, and freight. It is my duty to note that our embassy was never properly equipped to function effectively. . . . I do not intend to excuse myself for the things which were left undone, even without having the proper equipment on which to rely, but I cannot help alluding to what our action in Ghana could have been, if we had actually been in a position to accomplish all that was planned."[77]

This evaluation is made all the more poignant by the fact that Accra, the site of the first Brazilian legation in Black Africa, was raised to embassy status three months after its

76. Interview with Raymundo Souza Dantas, 14 September 1968.
77. Souza Dantas, *Africa difícil*, pp. 95–96.

installation in January 1961.[78] Quadros was sympathetic toward some of Nkrumah's philosophy and Goulart and his foreign ministers regularly reiterated numerous abstractions about the Third World, of which Ghana was vociferously attempting to establish itself as spokesman. Nevertheless, Brazilian-Ghanaian relations never realized their full potential, heralded in the more enthusiastic moments of 1961, despite the existence in and around Accra of well-respected communities composed of the descendants of former Brazilian slaves, upon which cultural exchanges could have been built. The omissions and failings in Ghana in spite of seemingly propitious circumstances are symptomatic of general Brazilian weaknesses and disadvantages in dealing with Afro-Asia. Clearly not everyone in the Foreign Ministry favored the "opening to Africa." Some regarded it as an extravagant and unproductive prodigality or flirtation with governments rolling headlong toward socialism. As often observable in Brazilian political life, a lack of consensus in an atmosphere of little urgency translated itself into impressive statements of intention accompanied by inaction. Lacking the necessary *cobertura*, or personal interest and support of influentials, without which little is accomplished in Brazilian administration (especially anything novel), the Afro-Asian "new look" and whatever imaginative ideas it embraced were parched by meaningless routine. They withered on the vine.

In the judgment of military officers responsible for the revolution of 31 March 1964, the independent foreign policy was the repository of many of the ills which justified the ouster of the constitutional government. Although the pro-Western response to the Cold War condemned the "neutralism" of the "independent" years, this veiled hostility toward neutralism was generalized to such an extent that it almost precluded cordial political relations with the Third World. Brazilian action in Afro-Asia was considered to be ideally an extension of Western influence and a contribution to the fight against the spread of communism, rather than an identification of interests or full solidarity.

Foreign Minister Vasco Leitão da Cunha, in a speech opening the general debate of the United Nations General Assembly's nineteenth session (3 December 1964), described the

78. Since 1948, Brazil has maintained a legation in Pretoria.

foreign policy of the new government as conforming to certain concentric circles of solidarity, passing, in order, from Latin America to the Western Hemisphere to the Western community to universalism (including Afro-Asia).[79] Clearly, identification with Afro-Asia was the most remote and tenuous, passing through three intervening "lines of solidarity" and specified in fourth place. Significantly, Leitão da Cunha began by quoting two excerpts from an important foreign policy address given by Castello Branco to Itamaraty on 31 July 1964. In his speech the Brazilian president had explained his conceptions of interdependence and the general national interest: "The interest of Brazil coincides in many cases, in concentric circles, with that of Latin America, the American continent, and the Western Community." In this original definitive statement, Afro-Asia's place was not specified. It was inserted only later under the heading "universalism" in the United Nations speech, for which Afro-Asian delegates were present. Castello Branco's passing mention of Africa, the Middle East, and Asia in his Itamaraty speech stressed trade relations and also "fraternal cooperation and full understanding between Brazil and the peoples who recently came into liberty *and are ready to maintain it*" (emphasis added). The president thereby underlined the subtle prerequisite that these nations be on guard against the extension of Communist imperialism within their regions.[80]

In accordance with this philosophy, the revolutionary government gave full moral support to the American position in Southeast Asia. It returned to the pre–1961 full defense of Nationalist China rather than supporting discussion of the admission of Peking into the United Nations as Goulart had done. As a consequence of these anti-Communist decisions, Brazil cut off relations with Cambodia, which had been initiated at the level of legation through Brazil's embassy in New Delhi on 9 May 1961, and later carried on through the embassy in Bangkok. Although this legation had never actually been fully installed, it was abolished by Decree No. 58,633 on 15 June 1966. Itamaraty alleged Cambodian lack of reci-

---

79. Brasil, Ministério das Relações Exteriores, Departamento Cultural e de Informações, *Textos e declarações sôbre política externa (de abril de 1964 a abril de 1965)*, pp. 99–101.

80. Ibid., pp. 13–14.

procity and cited the accusation that Cambodia was permitting the use of its territory as an infiltration route for North Vietnamese and Viet Cong units entering neighboring states.[81] In June 1964 the South Vietnamese government requested Brazilian aid through the latter's Bangkok embassy. In response, the Brazilian government donated five tons of medical and pharmaceutical supplies. These were delivered in September 1966, with the promise of additional aid, including five thousand sacks of coffee, as "a demonstration of the complete sympathy and moral support of the Brazilian government for the Vietnamese government, in view of the armed aggression which that country has been suffering at the hands of Communist regimes which threaten the peace and the security of the Free World."[82] Later that year the Brazilian mission to Saigon was given a permanent headquarters in that capital under a chargé d'affaires; it had previously operated out of the Brazilian embassy in Thailand. At the same time the Vietnamese ambassador in Washington was furnished with appropriate credentials to represent Saigon in Brazil.

The impact of security preoccupations and the military viewpoint reached its height in the African policy at this time. Foreign Ministry spokesmen clearly stated that any favorable position Brazil could gain in Africa should be used to propagandize Western political and economic philosophies to help combat infiltration of Marxist ideas into the weak states. Even if faint echoes of the bridge metaphor could be heard, it was also being made unmistakably explicit that this time Brazil stood well on the Western side of the hypothetical bridge—that Brazil was interpreting Western sentiments to Africa rather than vice versa.

Political and cultural differences aside, there remained possible a degree of economic cooperation with extrahemispheric developing nations, just as the military government

81. Information gathered at the Foreign Ministry's Division of Asia. In spite of this decree, Phnom Penh was not taken from the official diplomatic list, "Lista do pessoal no exterior."
82. Brasil, Ministério das Relações Exteriores, Relatório (1966), p. 84. The plane which made this delivery was at the same time the first Brazilian Air Force plane to circumnavigate the globe on that route, so the mission represented both an anti-Communist endeavor and a prestige factor for the Air Force.

had continued and even broadened trade with Eastern Europe. The mere fact, however, that Brazil and Afro-Asia face common problems of development does not imply identical or even largely congruent interests, and certainly not to the extent that Brazil could aspire to leadership of an Afro-Asian–Latin American alliance which would take on characteristics of an international class struggle. According to a peculiar definition by the revolutionary government, Brazil, with its centers of industrialization, was not an underdeveloped country, in spite of its low national income per capita and its illiteracy rate. Castello Branco argued, "More accurate, therefore, than to classify Brazil as an underdeveloped country would be to consider it as a nation still having regional pockets of underdevelopment."[83] Optimistic as this questionable assessment might have been, those who share it would be inclined to view the nations of the Third World primarily as commercial clients rather than as political partners in promoting major changes in the economic relations between developed and developing states. This was, in fact, the official viewpoint of Castello Branco's foreign policy decision-makers.

At first, apparent omission and neglect seemed to overcome any hope for dynamism in the Afro-Asian policy and spread suspicions of a tacit quarantine of Brazil from the Third World. But favorable signs to the contrary soon became noticeable in the Foreign Ministry if not on the part of the president of the republic and his military advisers. On the occasion of the official visit to Brazil of President Léopold Senghor of Senegal, in September 1964, cultural and commercial accords were signed and Brazilian-Senegalese relations strengthened on the basis of common bonds, both Negro and Latin. Through the cultural agreement, professors, scholarship holders, musicians and artists, and athletic teams have been exchanged. For the First Festival of Negro Arts in Dakar, in April 1966, the Ministry of Foreign Relations prepared a special publication highlighting the African contribution to Brazilian culture. Brazil participated in the festival with exhibitions and judges. Brazil has maintained close relations with Senegal since the establishment of a consulate in Dakar

83. Brasil, Ministério das Relações Exteriores, Departamento Cultural e de Informações, *Textos e declarações sôbre política externa (de abril de 1964 a abril de 1965)*, p. 37.

in 1920 (Brazil's first in Black Africa in this century), by virtue of its position as a stopover point on sea, and later air, routes to Europe. Conversely, Senegal's only diplomatic representation in Latin America is seated in Rio de Janeiro.

Although a trade mission of representatives from various governmental organizations visited Indonesia, Thailand, Ceylon, and India in 1963, only during the Castello Branco administration did Brazil seem to consider seriously the feasibility of expanding its exports to Afro-Asia. In June 1966, the National Confederation of Commerce and the National Association of Exporters of Industrial Products sent a private enterprise mission to the Middle East with the inaugural flight of Varig airlines to Beirut. Later that year commercial representatives from the United Arab Republic, Lebanon, and Kuwait paid a return visit to Brazil. The first two trade-promotion missions Brazil sent to Mid-Africa were those of 1965 and 1966. The first (lasting six weeks) passed through Senegal, Liberia, Ghana, Nigeria, Cameroon, and the Ivory Coast. The second included South Africa, Angola, Mozambique, Ghana, and the Ivory Coast. Both groups were sponsored principally by the Foreign Ministry, the Bank of Brazil, and the Ministry of Industry and Commerce. The first mission was made up as well by numerous representatives from private enterprise and led by Itamaraty's Assistant to the Secretary General for Economic Affairs. Common objectives were the exploratory study of increased commercial exchange between Brazil and Africa, discussion of possible governmental measures to facilitate it, and the establishment of contacts between Brazilian and African import-export firms. The 1965 venture was the first Brazilian trade mission of mixed composition to do simultaneous market research and promotion abroad. It carried specimen commercial treaties prepared by Itamaraty to be presented to Liberia, the Ivory Coast, and Cameroon for negotiation. The second, smaller mission, accompanied by the head of the Foreign Ministry's African Division, was of a more political nature. It examined the potential effects on relations with Black Africa of greater Brazilian trade with Portuguese Africa and the Republic of South Africa and studied controversial political conditions in southern Africa.

Another important political tour was undertaken in January 1966, by the Secretary-General for Eastern European and Asian Affairs and the Chief of the Division of Asia and Oceania to all Brazilian diplomatic missions in Asia, with the exclusion of Canberra. These men gathered data and opinions to frame an Asian policy to protect Brazilian interests as affected by the Vietnamese war. One result of this study was the aforementioned creation of a Brazilian embassy in Saigon, administratively subordinate to the Bangkok embassy.

With the inauguration of the Costa e Silva government in March 1967, signs of renewed interest in Afro-Asia multipled apace. New diplomatic and consular posts were created, with the intent of completing representation throughout Africa, including an honorary consulate installed in Abidjan in June 1966 and another in Monrovia in September 1967. In late 1967, embassies were placed in Addis Ababa and Nairobi, the first in East Africa. This move was apparently motivated by the Brazilian government's desire to monitor more closely the activities of the OAU and the United Nations' Economic Commission for Africa, to sound out opportunities for new markets, and to establish constant contact with Africa's principal coffee-exporting states. At the same time the Foreign Ministry's Divisions of Africa and the Middle East were separated from the Western European Bureau and taken to form a Bureau of African and Middle Eastern Affairs (Secretaria Geral Adjunta para a África e Oriente Médio). In October 1968, the president of the governmental Brazilian Coffee Institute headed a mission to Tanzania, Ethiopia, Kenya, and Uganda to convince East African producers and officials that expansion of world consumption and unity of producers constituted the most effective attack on the problem of coffee overproduction. Other indications of attention to Africa during 1968 included an official visit by the secretary-general of Senegal's Foreign Ministry; an exposition of Ghanaian art ("Aspects of the Culture of Ghana"), which toured major cities; the arrival of a high-level economic mission from Ghana for a two-week program; negotiations with the Democratic Republic of the Congo (now Zaire) at their request in order to initiate diplomatic relations at the ambassadorial level (eventually begun in May 1972); and the establishment of relations with the Sudan at an ambassadorial level via Brazil's Cairo embassy.

Commercial transactions with the Middle East gained tempo with the 1968 arrival of trade missions from Morocco and Algeria. The visit of Habib Bourguiba, foreign minister of Tunisia, resulted in the signing of a cultural treaty and an agreement waiving the necessity for visas on diplomatic and special passports. This was a preliminary step to the exchange of technicians and scientists, professors, artists, and athletes.

Asia was an area of high priority in the "Diplomacy of Prosperity," as evinced by Magalhães Pinto's visits to India, Pakistan, and Japan. He made these visits after attending the Second UNCTAD in New Delhi in February 1968, at which he had signed a cultural treaty with Pakistan and a commercial accord with India and had inaugurated the first meeting of the Brazilian-Japanese Mixed Economic Commission, created the previous year to oversee the expansion of trade and Japanese investment in Brazil. After election as president, Costa e Silva had also taken a trip to set in operation his new Asian policy by observing at first hand and making personal acquaintances with government officials in several countries. Trade missions from Pakistan, South Korea, and Japan, together with visits from Indira Gandhi, the prime minister of Thailand, Ceylon's minister of justice, and the vice-president of the Philippines, indicated an unprecedented degree of attention turned toward Asia. These missions were complemented by cultural treaties with Thailand and India and arrangements to locate a Brazilian embassy in Manila and a South Vietnamese embassy in Rio de Janeiro to allow more direct contact with those states and to round out Brazil's global network of representation.

If the 1961–1964 Afro-Asian policy was based on weak sentimental-cultural ties and ideological-political objectives, and the 1964–1965 biennium was characterized in the main by ostensible indifference or omission, the policy from 1966 to the present has a realistic, pragmatic, medium- and long-range set of objectives. The latest regimes have worked out their objectives as a function of their total economic development policies, without losing sight of limitations on interests, priorities, and capabilities in Afro-Asia. The first goal of this new Afro-Asian phase is for Brazil to win new markets, diversify exports, and expand the value of industrial sales abroad, as an adjunct to similar projects for Latin America and the North Atlantic area. It is hoped that Brazil can sell considerable quantities of manufactured goods in Afro-Asia, especially in Africa and Japan. The Foreign Ministry is promoting trade with these regions through published materials and studies for businessmen who want to capitalize on the export boom. The Bank of Brazil, largest commercial bank in the Southern Hemisphere, is considering the establishment of several new branches in Afro-Asia, as well as in the more traditional sites of international finance. The banking group Ipiranga has formed a trading company called Ipitrade to finance and encourage trade with Africa. Other such Afro-Asian ventures are expected under financial incentives offered by the Médici government. The year 1972 was picked for a decisive campaign to win a share of the African market for Brazilian manufacturers, utilizing trade missions and an official tour by Foreign Minister Gibson Barbosa and a high-ranking commercial retinue to West Africa and Zaire to propose facilities, finances, and technical aid. The government expects Afro-Asian acceptance of its campaign.

The second facet of Brazil's current diplomacy toward Afro-Asia is its promotion of unity among developing nations (under Brazilian leadership, when possible), for example, in negotiating within UNCTAD for concessions regarding terms of international trade and aid. President Médici has spoken even more clearly than Costa e Silva about the meaning of underdevelopment in relations between underdeveloped nations. It leads, according to Médici, to "active solidarity": "An ever larger share of the decision-making in the international community has befallen us, and we shall not fail to use it in favor of the peoples which, like ours, aspire to progress, to the full utilization of their resources, to access to the conquests of science and technology, to peaceful development, to the eradication of misery. A true peace demands the transformation of international structures. It cannot be the instrument of the maintenance and, much less, the broadening of the distance which presently separates rich nations from poor nations. The changing of the rules of international commerce is for that reason indispensible, for they have for a long time favored the developed countries and so affected the alteration of the mechanism of global distribution of scientific and technological progress. We cannot agree that the great scientific and technological revolution of our time should be made almost to the exclusive benefit of the most developed countries, as happened with the industrial revolution in the nineteenth century."[84]

Although this recent approach to Afro-Asia has no ideological or Third World overtones, its aggressiveness promises greater and more intense relations than achieved during the Quadros and Goulart years, when abundant verbiage about the so-called *política afro-asiática* produced rather little in either bilateral relations or international organizations. Brazil has now accepted the desirability of more vigorous diplomacy in Afro-Asia, having established a diplomatic and, to a lesser extent, a commercial network. It is now, under Médici, moving in the direction of an informed policy suitable to each case rather than predicated on either preconceived ideological abstractions or reflex actions traceable to policies pursued toward traditional allies.

84. "Discurso do Presidente da República."

4. Dimensions of Brazilian Relations with Afro-Asia

RECENT EFFORTS to concretize the notion of an international system have yielded increasingly sophisticated attempts to manipulate statistical data concerning the relations among nations in order to arrive at quantitative measures. Such measures can be employed to define either the characteristics of the international system or bilateral relations between a given pair of states. They can reveal regularities in what may otherwise seem only a bewildering perplexity of nearly simultaneous transactions of varying intensity.[1] The most comprehensive statistical investigation is the Dimensionality of Nations project (DON). Since its inception in 1962, it has tackled both cross-national classification of all nations (on the basis of 236 internal variables) and definition of the dimensions of interaction among nations, each for specified time periods.[2] When the massive data

---

1. See the statistical pattern-searching technique described and employed by Steven J. Brams in his "Flow and Form in the International System," and Brams, "Transaction Flows in the International System," pp. 880–98.

2. For background information on DON, see Rudolph J. Rummel, "The Dimensionality of Nations Project," pp. 109–29.

collection on these two phases of the project is complete, correlations between national attributes and international behavior will be run to discover any statistically significant relationships.

A major contribution of DON has been to identify and specify some measurements for the major dimensions of the dyadic behavior of nations, i.e., the behavior exhibited by two states as one acts in relationship to another, as in the dyad (Brazil→India). According to a summary of preliminary DON findings,

> The behavior of a nation towards another varies along eight major dimensions:
> salience—low to high salience involving treaties, translations of its literature, tourists, nonintergovernmental international organizations, etc.
> emigration and communication—low to high
> UN voting—none to high similarity in UN voting
> exports—none to relatively many
> foreign students—none to relatively many
> international organizations—few to many co-memberships
> official conflict behavior—none to much
> diplomatic representation—none to relatively high representation.[3]

Despite the scarcity of statistics on such transactions in Brazil, the application of some of these indicators to the analysis of Brazilian–Afro-Asian transaction flows can yield additional information pertinent to full examination of the development of relations. Available data lends itself to the measurement of four dimensions of Brazil's transactions with Afro-Asia: diplomatic representation, salience, emigration and communications, and exports.[4] By measuring the rela-

---

3. Rummel, "Some Empirical Findings on Nations and Their Behavior," p. 235.
4. No official figures exist concerning foreign students in Brazil. Ascertaining what percentage of Brazilian students abroad are in Afro-Asia would be a monumental task. Official conflict behavior toward Afro-Asia, as measured by either violence or negative communications, is negligible. Intergovernmental organization co-memberships, on which data are readily available, have been omitted, because each nation places differing emphasis on each membership it possesses

tions along these dimensions, we can ascertain Afro-Asia's relative position in Brazil's range of foreign relations at a given time. We can also determine patterns and regularities or change through time as congruent with or independent of Brazil's change of government. Thus we can get a rough measure of what could be termed Brazil's "level of attention" to Africa, the Middle East, and Asia, as indicated by variables shown to be most significant in describing dyadic relationships.[5]

Given the relatively low level of relations between Brazil and many Afro-Asian states, a variant regional approach, rather than a dyadic-type matrix, is employed. Seven world regions are delineated, largely on a geographical basis and perhaps somewhat arbitrarily: the United States (USA), other Western Hemisphere (OWH), Western Europe (WE), Eastern Europe (EE), sub-Saharan Africa (Africa), Asia and Oceania (Asia), and the Middle East and North Africa (ME).[6] I present and analyze the data on a regional level. Then, in order to place Afro-Asia in the context of the totality of Brazil's transactions on each particular indicator, I isolate the

---

according to the value it ascribes to that particular organization; i.e., not all nations in an organization are equally active and influential. Additionally, such shared membership figures would only represent channels for potential interaction. They would not accurately indicate an actual level of communications and influence exchange. It is known, however, that organizational ties "provide most nations with far greater access to the outside world than do diplomatic ties," as shown by Chadwick F. Alger and Brams in "Patterns of Representation in National Capitals and Intergovernmental Organizations," p. 662. An extensive comparison of United Nations voting records is not given here, but international issues central to Brazilian–Afro-Asian relations are analyzed in Chapters 5 and 6 with reference to the positions Brazil has held in United Nations debates and to its voting pattern.

5. A similar quantitative method is used to augment and interpret conventional historical data in Bruce M. Russett, *Community and Contention: Britain and America in the Twentieth Century*, although without the benefit of DON-identified variables and with a wider range of indicators.

6. The inclusion of the United States as a "region" is justified primarily because that nation plays such a disproportionately large role in these measures and certainly should not be grouped with Latin America. The inclusion of Japan, Australia, New Zealand, South Africa, and Israel in their respective geographic zones may be criticized from cultural, political, or economic points of view, but this classification follows the Foreign Ministry's administrative division of labor.

Afro-Asian nation scoring highest and explore significant patterns in the international relationships. In the final portion of this chapter, I investigate Brazil's relations with some of the most salient states.

Diplomatic and Consular Representation

If it is conceptualized that the diplomatic corps and staff of a state represent, in normal daily activity, the principal channels or units which the nation has at its disposal to communicate politically with the outside world, and if it is further recognized that for most nations the size of its diplomatic corps is restricted by economic or foreign policy considerations, it follows that each nation will tend to deploy its diplomats most heavily to capitals of highest priority in its foreign relations (i.e., those with the greatest workload) and then to capitals of lesser importance to its purposes, in descending order of priority. By comparing the diplomatic staff allocations which state A makes to state B, or to a region, with the total number of diplomats allocated worldwide, we obtain one measure of the relative political importance attributed by state A to state B or to any region in question.

Examination of the pattern of representation by region over time, shown in Table 4, reveals the gradualness with which changes in emphasis have come. Marked stability of relative position was most fixed from 1956 to 1958 and even into 1959. The most noticeable gross trends have been a decline in the percentage of Brazilian personnel in the United States and Western Europe, a constant level in Latin America, and an increase in the percentage stationed in Eastern Europe and Afro-Asia. The last is a consequence of the diversification of relations begun in 1959. All increases and decreases, however, are fluctuating rather than linear. Regarding the actual effects of Brazil's independent foreign policy on representation in Afro-Asia, although new embassies and legations were created and personnel sent, the percentage of individuals allocated to Asia, in reality, declined steadily between 1960 and 1964. The Middle East showed a slight relative gain of 2.0 percent and Africa increased only 1.8 percent in relative position, a modest amount in the latter, considering the few diplomats (3) in that region in 1960. For these three regions in 1956, we find a total allocation of 12.3 percent of all personnel in embassies and legations abroad; the corresponding figure for 1964 is only 13.9 percent, not a very impressive relative increase in bilateral diplomatic relations when juxtaposed with the enthusiastic statements of intention about Afro-Asia issuing from certain official sources during the 1961–1964 span. In the general expansion of Brazilian diplomatic representation from 1959 to 1964, it is not stretching the point too far to assert that Afro-Asian capitals were little

TABLE 4. Distribution of Brazilian Diplomatic Personnel in Embassies and Legations Abroad, by Region, 1956–68

Year	Total personnel	USA	OWH	WE	EE	Africa	Asia	ME	Total
1956	408	10.3	32.8	42.1	2.5	0.5	5.9	5.9	100.0
1957	426	11.0	32.9	42.0	2.6	0.5	6.3	4.7	100.0
1958	453	10.6	31.6	43.0	1.7	0.7	6.4	6.0	100.0
1959	492	10.0	34.3	39.6	2.9	0.6	7.3	5.3	100.0
1960	529	10.0	35.5	38.9	2.8	0.6	7.8	4.4	100.0
1961	510	8.0	31.0	42.8	3.3	1.4	7.6	5.9	100.0
1962	533	10.9	28.9	37.5	5.6	1.9	6.9	8.3	100.0
1963	758	12.7	29.3	38.8	5.9	2.0	5.4	5.9	100.0
1964	924	13.0	29.2	37.4	6.5	2.4	5.1	6.4	100.0
1965	802	10.6	28.4	36.9	7.4	2.6	6.9	7.2	100.0
1966	834	7.8	31.0	35.4	8.9	2.3	7.4	7.2	100.0
1967	920	6.9	31.8	33.8	9.2	2.2	7.8	8.3	100.0
1968	982	6.7	31.1	34.0	8.9	3.1	7.7	8.5	100.0

SOURCES: Compiled from the following mimeographed series lists: Brasil, Ministério das Relações Exteriores, "Lista do pessoal" (1956–1961); and Brasil, Ministério das Relações Exteriores, "Lista do pessoal no exterior" (1962–1968). Figures for each year are taken as close to mid-year as possible, given the intermittent publication of the "*Listas,*" and include personnel employed as non-professional assistants, as well as Brazilian diplomats. Consular personnel are excluded, as are honorary and in absentia representatives.

more than able to hold their relative positions either considered as a group or as individual regions, despite the fact that more personnel were deployed there as new posts were opened.

The situation after the 1964 revolution now appears in a slightly different perspective. Curiously, contrary to governmental statements idealizing the Western world and in spite of a slight decrease in personnel abroad, the figures for 1965 and 1966, when compared with those for 1964 or even 1963, demonstrate small but definite general decreases in the proportion stationed in the United States and Western Europe and general increases in Eastern Europe and Afro-Asia. Under the revolutionary government, the percentages allocated to the United States and Western Europe in 1966 marked the lowest points from 1956 to 1966. Those to Eastern Europe and Afro-Asia attained figures higher than or nearly as high as those observed at any other time during the same decade. The years of 1967 and 1968 illustrate the political results of the diplomacy of prosperity—again with slow declines evident in the United States and Western Europe, and slight gains for the other five regions. By 1968, diplomatic personnel in Afro-Asia constituted 19.3 percent of all those abroad (almost one-fifth) and embodied a considerable increase from the 13.9 percent figure of 1964. The allocated percentage for Afro-Asia grew much more rapidly between 1964 and 1968 than during the *política externa independente*.

Within Afro-Asia, rather high concentrations of personnel in prominent capitals has been the rule, with lesser states receiving meager or token (cumulative) representation. In August 1968, for example, the Tokyo embassy employed one-quarter of all Brazilian diplomatic personnel in Asia, while Bangkok accounted for one-eighth and Taipei, New Delhi, and Seoul each constituted about one-tenth of the total. In the Middle East, representation is somewhat more dispersed and even: Beirut leads with 17 percent, followed by Cairo (16), Tel-Aviv (13), Damascus (12), and Ankara (10). In both regions, five embassies employ over two-thirds of the Brazilian diplomatic personnel. A diplomatic representation of only 30 persons (including assistants) was found in sub-Saharan Africa, a decided increase over previous years but still less than the staff maintained at such well-established embassies as London (45), Montevideo (42), Paris (38), Buenos Aires (38), Bonn (31), and only 1 more than the staff in Lisbon. The African embassies and the Pretoria legation each had 5 or 6 on staff, except Addis Ababa with 3.[7] Because of this paucity of representation (only 11 diplomats, if assistants are excluded), many of Brazil's important political contacts with Africa have been effected through the United Nations. Although the world organization will continue to be

7. All figures in this paragraph were taken from Brasil, Ministério das Relações Exteriores, *"Lista do pessoal no exterior"* (August 1968).

the site of much communication of this nature, Costa e Silva's diplomatic expansion program was designed to allow more direct, bilateral ties with a greater part of the Afro-Asian bloc.

Consular posts are established in a country as the transaction volume increases and justifies the addition of specialized nondiplomatic staff. Since the transaction level between Brazil and Afro-Asia is a rather small fraction of Brazil's worldwide transactions, few consulates have been

TABLE 5. Distribution of Brazilian Consular Personnel in Consulates and Consulates-General Abroad, by Region, 1956–68

Year	Total personnel	USA	OWH	WE	EE	Africa	Asia	ME	Total
1956	385	21.8	18.7	52.5	0.0	1.3	2.8	2.9	100.0
1957	379	20.6	19.3	53.0	0.0	1.3	3.2	2.6	100.0
1958	403	19.4	19.6	52.4	0.0	1.0	3.9	3.7	100.0
1959	405	19.7	20.0	51.1	0.0	1.2	3.8	4.2	100.0
1960	423	19.4	19.1	50.8	0.5	1.2	4.5	4.5	100.0
1961	439	19.1	19.6	50.3	0.7	1.8	4.6	3.9	100.0
1962	419	21.7	19.3	49.3	0.5	3.1	4.1	2.0	100.0
1963	408	20.3	17.4	52.2	0.7	3.2	4.0	2.2	100.0
1964	440	19.5	18.6	52.3	0.9	3.2	3.9	1.6	100.0
1965	450	19.8	20.9	50.0	1.1	3.1	3.8	1.3	100.0
1966	501	21.9	22.5	47.0	1.0	2.8	3.2	1.6	100.0
1967	509	22.8	21.0	47.9	1.0	2.6	4.1	0.6	100.0
1968	539	24.7	22.6	43.0	0.9	2.8	5.8	0.2	100.0

SOURCE: Compiled from the following mimeographed series lists: Brasil, Ministério das Relações Exteriores, "Lista do pessoal" (1956–1961); and Brasil, Ministério das Relações Exteriores, "Lista do pessoal no exterior" (1962–1968). Figures for each year are taken as close to mid-year as possible, given the intermittent publication of the "Listas," and include nonprofessional support personnel employed, as well as Brazilian consular officials. Diplomatic personnel are excluded.

established in these areas. Diplomatic intercourse has been the predominant form of relations, with the exceptions of several states which support trade flows with Brazil. Examination of the consular network through time (Table 5) reveals generally lower proportions of personnel in Afro-Asia than does the diplomatic chart (with some exceptions in Africa), partly because in countries of little consular traffic, consular functions are taken over by the embassy. This, for example, is the cause for the Middle East's low percentage in 1967 and 1968.

By consolidating the diplomatic and consular data (Table 6), we obtain a more complete measure of the percentage enjoyed by Afro-Asia of the Foreign Ministry's personnel resources allocated abroad from 1956 to 1968. We also thus circumvent to some degree the problem of consolidation of diplomatic and consular functions. This combined set of statistics shows that, as gauged by the Foreign Ministry's choices

TABLE 6. Brazilian Diplomatic and Consular Personnel Allocated to Africa, Asia, and the Middle East, 1956–68

Year	Total personnel	Percentage of all personnel abroad			
		Africa	Asia	ME	Total
1956	77	0.9	4.4	4.4	9.7
1957	76	0.9	4.8	3.7	9.4
1958	94	0.8	4.8	5.0	10.6
1959	102	0.9	5.7	4.8	11.4
1960	110	0.8	6.3	4.4	11.5
1961	121	1.6	6.2	5.0	12.8
1962	129	2.4	5.7	5.5	13.6
1963	139	2.4	4.9	4.6	11.9
1964	166	2.6	4.7	4.8	12.1
1965	171	2.8	5.7	5.1	13.6
1966	179	2.5	5.8	5.1	13.4
1967	205	2.3	6.5	5.5	14.3
1968	237	3.0	7.0	5.5	15.5

SOURCE: Compiled from the following mimeographed series lists: Brasil, Ministério das Relações Exteriores, "Lista do pessoal" (1956–1961); and Brasil, Ministério das Relações Exteriores, "Lista do pessoal no exterior." Figures for each year are taken as close to mid-year as possible, given the intermittent publication of the "Listas," and include nonprofessional support personnel employed, as well as Brazilian diplomatic and consular officials.

of deployment of the personnel under its control, Brazil's channels of communication to Afro-Asia were wider in 1967 and 1968 than at any previous time during the period under study. Between 1966 and 1968, the number of representatives present in Afro-Asia increased 32.4 percent. The much-vaunted opening to Afro-Asia yielded an increase of only 17.3 percent between 1960 and 1962, with only 19 more individuals present in Afro-Asia in 1962 than in 1960. These findings, however, unfortunately do not allow further inferences about either the volume or the content of political transactions flowing through the institutional provisions which were enlarged after 1966. It is interesting nonetheless that in August 1968, 45.1 percent of Brazil's representation in Afro-Asia was located in Asia and Oceania, 35.5 percent in the Middle East, and 19.4 percent in Africa. In the same month, 30.8 percent of the Asian personnel were found in Japan, and 44.5 percent of those in sub-Saharan Africa were in either South Africa or Portuguese Africa. The latter fact has been noted by Africans engaged in eliminating colonialism and racial discrimination from the continent and suspicious of Brazil's defense of Portugal and its "wait and see" attitude toward South Africa.[8] If all personnel in South Africa, Portuguese Africa, Israel, Japan, and Australia are subtracted from the statistics for geographically defined Afro-Asia, the percentage of all personnel worldwide which was present in 1968 in the "Third World" or "developing Afro-Asia" was a mere 10.6 percent. It was scattered among 22 embassies, 10 cumulative embassies and legations, 1 consulate-general, and 2 consulates (not including some honorary consulates), the latter two existing in name only and without staff.[9]

Some conception of the other side of the relationship can be gained from the nature of Afro-Asian representation in Brazil. In mid-1968, Afro-Asian states counted 140 diplomatic and consular representatives in Brazil, including 12 honorary consuls. Of this number, 59.2 percent were accredited from Asia, 28.6 percent from the Middle East, and 12.2 percent from Africa. Japan had the most numerous representation, making up 29.3 percent of all Afro-Asian representatives and 49.5 percent of those from Asia. Japan has an important consular network extending throughout Brazil.

The typical Afro-Asian state (Japan excepted) having representation in Brazil supports an embassy in Rio de Janeiro with a staff of 4 diplomatic or consular personnel and headed by an ambassador also accredited to other South American states. Thus, for smaller Afro-Asian states, the Rio de Janeiro

---

8. Incidentally, the total of Brazilian diplomatic and consular personnel in Portugal was 2.3 times that of all in Black Africa, excluding South Africa and the Portuguese colonies, a fact which indicates the much greater saliency of Portugal and is quite significant in the consideration of Brazilian policy toward questions affecting Portuguese Africa.

9. Figures calculated from Brasil, Ministério das Relações Exteriores, "Lista do pessoal no exterior" (August 1968).

embassy serves as a "listening post" for Latin America. In several cases it is the first embassy established on Latin American soil. Five states (Lebanon, Syria, Israel, South Africa, and Nationalist China) make use of honorary consulates to extend their representation. Only one state, South Africa, maintains relations at the level of legation; in turn, Pretoria is the site of Brazil's only legation in Afro-Asia. Embassies with larger than average diplomatic staffs (5 or more) are those of Nigeria, the United Arab Republic, Japan, Nationalist China, South Korea, the Philippines, and India. Compared with the total number of diplomatic officials Brazil received in Rio de Janeiro and Brasília, diplomatic officials from Afro-Asia's developing areas numbered only 58, merely 8.8 percent of the total, fewer than those representing the United States in Rio de Janeiro and Brasília, although these Afro-Asian missions compose 27 percent of all foreign missions physically present.[10]

Salience

Transactions which the DON project has identified as indicators on the salience dimension include official decorations, treaties, and tourist travel, all measuring the degree of prominence of one country in the relations of another. Brazil, like many nations of Latin culture, extensively uses the awarding of medals to distinguished foreign citizens as a means of generating diffuse good will and recognizing individual contributions to international understanding; its ulterior motive is to strengthen relations between Brazil and the recipient's homeland. An analysis of patterns emerging from this conscious, intentional bestowing of awards, with attention to the geographical areas favored, shows to what extent awards have been employed as foreign policy instruments in Afro-Asia, as compared with the other four regions.

The National Order of the Southern Cross, with various degrees or ranks, is the highest decoration with which Brazil honors a foreigner. Between 1 January 1956 and 31 December 1967, approximately 2,600 of these awards were bestowed (see

10. Statistics calculated from Brasil, Ministério das Relações Exteriores, *Lista Diplomática, Julho de 1968*; and Brasil, Ministério das Relações Exteriores, Departamento Consular e de Imigração, Divisão Consular, *Lista, Corpo consular estrangeiro, junho de 1968*.

Table 7). The majority of these were received by citizens of other Latin nations, either in the Western Hemisphere or Western Europe, with West Germany, Great Britain, and the United States also figuring high. In the twelve years shown, Afro-Asia ranked low in its percentage of all awards granted, with a total of 10.4 percent. The seven highest-ranking Afro-Asian states combined accepted 74.2 percent—Japan (35),

TABLE 7. Conferrals of the Ordem Nacional do Cruzeiro do Sul, by Region, 1956–67

Year	Total conferrals	\multicolumn{7}{c}{Percentage distribution by region}
		USA	OWH	WE	EE	Africa	Asia	ME	Total
1956	194	8.2	41.2	44.9	0.0	0.5	2.6	2.6	100.0
1957	210	9.1	18.1	61.9	1.0	0.0	3.3	6.6	100.0
1958	401	6.2	33.4	52.4	0.0	2.0	3.5	2.5	100.0
1959	208	6.3	27.9	53.4	0.0	0.0	11.0	1.4	100.0
1960	238	10.1	31.1	53.4	0.8	0.0	2.9	1.7	100.0
1961	167	1.8	48.0	19.7	10.7	7.2	9.6	3.0	100.0
1962	254	4.3	14.6	76.8	1.2	2.3	0.4	0.4	100.0
1963	233	6.0	30.0	31.3	20.6	0.0	5.6	6.5	100.0
1964	172	8.1	27.3	48.3	3.5	2.9	5.8	4.1	100.0
1965	136	4.4	22.1	57.4	0.0	0.7	2.9	12.5	100.0
1966	199	11.6	35.2	47.2	0.0	0.5	4.0	1.5	100.0
1967	182	3.3	23.1	49.5	0.5	1.1	19.8	2.7	100.0

SOURCE: Compiled from Brasil, Ministério das Relações Exteriores, Ceremonial, "Lista dos agraciados com a Ordem Nacional do Cruzeiro do Sul, atualizado até dezembro de 1967." The compilation includes only those surviving, to the knowledge of the Foreign Ministry, on 31 December 1967. An advance in rank (second award to same individual) is regarded as a separate award in this table.

Lebanon (9), Iran (7.4), Israel (6), United Arab Republic (5.6), Indonesia (5.6), and Ethiopia (5.6). Remaining states whose citizens have received the Cruzeiro do Sul are Syria, Morocco, Turkey, Senegal, Ghana, Nigeria, Sierra Leone, Tanzania, South Korea, Thailand, Pakistan, and India. Most of these conferrals were made to government officials, often as a result of official visits. Half of all the awards granted to Africans were given in 1961 and 1962, presumably as part of the "opening to Africa" program. Similarly, the high number of medals given to Asians in 1967 (36, or 25 percent of all awards received by Asians between 1956 and 1967) could be a consequence of Itamaraty's new interest in that continent, an effort to improve Brazil's image across official channels.

Although treaties are essentially institutionalized agreements through which a greater or lesser flow of transactions may be achieved, and to which much or little attention may be paid, the recognition that they do serve as formal channels for strengthening relations leads to the conclusion that the signing of an agreement with a specific foreign country represents a deliberate decision to broaden or consolidate formal

TABLE 8. Bilateral Agreements Concluded by Brazil since 1 January 1950 and in Effect on 1 June 1968, by Region

Region	Number of Agreements	Percent of Total
USA	48	15.3
OWH	92	29.3
WE	119	37.7
EE	27	8.6
Africa	3	0.9
Asia	13	4.1
ME	13	4.1
Total	315	100.0

SOURCE: The official treaty list: Brasil, Ministério das Relações Exteriores, Divisão de Atos Internacionais, "Relação dos acôrdos em vigor, por países." Included in the compilation are *tratados, acôrdos, protocolos, convenções, convênios, ajustes, notas reversais*, and *trocas de notas*.

ties with that country within the field of activity specified by the document. Since this element of independent choice is present, despite differences in economic and political import between a treaty with, for example, Senegal and one with a major power, bilateral treaties serve as one indicator of saliency. Apart from problems introduced by differences in volume of transaction flows in trade, aid, etc., measured elsewhere in this chapter, the more treaties state A has with state B, the more salient B is to A.

As evident in Table 8, only 9.1 percent of all the bilateral agreements to which Brazil was a signatory concluded since 1 January 1950 and in effect on 1 June 1968 were signed with Afro-Asian states. If we deduct the 10 treaties with Japan and the 7 with Israel from the totals for Asia and the Middle East, respectively, only 12 treaties or 3.8 percent of all concluded remain as the total for developing Afro-Asia.[11] This low incidence attests to the lack of substantial volume in Brazilian dealings with developing Afro-Asia, and reflects the existence of insufficient intercourse to require regulation by mutual consent.

Most of the extant agreements are commercial and cultural, with Cameroon, Senegal, the United Arab Republic, Lebanon, Turkey, Iran, Nationalist China, and Korea. Until the present, cultural agreements were those most commonly completed with Afro-Asian nations, but more tangible commercial agreements are now ultimately sought by the Foreign Ministry to further trade relations. Between 1941 and the end of 1965, Brazil signed 34 cultural accords. Seven of these were with Afro-Asian states, a share of over one-fifth, which is considerably greater than the 9.1 percent participation by Afro-Asia in agreements of all sorts from 1950 to 1968.[12] All of the numerous treaties signed with Afro-Asian states since 1968 share the objective of providing ready institutional support for the greater activity in Afro-Asia anticipated with the growth of Brazilian representation and trade promotion there.

Although determined primarily by factors other than the state of political relations between governments (given at least a satisfactory state of amicability), the number of tourists from state A which visit state B has been demonstrated by DON to be the most reliable indicator of the salience of B to A. Statistics on the number of Brazilian tourists visiting foreign nations have not yet been collected, but Embratur (a government-sponsored autonomous agency promoting tourism) has taken a provisional survey of the number and nationalities of foreign tourists entering Brazil at border checkpoints between 1962 and 1966. These statistics, shown in Table 9, include all foreigners entering on a "tourist" visa.

11. Ten agreements now in effect were concluded before 1950, with Afghanistan, Nationalist China, Iran, Lebanon, Liberia, South Africa, Turkey, and Japan. The year 1950 was chosen as a cut-off date because it coincided roughly with the granting of independence to colonial peoples which began following World War II. Had the calculation been based upon the totality of Brazil's agreements now in effect (some dating from the early days of the First Republic), Afro-Asia's share would have been considerably reduced.

12. Brasil, Ministério das Relações Exteriores, *Acôrdos culturais, Atualizado até dezembro de 1965.*

They exclude diplomatic personnel, businessmen, official delegations, and students. As would be expected, nearly all of the tourist flow originates in the United States, Western Europe, and Latin America, the first two being developed regions which contribute disproportionately to world tourist traffic, and the latter ranking high because of its geographical proximity. Afro-Asia is the origin of only 2.0 percent to 4.3 percent

TABLE 9. Foreign Tourists Entering Brazil, by Region of Nationality, 1962–66

Year	Total tourists	USA	OWH	WE	EE	Africa	Asia	ME	Total
1962	98,371	15.3	65.9	16.5	0.3	0.2	0.8	1.0	100.0
1963	104,809	15.4	64.9	17.0	0.5	0.1	1.0	1.1	100.0
1964	125,118	24.6	49.3	23.5	0.3	0.2	0.8	1.3	100.0
1965	102,919	23.8	48.5	24.9	0.4	0.2	1.2	1.0	100.0
1966	133,336	22.9	44.5	27.6	0.6	0.3	2.1	2.0	100.0

SOURCE: Emprêsa Brasileira de Turismo, "Dados estatísticos." According to an Embratur estimate, the statistics account for at least 95 percent of the actual total of foreign tourists entering Brazil by air, sea, or land.

of all foreign tourists, not surprisingly, because the relatively few travelers from those continents would most probably frequent the metropolitan centers. Thus the maximum inflow of tourists from each of these areas to Brazil is also quite small in absolute terms; in 1966, when Afro-Asian tourists reached a high of 4.4 percent, the following numbers were registered: Africa, 399; Asia, 2,838; and the Middle East, 2,665. All of Afro-Asia taken together averaged approximately 3,100 tourists annually for the period, which is one-tenth the number which arrived from the United States in 1966.

Besides making clear the low salience which Brazil has for Afro-Asian countries, the statistics show a high degree of concentration of national origin among African and Asian tourists, with the Middle Eastern travelers slightly more evenly distributed. From 1962 to 1966, between 97.6 and 100 percent of the African visitors came from the Republic of South Africa. The national distributions for Asia and the Mideast are given in Table 10.

Japan supplied an average of nearly two-thirds of all Asian tourists, in keeping with the size and importance of the

Japanese colony in and around São Paulo. Japan's income level, which allows more Japanese citizens the opportunity to travel abroad than citizens of most Asian nations, also contributes. Australia and Japan combined have consistently furnished between 70 and 80 percent of all Asian tourists visiting Brazil, or 77.5 percent of the five-year Asian total. The volume of tourists from other Asian countries in

TABLE 10. National Origin of Asian and Middle Eastern Tourists Entering Brazil, 1962–1966

Country	Yearly Percentage of Regional Contribution				
	1962	1963	1964	1965	1966
Asia					
Japan	61.4	68.7	55.9	56.5	69.7
Australia	11.3	11.5	19.0	17.3	10.1
Nationalist China	8.2	7.2	5.1	14.2	7.5
Philippines	13.2	3.4	5.4	5.6	3.4
India	1.8	3.7	6.9	4.1	3.6
Total	95.9	94.5	92.3	97.7	94.3
Middle East					
Israel	39.5	39.7	39.6	41.2	34.7
Lebanon	36.0	32.7	22.4	23.0	37.3
Jordan	1.6	3.6	5.0	7.4	10.5
Iran	4.6	4.0	17.6	4.1	4.2
Turkey	5.5	5.4	7.4	8.3	4.2
Syria	7.4	10.4	6.1	0.5	2.7
Total	94.6	95.8	98.1	84.5	93.6

SOURCE: Emprêsa Brasileira de Turismo, "Dados estatísticos."

the entire period was quite reduced; Nationalist China (580), the Philippines (358), and India (272) were the only ones with totals over 100. Similarly, Israel and Lebanon stood out distinctly as the Middle Eastern states which contributed most heavily, together averaging 70 percent yearly. Nevertheless, more Middle Eastern than Asian states had over 100 tourists for the period 1962–1966: Iran (536), Jordan (495), Turkey (436), Syria (369), Saudi Arabia (261), and the United Arab Republic (138).

Emigration and Communications

The most accurate indicator for the communications dimension is emigrants A→B/A's population, but complete statistics on emigration from Brazil to Afro-Asia are practically unobtainable and, if located, would surely be so diminutive as to be devoid of significance. On the other hand, Afro-Asians have immigrated into Brazil in the thirteen years under study. According to official immigration data, of the total immigration of 276,874 which occurred between 1956 and 1961, 20.2 percent came from Afro-Asia. Of this latter group of a little over 56,000, 70 percent was Japanese, 9.8 percent Lebanese, 5.8 percent Israelis, and 4.9 percent Chinese. The remaining 9.5 percent was scattered among 23 nations, with most coming from the Middle East (the United Arab Republic, Syria, Iran, Morocco, and Turkey). The African nation with the most immigrants in the above period was the Republic of South Africa, with 111. Only 11 other immigrants from Black Africa were registered—from Sudan and Ethiopia.[13]

Clearly, the most highly ranked nations on the communications dimension, using the immigration indicator, are Japan, Lebanon, and Israel. The Japanese community has already been described, but it is necessary as well to note that the sizable numbers of Mideastern immigrants have formed important, organized Jewish and Arab communities in large Brazilian cities.[14] In all three cases there appears to be a significant positive relationship between immigration on one hand and intensified general relations on the other, including salience, diplomatic relations, and exports. Combined, Japan, Israel, and Lebanon accounted for 85.6 percent of all Afro-Asian immigrants, 1956 to 1961, 61.7 percent of all Afro-Asian tourists received, 1962 to 1966, and 50 percent of all Cruzeiro do Sul awards to Afro-Asian citizens from 1956 to 1967. As seen below, they also account for a high percentage of the total communications flow to Afro-Asia.

A second emigration and communications indicator, statistics on international telephone and telegraph traffic, also serves to measure the extent and nature of communication

13. Brasil, Instituto Nacional de Imigração e Colonização, Departamento de Estudos e Planejamento, Divisão de Estatística, "Informações estatísticas—Imigração."
14. Since 1961, the Japanese influx has dwindled considerably, but Brazil still keeps an Immigrant Selection Service for the Far East in its Tokyo embassy and in the consulate-general in Kobe, the only such agencies it has in Afro-Asia.

between Brazil and Afro-Asia.[15] The telephone statistics presented in Table 11 represent the international traffic handled by all International Telephone and Telegraph, S.A. (ITT) agencies throughout Brazil. But, since they include only 93 percent of all Brazilian international calls, they can

TABLE 11. Regional Distribution of International Telephone Traffic to and from Brazil, January 1966–June 1968

Year	Total calls	USA	OWH	WE	EE	Africa	Asia	ME	Total
Outgoing from Brazil									
1966	38,978	55.45	27.58	15.69	0.08	0.05	0.41	0.74	100.0
1967	45,674	51.74	27.57	18.91	0.12	0.07	0.75	0.84	100.0
1968a	26,426	49.68	25.77	22.90	0.11	0.06	0.85	0.63	100.0
Incoming to Brazil									
1966	45,679	58.30	27.33	13.23	0.20	0.08	0.42	0.44	100.0
1967	49,682	57.13	26.07	15.59	0.19	0.05	0.42	0.55	100.0
1968a	28,264	54.94	27.20	16.55	0.19	0.06	0.59	0.47	100.0

SOURCE: Statistics obtained at the Rio de Janeiro office of ITT, representing 93 percent of all Brazilian international telephone calls.
a. January–June.

suggest only ratio relationships rather than correct absolute totals of all message units actually sent and received by Brazil between January 1966 and June 1968.[16] Afro-Asian participation in these communications figures is by far the lowest encountered on any of the measures, reaching a peak of only

15. Mail A→B/A's mail to all foreign nations is also used as a DON communications measure, but in Brazil no records are kept of the destination of outgoing mail, nor does Brazil submit to the Universal Postal Union any data which would be adaptable to this measure. Such persistent difficulties limit the application of the DON approach to studies of transactions between developing nations, where interest in producing such statistics (either accurately or at all) is minimal. Further, the availability of data restricted the time periods which could be covered with DON techniques.
16. The worldwide telecommunications network of ITT makes its records suitable for such analysis. However, ITT does enjoy exclusive rights to traffic from Brazil to the United States, so the United States–bound figures are representative of the true total but indicate a higher percentage of all calls than those actually sent to the United States, given the missing 7 percent scattered in some manner among the six other regions.

1.66 percent in 1967 on calls sent and a peak of 1.12 percent in the first six months of 1968 on calls received. Further, the familiar pattern of predominance exercised by several countries reappears. In 1966, Lebanon received 59.2 percent of all calls to the Mideast and sent 46.8 percent of all Mideastern calls to Brazil. The corresponding figures for Israel are 36.3 percent and 39.4 percent, respectively. The 1967 traffic shows similar patterns. For 1966 and 1967 these two nations together averaged about 95 percent of the traffic from Brazil to the Mideast and 82 percent of the traffic in the opposite direction. For these same years, Japan accounted for 78 percent of the Asian-bound calls from Brazil and 93 percent of all Asian calls to Brazil. Its only two rivals were Hong Kong (9.9 and 4.3 percent) and Australia (6.5 and 0.5 percent). The three Asian countries totaled 94.4 percent of all Asian calls from Brazil and 97.4 percent of all to Brazil. Calls to and from Africa had more scattered destinations and origins but were too few to analyze meaningfully.

Available telegraph statistics, also from all ITT agencies in Brazil, are less comprehensive, composing only 38.5 percent of all Brazilian international telegraph traffic inflow and outflow. Nonetheless, because the ITT agencies handling international traffic are dispersed in principal Brazilian cities, these figures may also be taken as samples suggestive of ratio relationships. Presented in Table 12, the telegraph figures show greater percentage consistency within region through time than do the telephone statistics, partly by virtue of the higher total message load. Because of this consistency, more extensive use may be taken as a better indicator of relative levels of message flow. Again African traffic is negligible, averaging only 0.3 percent of total outflow and 0.1 percent of inflow. Outgoing telegraph messages are directed more to Asia, and most incoming originate in the Middle East. The statistics on telephone traffic show a more evenly balanced flow in both directions. The Afro-Asian share of all traffic is slightly higher, a peak of 3.3 percent of all messages sent in the first half of 1968, and an inflow peak of 2.2 percent in 1967. The same high degree of concentration persists, with Japan receiving 77.5 percent of all Brazilian messages to Asia and sending 83 percent of all Asian messages to Brazil in 1966 and 1967, followed by Australia (5.5 and 3.5 percent) and Hong Kong (4.3 and 0.3 percent), an aggregate total of 87.3 percent of all messages sent to Asia and 86.8 percent of all Asian messages received by Brazil. In the Middle East, Israel dominated the traffic in 1966 and 1967, with 67 percent of all Brazilian telegrams to the region and 79.3 percent of all Mideast telegrams to Brazil, followed by Lebanon (15.4 and 1.0 percent) and the United Arab Republic (6.5 and 15.7

TABLE 12. Regional Distribution of International Telegraph Traffic to and from Brazil, July 1965–June 1968

Year	Total telegrams	USA	OWH	WE	EE	Africa	Asia	ME	Total
Outgoing from Brazil									
1965[a]	139,710	39.7	23.8	33.1	0.7	0.3	1.7	0.7	100.0
1966	285,050	38.6	23.0	34.8	0.6	0.3	2.0	0.7	100.0
1967	288,284	36.5	23.1	36.4	0.8	0.3	2.0	0.9	100.0
1968[b]	158,317	36.3	23.3	36.2	0.9	0.3	2.2	0.8	100.0
Incoming to Brazil									
1965[a]	168,258	41.1	23.4	33.1	0.6	0.1	0.5	1.2	100.0
1966	338,412	42.3	21.3	33.9	0.6	0.1	0.6	1.2	100.0
1967	351,029	41.4	20.7	35.1	0.6	0.1	0.6	1.5	100.0
1968[b]	196,379	42.3	20.4	34.8	0.5	0.1	0.7	1.2	100.0

SOURCE: Statistics obtained at the Rio de Janeiro office of ITT, representing 38.5 percent of all Brazilian international telegraph messages.
a. July–December.
b. January–June.

percent), an aggregate total of 88.9 percent of all outgoing telegrams and 96 percent of all incoming telegrams. South Africa in the same years averaged 55 percent of the African-bound flow and only 2.4 percent of the traffic from Africa to Brazil.

The emigration and communications dimension of Brazilian–Afro-Asian relations reveals a low level of interaction, in both absolute and relative terms. If Israel, Australia, Japan, and South Africa are excluded as developed nations, the developing Afro-Asian states accounted for merely 4.9 percent of total immigration between 1956 and 1961 (mostly from Arab nations and China) and only 0.48 percent of all incoming telegrams and 0.7 percent of all outgoing telegrams in 1967.

Exports

A goal of Itamaraty since the Kubitschek government, and independent of regime changes, has been the winning of a place for Brazilian exports in Afro-Asian markets. More recently, this goal has become an important component of both the diplomacy of prosperity and that of the Médici government, and so deserves detailed examination. With Operação Brasil-Ásia and the Gondim Mission of 1959, Brazil's most plausible initial prospects seemed to be in South Asia, but Quadros' spotlighting of Africa soon pre-empted the center of attention from Asia and struck the imagination of a few venturesome industrialists and economists. They held that as long as the domestic market remained one of restricted demand, Brazil's industrialization was hampered. If manufactures could be sold to Africa, not only could the rate of industrialization be accelerated, but the country would also benefit from higher export and foreign exchange earnings (along with stabler prices) and enjoy a wider range of products than the domestic market alone would stimulate, and at a lower cost of production. Any increase in sales of raw materials, of course, would also be welcomed.[17] For several years these arguments fell on deaf ears and were considered idealistic by most exporters. They were firmly oriented toward traditional buyers and reluctant to gamble as long as the American and Latin American Free Trade Association markets remained favorable.

In the interim, the Foreign Ministry continued studies on the problem, which still remained relegated to the status of a curiosity item during most of Goulart's term. The first two commercial missions to sub-Saharan Africa and other inquiries defined the limits of Brazilian trade possibilities. Several obstacles interposed themselves, the most obvious of which was the low value of the sporadic commercial exchange then actually carried on with Africa, affording few existing links on either side upon which to build flourishing trade. In most cases, Brazilian penetration would be forced to begin almost from nothing. A further difficulty in trade expansion has been determining which African goods could be purchased by Brazil. Most African countries prefer bi-

---

17. Ignácio M. Rangel, "A África e outros novos mercados."

lateral exchange agreements rather than convertible currency arrangements, since they have foreign exchange deficiencies. Lack of return freight also has created greater shipping expenses.

Economists customarily emphasize the noncomplementary nature of the Brazilian and African economies, competitive in coffee, cocoa, timber, certain ores, diamonds, and other basic products. This evaluation conceals the wide range of other important products which could profitably form the core of a dynamic trade flow. It ignores the fact that Brazilian-African trade has traditionally been based upon exchanges of Brazilian rice, corn, sugar, tea, menthol, nuts, tobacco, cotton, and sisal for African copper, asbestos, cobalt, and phosphates, all raw materials needed by Brazil's industrial park. According to trade reports, an industrializing Brazil could also find in Africa excellent sources of supply for its growing demands for crude petroleum, aluminum, natural rubber, cassiterite, zinc, tungsten, lead, vegetable and essential oils, pyrethrum, calcium phosphates, soda ash, gum arabic, tanning extracts, and cloves, in sufficient quantity to easily finance African imports of Brazilian goods up to a value of $250 million.[18] In return, the commercial missions to Africa discovered, the nations across the South Atlantic expressed a lively interest in acquiring from Brazil the following manufactured and semimanufactured items: fabrics, clothing, shoes, refrigerators, stoves, household appliances, lathes and machine tools, steel pipe, electrical and construction materials, agricultural machinery, canned goods, paints, and chemical and pharmaceutical products.[19] This potential sales list contains ample possibilities for cooperation, since Brazil and Africa are both attempting to diversify their trade.

Even granted this substantial list of commodities, provisional as it may be, serious impediments remain, not the least of which is the somewhat oligopolistic control over African trade exercised by a few trading companies from the former colonial powers. Such well-established, powerful groups as

18. Bazílio de Carvalho Sampaio, "Promoção das exportações brasileiras e do frete em navios do Lóide brasileiro—Relatório pelo CEPEX, MRE, e Lóide."
19. Mário Borges da Fonseca, "Substancial mercado para as exportações brasileiras na Africa," p. 206.

Unilever and Compagnie Française de L'Afrique Ocidentale maintain a firm grip on the African market in a wide range of products, enjoying as well the brand preferences of the consumers, habituated to the articles traditionally offered. In several cases, Brazilian sales to West Africa had to be consummated through the main offices of these British and French firms, which tend to favor business with their own nationals. This resistance to redirection of commercial practices is less marked in states in which trade has been nationalized in government hands, as in Ghana.

Another difficulty in the way of greater Brazilian-African trade flows has been preferential tariff treatment accorded many African states by either the European Common Market or (earlier) the British Commonwealth. This arrangement, from the Brazilian point of view, not only impedes sales of Brazilian finished goods to Africa but also permits competitive African raw materials to enter European ports without the customs duties faced by similar Brazilian products. The Associated African States and the Malagasy Republic, composed of the twelve former French colonies, plus Togo, Cameroon, Zaire, Ruanda, Burundi, and Somalia, enjoy such advantages in importing European articles that outside competition has been largely excluded. Since agreements between Great Britain and African nations of the Commonwealth were designed primarily to protect African goods arriving in Great Britain rather than British exports to Africa, Brazilian prospects for exports to commonwealth members were more favorable and have aroused great recent interest with the Foreign Ministry. This knowledge spurred the 1967 creation of the embassy in Nairobi. Trade missions are now planned for the East African region, as are economic and commercial departments for various embassies in sub-Saharan Africa.[20]

Within the limitations imposed by the foregoing restrictions, the Foreign Ministry considers that several mid-African nations offer conditions which could lead to "a regular and

20. In 1968 the Bank of Brazil had seventeen trade specialists working for the Foreign Ministry, on a requisition basis, in embassies and consulates abroad in what were considered key areas for trade expansion. The only Afro-Asian post provided with such a specialist was the consulate-general in Lourenço Marques, Mozambique. Commercial promotion does exist in other Afro-Asian posts, but with specialists of lesser rank from other government ministries.

continuous commercial exchange" across the South Atlantic, in addition to the established trade with South Africa.[21] The most attractive new market for Brazil has been Nigeria, with its population of 60 million, an impressive economic potential, a minimum of preferential ties to Europe, and colonies of Brazilian descendants. Itamaraty hopes to build a substantial exchange of manufactures for Nigerian petroleum and natural rubber, but has been troubled by a persistent trade deficit of great proportions (515 to 1 in 1967–1968) because of few Nigerian purchases in Brazil.

Nigeria is already the site of a unique Brazilian venture. In 1962, President Pery Igel and Director Rubem Rogério of Ultragas, a large São Paulo–centered company processing, bottling, and distributing natural gas, took the initiative with Mobil Mediterranean and Oiven Lorensen of Norway to form in Nigeria the Pan African Gas Distributors, with the commercial name of Sungas. This company, administered by Ultragas of Brazil, has become one of the largest of its kind in Nigeria.[22] Initially importing all equipment from Brazil, Rogério discovered that the 1,200 tons of industrial goods—stoves, gas refrigerators, gas bottles, washing machines, sewing machines, fans, mixers, and blenders—which he exported to Nigeria sold easily. Success made him an enthusiast for increased Brazilian-African trade, even in the face of transportation problems caused by lack of a regular sea route to West Africa. Rogério recommended establishment of a sea route because it would encourage trade in the long run even if several of the first voyages had to be made with little cargo.[23]

The next most appealing area, in the view of the Foreign Ministry, includes Zaire and Zambia, which can supply Brazil with important nonferrous metals. The final major new market to be penetrated is English-speaking East Africa (Kenya, Uganda, and Tanzania), a region which formerly possessed only the most remote, indirect maritime connections with Brazil.

21. Brasil, Ministério das Relações Exteriores, Departamento Cultural e de Informações, *Textos e declarações sôbre política externa (de abril de 1964 a abril de 1965)*, p. 128.
22. Interview with Casério B. Ceschin, 16 September 1968.
23. Brasil, Ministério das Relações Exteriores, Divisão de Estudos Econômicos, "Intercâmbio Brasil-África," pp. 4–7.

This recurring problem of transportation facilities constituted a serious impediment in trade expansion until the Foreign Ministry prevailed upon the Brazilian Lloyd Lines to charter new routes to Afro-Asia in order to expedite programs generated by the diplomacy of prosperity. The lack of regular, direct sea routes had greatly increased delay and transportation costs to delivery points, as goods for Africa had to be transshipped via New Orleans, New York, Tangiers, Dakar, or Cape Town. This unpredictability had not only discouraged Brazilian exporters with ambitions to trade with Africa, but had also left African purchasers in doubt concerning the future acquisition of repairs or spare parts. To expedite steady trade, the Lloyd Lines started a monthly West Africa route in February 1968. Scheduled stops are now made in Dakar, Monrovia, Tema, Takoradi, Lagos, Luanda, and Lobito. Optional ports are included when additional service is required. East Africa is to be served from ports in South Africa and Mozambique until such a volume is attained as merits a direct linkage.[24]

São Paulo industrial organizations have shown the greatest private sector interest in Africa, dating to the 1968 creation of the Afro-Brazilian Chamber of Commerce there. The Chamber of Commerce was organized through the initiative of exporters and with the backing of the Bank of Brazil. Its financial backers are counting on the proffered collaboration of African embassies, the São Paulo Confederation of Commerce, and the National Association of Exporters of Industrial Products. The São Paulo Industrial Center conducted studies on trade expansion with Africa, focusing on Senegal, the Ivory Coast, Ghana, Nigeria, Cameroon, and other countries visited by Foreign Minister Gibson Barbosa in October–November 1972 as part of a major campaign to widen cultural, trade, financial, and technical relations with West Africa. This visit yielded nine joint declarations on common policy in developmental matters, six cultural treaties,

24. Not only did cargoes face circuitous routes before recent changes, but as late as 1965 West Africans who desired to trade with Brazil found it necessary to travel to Dakar to have trade documents officialized, because the Brazilian embassies in Accra and Lagos had no consular service. Since that time, the embassy in the Nigerian capital has been charged with consular duties, as well as given trade-promotion functions.

five treaties on technical cooperation, and a trade agreement with Nigeria. The latter lists a wide variety of items to be exchanged by Brazil and Nigeria, both in the raw material and manufactured lines. Brazilian government officials view the trip as highly successful and promising of future receptivity to their ventures in the region.

It is true that "Brazil faces Africa," yet only recently have direct transportation routes come into existence. In the case of Asia, much greater distances intervene to reduce the frequency and magnitude of commercial relations and there are few noncommercial ties which could stimulate trade. As with Africa, the economies are partially noncomplementary, but Brazil has sold coffee, sugar, frozen and canned meat, iron ore, essential oils, textiles, watches, machine tools, electrical domestic appliances, Diesel and electric motors, and drugs to Asia, while importing tin, natural rubber, gums and resins, and industrial products (from Japan). With the outstanding exception of Japan, these exchanges have been intermittent and irregular, since Brazil's only real commercial efforts to date have centered in Japan and Hong Kong. Brazil's products are not well known outside those areas and suffer greatly in quality competition with those of better-known suppliers such as Japan, Hong Kong, Communist China, Great Britain, and the United States, which are furnished with adequate means for distribution and service. Brazil also has been unable to offer attractive credit facilities on equal terms with these nations.

The long-term prospects for Asian trade appear to be improving under government incentive. The broadening of commercial promotion (including participation in trade fairs) and the October 1967 inauguration of Lloyd's Far East route, the first regular Brazilian maritime communication with Asia, have helped. This line now stops in Durban, Lourenço Marques, Singapore, Bangkok, Hong Kong, Kobe, Keelung, Magoya, Yawata, and Yokohama. Every other month the route includes Sydney and Melbourne, with possible service for Pakistan and India if sufficient trade develops through the mechanism of recent treaties. Like the new African line, the Oriental experiment will carry floating demonstrations of Brazilian products, including catalogs. It will function with the support of diplomatic missions in Asia. Representatives of the Bank of Brazil and the National Confederation of Industry will accompany the floating exhibit.

The Middle East has been the area of Afro-Asia in which the least has been done for export promotion, although trade with Lebanon was advanced with the establishment of an entrepôt in Beirut's free port by the Brazilian Coffee Institute and a Varig airline route to the same city (1966). Itamaraty also maintains a commercial promotion service through its Beirut embassy. Brazil purchases half of its petroleum imports from the Middle East, largely in trade for coffee, but finds that it has few products to offer the best petroleum producers (Saudi Arabia, Iraq, Kuwait) and so suffers an unfavorable credit balance. Conversely, where its coffee sales are most successful (Lebanon), it finds little to buy and accumulates an undesirably large surplus balance. The only Mideastern nations with which Brazil had trade treaties by 1968 were Lebanon and Israel, in spite of years of diplomatic presence in other countries of the Levant and Maghreb. Brazil has yet to conduct serious studies of the economies and commercial structures of most states in these regions.[25] To date, few trade missions have visited the Middle East. The first was composed in its entirety of representatives from the National Confederation of Commerce and National Association of Exporters of Industrial Products. The trade mission visited Lebanon, Syria, Jordan, and the United Arab Republic in June 1966, in the unsuccessful attempt to obtain a Beirut entrepôt for distribution of Brazilian manufactures throughout the Middle East. Since then attention has shifted to the Persian Gulf region, Morocco, and Algeria.

A potentially profitable way to balance the transaction flows was seen in 1971 when Petrobrás signed an agreement with Iraq's state oil company to purchase Iraqi oil with Brazilian manufactured goods, such as the $1 million worth of automobiles to be included as part of the first trial transaction of $5 million. This technique, if successful, could alleviate the imbalance in what is now the most serious region of habitually unfavorable balance of payments and could serve as a pattern for use elsewhere.

25. Brasil, Ministério das Relações Exteriores, Secretário Geral Adjunto para a África e Oriente Próximo, "Promoção comercial brasileira no Oriente Próximo."

Officials of the Bank of Brazil's Export Promotion Center are confident that the new promotional and transportation measures will eventuate in a greater share for Afro-Asia of Brazil's gross export volume. They also believe it will help stimulate a decided rise in that proportion of Brazil's export value composed of manufactured and semimanufactured items. They are encouraged by Japan's and Australia's initiatives, through the UNCTAD, in granting tariff preferences for quotas of manufactured articles from developing nations, and they have striven to make industrialists aware of this opportunity.[26] In the final analysis, the increase of industrial exports to Afro-Asia is contingent upon the development of an aggressive export mentality among Brazilian industrialists and businessmen. A lack of this mentality has invariably been singled out by the early trade missions as a prime factor impeding more dynamic trade expansion in Afro-Asia. The director of the Foreign Trade Department of the São Paulo Confederation of Commerce in 1968 reported receiving a "great volume" of inquiries from Afro-Asian importers (mostly from Hong Kong and Japan) interested in Brazilian products, but the customary circulation of such inquiries at that time brought little response from Brazilian exporters.[27] A modification of this passive attitude was indispensable to the attainment of the government's objective of trade development and diversification into new markets. Under the Médici government's aggressive export-promotion campaign, much progress in this direction has been made, especially in the São Paulo area.

Patterns apparent in the regional distribution of Brazilian exports between 1956 and 1967 (Table 13) show a gradual tendency away from previous reliance on traditional markets in the United States and Western Europe towards trade diversification through sales to Eastern Europe and Afro-Asia. The position of Latin America has fluctuated through time to the extent that no clear trends may be discerned other than the low trough from 1959 to 1963. The United States has plainly given way to Western Europe as the dominant customer, reversing a long-standing rank order. The most significant change in the other four geographical areas, generically re-

26. Interview with Bazílio de Carvalho Sampaio, 8 October 1968.
27. Interview with Gilberto Machado, 6 August 1968.

ferred to as "new markets," has been the increase in trade with Eastern Europe—a 181-percent growth in dollar value from 1958 to 1967—in a decade when the value of trade with Afro-Asia increased by only 53.5 percent. Although the value of all exports to Afro-Asia exceeded that to Eastern Europe by nearly $32 million in 1958, by 1967 the value of goods shipped to Eastern Europe nearly equaled that of exports going to Afro-Asia.

TABLE 13. Distribution of Brazilian Exports, by Region of Destination, 1956–67

Year	Dollar value (in billions)	USA	OWH	WE	EE	Africa	Asia	ME	Total
1956	1.48	49.5	8.2	34.0	3.7	0.5	3.4	0.7	100.0
1957	1.39	47.4	11.6	32.8	3.1	0.4	3.3	1.4	100.0
1958	1.24	43.0	14.5	33.1	3.3	0.7	3.8	1.6	100.0
1959	1.28	46.2	9.2	34.8	4.6	0.4	3.5	1.3	100.0
1960	1.27	44.4	9.2	35.2	6.2	0.6	3.6	0.8	100.0
1961	1.40	40.1	9.6	37.8	5.7	0.6	5.1	1.1	100.0
1962	1.21	40.0	8.5	39.5	6.2	0.6	4.3	0.9	100.0
1963	1.41	37.8	7.7	42.2	7.2	0.7	3.4	1.0	100.0
1964	1.43	33.2	11.4	42.2	7.1	0.6	3.6	1.9	100.0
1965	1.60	32.6	14.3	41.2	6.4	1.1	3.2	1.2	100.0
1966	1.74	33.4	12.3	40.0	7.1	1.0	4.4	1.8	100.0
1967	1.65	33.1	11.0	41.9	7.0	0.8	4.4	1.8	100.0

SOURCE: Brasil, Ministério da Fazenda, Serviço de Estatística Econômica e Financeira, *Comércio exterior do Brasil—Exportação.*

The Afro-Asian component of Brazilian exports remained relatively unimportant, fluctuating between a low of 4.6 percent (1956) and a high of 7.2 percent (1966), with Asia yearly making up six-tenths or more of these aggregate percentages. Examination of the degree of export concentration by region shows a great amount of national variation between years, but several nations consistently retained their high-ranking positions for at least five years. Table 14 shows the rankings of the major trading partners in Asia and the Middle East from 1962 to 1967. It reveals that Japan and Hong Kong are the only important markets in Asia, and Lebanon, Algeria, and Morocco lead the Mideast. Africa's statistics indicate that South Africa is the principal customer by a wide margin, receiving up to 97.5 percent of all exports to sub-Saharan Africa. Sales to other African nations have been occasional and of low value. Even when South Africa is tallied, sales to sub-Saharan Africa in 1967 amounted to only $13 million, or about one-third the value of Brazilian exports to Belgium and Luxemburg. The five top-ranking states in 1964 and 1967 (Japan, Lebanon, South Africa, Hong Kong, and Algeria) accounted for, respectively, 81 percent and 79 percent of all Brazilian sales to Afro-Asia in those two years. This was not atypical since the five largest purchasers have usually im-

TABLE 14. Destination of Brazilian Exports to Asia and the Middle East, 1962–67

	Yearly percentage of regional contribution					
	1962	1963	1964	1965	1966	1967
Asia						
Japan	55.7	65.0	54.3	59.0	53.8	76.2
Hong Kong	26.6	18.3	30.9	28.0	26.8	9.1
Australia	4.3	4.4	4.5	5.0	2.0	2.4
Nationalist China	5.6	0.2	5.3	3.1	2.2	2.5
India	0.4	0.3	0.2	0.4	9.5	4.3
Total	92.6	88.2	95.2	95.5	94.3	94.5
Middle East						
Lebanon	48.5	49.1	33.8	24.2	58.7	38.7
Algeria	4.4	10.0	33.7	1.8	10.5	21.0
Morocco	11.2	10.3	5.8	9.1	2.4	21.0
Tunisia	6.0	5.0	12.5	12.0	9.2	8.6
Israel	15.6	4.9	1.8	12.5	6.2	5.0
Syria	2.4	10.8	0.7	5.5	5.9	0.0
Total	88.1	90.1	88.3	65.1	92.9	94.3

SOURCE: Brasil, Ministério da Fazenda, Serviço de Estatística Econômica e Financeira, *Comércio exterior do Brasil—Exportação*.

ported about four-fifths of the aggregate total for the three regions. If we exclude Japan, Australia, New Zealand, South Africa, and Israel in determining the magnitude of Brazil's exports to developing Afro-Asia or the Third World in 1967, we are left with a figure of $45.2 million, only 2.7 percent of Brazil's global total.

For Brazil's main partners in Afro-Asia, trade with Brazil represents a minute percentage of their global imports and even less of their exports. Japan, South Africa, and Lebanon from 1962 to 1966 counted Brazil as the source of about 0.5 percent of their imports; Hong Kong could claim Brazil for approximately 1.0 percent. Only Japan sent as much as an average of 0.5 percent of its exports to Brazil, whereas the remaining three never sent Brazil over 0.06 percent of their export total during the four years.[28]

When compared with the export patterns of Latin America taken as a region, the Brazilian statistics adhere rather closely to the norm for exports to Afro-Asia, excluding Communist China. As an economic region, from 1965 to 1967, Latin America sent, respectively, 6.6 percent, 6.5 percent, and 7.0 percent of its export total to Afro-Asia, while in the same years Brazil registered 5.5 percent, 7.2 percent, and 7.0 percent. Brazil directs a slightly higher percentage of its trade to Africa and the Middle East and less to Asia than does Latin America. Brazil concentrates its Asian sales much less on Japan and relies for its African exports much more on South Africa.[29]

It is not the present level of sales to Afro-Asia which has attracted Brazilian attention, but rather the potentialities for future sales of manufactures and semimanufactures, items whose share in total export value has risen steadily since 1960, reaching 15 percent and $412.8 million in 1970 and ranking second only to coffee (at 34 percent). To all indications this share will continue to grow rapidly with the program of government incentives for exportation of manufactures and with further industrialization. The International Bank for Reconstruction and Development in 1971 predicted the 1976 sale of over $2 billion in these manufactures categories.

Up to the present, despite earlier opinions by some diplomats and exporters, Afro-Asia has not proven to be the "natural outlet" for these manufactures, which have been going instead to Latin America, the United States, and Western Europe. Trade between Brazil and Afro-Asia continues to be heavily dominated by raw materials. Japan is the sole anomaly. Most of the manufactures sold in Africa have gone to the Republic of South Africa, while in the Middle East, Lebanon, Algeria, Morocco, and Iraq have shown new interest but modest purchases in the past. None of the percentages or absolute values of manufactures purchased by Afro-Asia from

---

28. United Nations, Department of Economic and Social Affairs, Statistical Office, *Yearbook of International Trade Statistics, 1966.*

29. United Nations, Department of Economic and Social Affairs, Statistical Office, *Monthly Bulletin of Statistics.*

Brazil would be conducive to optimism concerning quick success in expanding regular sales, especially outside Hong Kong (an entrepôt) or outside Japan, India, Australia, and South Africa, which are in various stages of industrialization where complementarity is more easily found. The persistence and ingenuity of the Brazilians in exploring all possible approaches, however, just may lead to some surprising deals in the future and the expansion of a steady trade.[30]

Dimensional Summary

This chapter demonstrates the usefulness of a quantitative approach in the study of foreign policy as an additional analytical tool which can gauge generalized uniformities of the behavior of one state toward other states and which can detect the strength, extent, and direction of a state's behavioral changes. By using applicable measures from the DON project, I define the various levels of prominence in Brazilian foreign relations held by each of the seven specified geographical regions under study. By focusing on the positions held by Africa, the Middle East, and Asia, I analyze each dimension of Brazil's international behavior towards Afro-Asia within the general context of its gamut of bilateral behavior relationships with all states. The levels of prominence of Afro-Asia or the degree of Brazilian attention to Afro-Asia may therefore be expressed as percentages of Brazil's global transactions or as ratio relationships in comparison with other regions (see Table 15).

The figures which measure Brazil's actions toward Afro-Asian nations indicate a low relative prominence for Afro-

30. A general notion of the relative importance attached to various Afro-Asian countries as prospective trading partners by trade-promotion officials is obtained from a Bank of Brazil request to the International Trade Center (UNCTAD-GATT) in Geneva for market research in Afro-Asia on specified Brazilian industrial products, including clothing, domestic appliances, drugs, paint, chemicals, machine tools, pumps, agricultural machinery, and road-building equipment. The countries or areas specified, in descending order of priority, are South Africa, Mozambique, Rhodesia, Israel, the Philippines, India, Nigeria, Singapore, Lebanon, Kenya, Hong Kong, Iran, Malaysia, Thailand, Ethiopia, Pakistan, Morocco, Ghana, region of the Persian Gulf, Liberia, Ivory Coast, Nationalist China, and Senegal. Japan is not included because Brazilian-Japanese commercial relations are well developed. See Sampaio, "Promoção das exportações brasileiras e do frete em navios do Lóide brasileiro—Relatório pelo CEPEX, MRE, e Lóide."

Asia in the whole scheme of Brazilian foreign relations. The highest level of prominence is in diplomatic representation, followed by the category diplomatic and consular personnel. Both are functions of Foreign Ministry interest in Afro-Asia, which, as we have seen, varied through the 1956 to 1968 period, reaching its height in 1968. The first five categories reveal the level of government-initiated or intergovernmental activity (administrative behavior). Columns six and seven indicate the more limited extent of largely private commer-

TABLE 15. Brazilian Transactions with Afro-Asia, on Selected Measures, Expressed as Percentages of Brazil's Global Transactions

Region	Diplomatic representation (1968)	Diplomatic and consular representation (1968)	Cruzeiro do Sul awards (1956–1967)	Treaties (1950–1968)	Consular representation (1968)	Exports (1967)	Outgoing telegrams (1967)
Asia and Oceania	7.7	7.0	5.6	4.1	5.8	4.4	2.0
Mideast and North Africa	8.5	5.5	3.4	4.1	0.2	1.8	0.9
Sub-Saharan Africa	3.1	3.0	1.2	0.9	2.8	0.8	0.3
Total	19.3	15.5	10.2	9.1	8.8	7.0	3.2

cial and communications activity (private international relations, in Rummel's terms). The fact that all the measures of government-initiated activity rank above "exports" and "telegrams" would seem to signify that Brazilian–Afro-Asian relations are in a state of development in which intergovernmental or political relations are more salient than such society-wide, relatively noninstitutional ties as trade, mail, student and tourist exchange, translations of literature. The chief exception to this rule may be emigration from Afro-Asia to Brazil, a flow which has not been reciprocal and which in the past has principally involved Japan and the Levant. This influx of immigrants appears to have heightened the salience of Japan, Lebanon, and Israel for Brazil, just as the presence of many Portuguese immigrants underlies in part the particular attention which Itamaraty has been giving to the events in Portuguese Africa.

On practically all measures, Asia ranks first in degree of prominence, followed by the Middle East, then Africa. In only two instances is this order broken: in both diplomatic and in consular representation it is broken because of the administrative expedient of charging most Middle Eastern embassies with consular functions rather than establishing separate consulates to handle the present level of transactions. Within each geographical region the transaction flow is directed largely to one or two states, namely Japan, Israel, Lebanon, and South Africa. Brazil maintains significant bilateral relations with these states. With the majority of the developing nations of the Third World, relations have been somewhat more intense and conflict and cooperation more evident in international organizations, especially in the United Nations and its specialized agencies, as well as the UNCTAD. In the following pages the bilateral relations with some of these more salient states are briefly examined. In subsequent chapters the discussion shifts to two issues which have been pivotal in multilateral relations between Brazil and developing Afro-Asia: colonialism and economic development.

Three Case Studies

Three of the Afro-Asian nations with which Brazil has had the closest contact, as measured by the DON dimensions, are not members of the Afro-Asian group caucusing in the United Nations nor can they be classed economically as members of the Third World in a developmental sense. As Russett demonstrates conclusively in empirically defining international regions, in many respects Japan, Israel, and South Africa are quite atypical politically, culturally, and economically of the geographic regions in which they are situated. On the basis of their trade and cultural and political relations, each is closely linked with the Western community. According to Russett: "Israel, and more surprisingly Japan . . . belong with the European countries on every criterion except proximity (and Israel is not really so distant). . . . If the world of the next several decades is to see a very general kind of agreement and common interest among the Western industrialized countries, with interests that come increasingly into conflict with the non-Western underdeveloped nations of Asia and Africa, Israel and Japan, now 'have' states, are much more likely to be aligned with their rich developed fellows than with their geographical neighbors."[31]

South Africa, in many ways an internationally isolated outcast from even the old Commonwealth groupings, is a case sui generis which defies general classification, although the politically dominant segments of the population are largely Western European and the economy is considered "developed" by United Nations evaluation. With respect to South Africa, Russett concludes, "It is of course precisely the efforts of its white government to keep the country from becoming socially and culturally Afro-Asian that has produced the present political tension."[32]

Because of the peculiar circumstances and the political implications surrounding the South African case, relations between Brazil and Pretoria are discussed at more length in Chapter 5. The nature of Brazil's relations not only with Japan and Israel but also with India are briefly examined in order to illustrate various facets of Brazilian policy toward Afro-Asian states at diverse levels of development as well as to emphasize the unique characteristics which determine each case.

Japan.—Close relations with Japan date from the first wave of Japanese immigrants which entered Brazil in 1908, a circumstance which heavily influenced the subsequent development of relations between Tokyo and Rio de Janeiro. The wave of immigration led most immediately to the creation of a Brazilian embassy in the Japanese capital in 1909 and, secondly, to the development of an accompanying embryonic flow of trade. The economic importance of the large immigrant colony and the favorable image it now enjoys among the Brazilian public, as noted previously, contribute a positive spillover to relations between the two nations. In the words of Crown Prince Akihito in an address to the Brazilian Congress in 1967, "I think that the strong links between our countries have a special characteristic not found in Japanese relations with other nations—a characteristic which had its origin in the year 1908 when Brazil opened its doors to Japa-

---

31. Russett, *International Regions and the International System: A Study in Political Ecology*, p. 178.
32. Ibid., p. 31.

nese immigrants whose descendants here now number 600,000."[33]

Most tangibly, the colony's presence has facilitated the cultural programs of the Japanese embassy and the consulate-general in São Paulo, with the collaboration of groups such as the Sociedade Paulista de Cultura Japonêsa (Japanese Cultural Society of São Paulo), the central organ of the immigrant groups. This organization's purpose is to raise the cultural level of the colony and promote Brazilian-Japanese relations. A sister organization, the Aliança Cultural Brasil-Japão (Brazilian-Japanese Cultural Alliance), is composed largely of Brazilians. Similar associations are active in most centers of Japanese settlement in the states of São Paulo and Paraná. Many involve Brazilians of other than Japanese descent although Japanese immigrants and their descendants predominate.[34]

Besides providing a diffuse feeling of good will, the colony's existence has yielded some concrete benefits for Brazilian-Japanese relations, not the least of which was the establishment of the Usinas Siderúrgicas de Minas Gerais (USIMINAS) under the guiding hand of Yukishigue Tamura, the first of four Japanese descendants to be elected to the position of federal deputy. This steel-producing company, the largest single Japanese investment in Brazil, was begun in 1957 in Minas Gerais as a mixed-capital joint venture with 40 percent participation on the part of the Japanese government. (This proportion has since been effectively reduced because the company has grown at the same time that Japanese capital investment has remained constant.) USIMINAS is now the second largest steel-producing center in Brazil, with an output exceeded only by the Volta Redonda complex.

Although companies such as Kanêbo do Brasil and Lâmpadas Sadokin are based on Japanese-Nissei cooperation, with Japanese technical assistance, local Nissei capital, and mixed management, such examples are few. They account for a small fraction of the Japanese investment in Brazil, which started in 1954 and has been expanding steadily since that date. Of all independent capital entering Brazil between 1963

33. *Brazil International Report* (June 1967): 2.
34. Interview with Yoshinori Nuimura, 21 June 1968.

and 1967, including that furnished by international institutions, Japan supplied 14 percent of all direct investment in currency and equipment and 6 percent of all loans in currency and for the financing of imports.[35] In 1968, 70 Japanese firms had a total of $230 million invested in Brazil, or fully 38 percent of all the Japanese capital invested outside the home islands.[36] The 35 large Japanese factories then in Brazil contrasted sharply with the few existing in Argentina (2), Peru (4), and other South American countries.[37] One of these factories, that of Ishikawajima Harima Heavy Industries of Brazil in Rio de Janeiro, is the largest shipyard in the Southern Hemisphere. In 1968 it completed construction of the heaviest vessel ever built in Brazil, launched in the presence of the ambassador of Japan. Other important firms are found in the fields of textiles, electronics, machinery, agriculture, photography, and finance, with the range of products and services becoming more diversified into paper pulp and steel mills, cement and textile factories, and hydroelectric complexes.

The shape of things to come was revealed by the December 1971 mission to Brazil of twenty presidents and executive directors of the largest Japanese companies, anxious to invest overseas since the Tokyo government relaxed restrictions several years ago on capital outflow and encouraged the establishment abroad of companies to manufacture for export to Western Europe and the United States. This scheme combines well with Brazilian intentions and their open invitation to all firms, however polluting, to begin operations in Brazil. It can be anticipated, in the context of Japanese expansion into Latin America, that Japanese investment in Brazil will rise well above the $360.6 million of 1970 and the over 100 subsidiaries active in 1972.[38]

Although Brazil is involved in a much greater percentage of Japan's total foreign investment than in its total foreign trade, commercial interchange is assuming greater weight for both states. Between 1964 and 1967, Japan climbed rapidly from twelfth to seventh in rank among the principal pur-

35. Banco Central do Brasil, *Relatório* (1967), p. 316.
36. Ikuzo Hirokawa, "As indústrias japonêsas no Brasil," p. 2.
37. Interview with Ikuzo Hirokawa, 20 June 1968.
38. "Latins Assess Japan's New Presence," *New York Times*, 21 June 1971, p. 8.

chasers of Brazilian exports, winning sixth place in 1969 and 1970. Brazil has continued as Japan's most important trading partner in Latin America. The trade is based principally on the exchange of Brazilian coffee, sugar, hematite, pig iron, and cotton for a wide variety of Japanese manufactured goods. Since the upsurge in the intensity of relations between the two countries, starting about 1956, a frequent reciprocal exchange of official trade missions (often at ministerial level) has proceeded on a regular basis, along with goodwill and cultural missions. Within the background of Japan's need for raw materials (deriving from its ecological situation) and of Brazil's requirements for manufactured products and capital goods (likely to increase with the growth of industrialization), future prospects for intensified trade appear promising and have aroused interest in both countries. Also arousing interest have been the discussions about new Japanese investments, carried on within the framework of the Brazilian-Japanese Joint Economic Commission inaugurated in February 1968. On his return from a trip to Tokyo in February 1972, Minister of Planning Paulo dos Reis Veloso predicted that the 1975 flow of trade will be 3 times that of 1970 (which saw exports to Japan of $144.9 million, 2.5 times the 1967 value). The balance of trade has consistently been in Brazil's favor. The Bank of Brazil and the private Bank of the State of São Paulo opened branches in Tokyo in 1972, the first major Latin American financial institutions to have agencies in Japan. This expansion gives some indication of the importance Brazil places on Japan as a trading partner.

Plans have been forwarded to use Japanese skills in the expansion and diversification of Brazil's trade. In 1968 Caio de Alcântara Machado, president of the Brazilian Coffee Institute, personally visited Tokyo to negotiate an agreement with the Mitsubishi industrial complex. The latter firm was to become the sales agent for Brazilian coffee throughout Asia (with the exceptions of Australia and New Zealand). According to the Brazilian Coffee Institute, this agreement was designed to rapidly double Asian coffee sales by allowing Brazilian exporters to take advantage of Mitsubishi credit and distribution facilities.[39] The Foreign Ministry's Secretary-General for Commercial Promotion also requested that two

39. *Jornal do Brasil*, 4 September 1968, p. 17.

Japanese experts in world commerce tour Brazil to encourage an aggressive, informed export mentality among businessmen.[40] The last several years have seen discussion of the formation of trading companies on the Japanese model to promote Brazil's foreign trade.

The most notable Japanese contributions to Brazilian development in the area of technical assistance have been in the forms of technical experts and scholarships for study in Japan. From 1961 to 1968 approximately 400 Japanese specialists were furnished, upon Brazilian request, in such fields as tropical medicine, agriculture, telecommunications, electric power generation, and textiles. Japan has exhibited special interest in recent Brazilian efforts to develop the Northeast and Amazon regions.[41]

According to enthusiasts of this partnership, there exists a natural complementarity between economically developed Japan, with its high population density, and developing Brazil, with very low population densities in the virgin Amazon and Center-West regions. This complementarity could best reach fruition through establishment of centers of Japanese colonization in frontier zones.[42] As part of the program to integrate frontier areas into national life in the face of the reluctance of native Brazilians to migrate inland from the coast, the federal government and various state governments have already established two dozen such nuclei in the regions served by the Agency for the Development of the Amazon (SUDAM) and the Agency for the Development of the Northeast (SUDENE). The governments are considering the possibilities for new centers in view of the interest in this enterprise demonstrated by Japanese colony representatives in São Paulo. Future expansion in this direction of rural colonization will emphasize the immigration of Japanese with technical or agricultural experience, but it must contend with the Foreign Ministry's firm decision to keep Amazon colonization in national hands. Illustrative of this jealous safeguarding of the national sovereignty were the establishment of an Amazon Division in Itamaraty and the 1968 Foreign Ministry veto of

40. *Correio da Manhã*, 24 October 1968, economics sec., p. 7.
41. Consulado Geral do Japão (São Paulo), "Emigração japonêsa no Brasil," p. 3.
42. Interview with Manoel Orlando Ferreira, 21 May 1968.

an official Japanese request to send a scientific expedition into the Amazon, amid speculations in certain quarters that the Japanese would attempt to obtain a foothold in the little-explored region.[43] This development is perhaps best understood in conjunction with the unfavorable Brazilian reaction to the Hudson Institute for Defense Analysis report outlining a plan for international development of the Amazon Basin, as well as some Brazilians' lingering suspicion when they recall Japanese plans for expansion in Latin America prior to World War II and fear a recurrence at Brazilian expense.

Great language differences, compounded by the obscurity of Japanese and Portuguese among international languages, have kept to small numbers the flow of students between Brazil and Japan. According to one estimate, only one or two Japanese yearly travel to Brazil to pursue their studies, while fewer than ten Brazilians annually go to Japan to study at their own expense.[44] In order to strengthen Japanese-Brazilian relations through the descendants in Brazil, Japan's provinces offer graduate fellowships to the children of emigrants from each Japanese province, and the Tokyo government yearly offers eight fellowships of three-years duration. In practice, the latter fellowships are distributed to three native Brazilians and five Japanese descendants. In addition, six enterprises in Japan maintain industrial scholarships for Brazilians and the Japanese Foreign Ministry offers colony leaders three or four trips to Japan each year. In this way the total number of Brazilians going to Japan to study oscillates between fifty and sixty per year. Universities and schools in the United States and Western Europe exert much greater attraction for Brazilian students.[45]

The 28 June 1968 inauguration of the twice-weekly Varig flight to Tokyo via the United States, carrying Senhora Costa e Silva and Minister of Planning Hélio Beltrão, represented not only the initial scheduling of a Brazilian airline to Asia but also indicated the increasing volume of travel between Brazil and Japan.[46] Antedating the establishment of a Japa-

43. *O Jornal*, 25 September 1968.
44. Interview with Yoshinori Nuimura, 21 June 1968.
45. Interview with Hiroshi Saito, 20 June 1968.
46. In advertising the new route, Varig concentrated on informing Japanese immigrants of the new ease and speed in visiting their

nese air route to South America, the Varig effort was one of several manifestations of heightened Brazilian interest in relations with Japan. That country will certainly remain at a higher level of saliency in Brazilian foreign relations than any other Asian nation for some time to come.

Israel.—Relations with Israel can be traced from 29 November 1947, the date of the partition of Palestine. Former Foreign Minister Oswaldo Aranha, while president of the United Nations General Assembly, actively defended the creation of a Jewish nation-state, for which he is still remembered among the Israelis. Until 1962 Brazilian-Israeli relations followed a friendly but routine course, predicated largely on the sizable number of Jews residing in Brazil and upon Israel's status as the Christian Holy Land. Religious considerations, from the beginning in the forefront in Brazil's posture toward Israel, were evident in Itamaraty's early advocacy of international status for Jerusalem. This policy was in line with the policy of the Vatican, and its recognition of Tel Aviv rather than Jerusalem as Israel's capital. Not only were Brazilian representatives sent to Tel Aviv, but the embassy personnel were also carefully instructed not to visit partitioned Jerusalem in an official capacity, to lend as much endorsement as possible to a possible future special international status for the beleaguered Holy City.[47] The 1958 creation of a consulate-general in Jerusalem also followed the political-religious objective of giving to Christianity, in the words of the Foreign Minister, "a demonstration that Brazil understands the importance of its role as the largest Catholic power in the world. . . ."[48]

In 1962, with the signature of a Basic Agreement on Technical Cooperation, Israel began a program of foreign aid to Brazil, similar to projects already undertaken in Afro-Asia to gain support for the Israeli position in the Middle East conflict and in response to successful Arab appeals to neutralist nations. Israeli assistance to Brazil has been concentrated in the Northeast's drought polygon in conjunction with the

---

former homeland, even utilizing television commercials completely in Japanese in major Brazilian cities.

47. *Revista brasileira de política internacional*, 1, No. 3 (September 1958): 167.

48. Ibid. In the subsequent years, this post has not had an official designated to fill it.

National Office for Anti-Drought Projects (DNOCS) and SUDENE. In Rio Grande do Sul, Israeli assistance has taken the form of joint field research by Israeli and Brazilian scientists on water exploration, irrigation, and development of strains of hybrid seeds suited to the local climate, all skills which the Israelis have been able to develop in the demanding ecology of their native land. Technical advice has also been furnished Brazil in establishing experimental agricultural cooperatives to colonize rural areas in the interiors of such states as Ceará, Piauí, and Rio Grande do Norte. These farms are expected to serve as pilot projects for later duplication elsewhere as part of the federal government's programs to utilize presently barren land and to encourage the population to leave the heavily inhabited seacoast. As an adjunct to the field-oriented programs, Israel has given over seventy fellowships to Brazilians for graduate study of agriculture in Israel. Plans are also going forward for greater cultural exchange under a 1959 treaty and for a direct twice-weekly air route between Israel and Brazil. All of these developments reveal an upsurge in Israeli interest in Latin America, signaled in part by the 1966 visit of President Zalman Shazar, the first Israeli head of state to visit Brazil.

New and significant avenues of cooperation were opened by the series of discussions and agreements culminating in the May 1967 "Agreement on the Use of Nuclear Energy for Peaceful Purposes." This agreement is to provide for exchange of technicians and information between the two countries. Both Brazil and Israel opposed the Nuclear Non-Proliferation Treaty as restrictive of their autonomous development of nuclear technology for peaceful purposes and announced intentions to diversify as much as possible their foreign sources of nuclear supply and assistance. Areas of nuclear collaboration already include the radiation of foods and seeds for preservation, sterilization of harmful insects, use of radio-isotopes to discover underground water, studies on the prospecting and processing of uranium and other fissionable materials, and experimentation with different types of reactors.[49] Other fields are to be explored by future agreement.

49. Brasil, Ministério das Relações Exteriores, Secretaria Geral Adjunta para o Planejamento Político, *Documentos de política externa (de 15 de março a 15 de outubro de 1967)*, p. 19.

In 1968 Israeli scientists were working under this agreement in São Paulo, Piracicaba, and Recife.[50]

Regarding Arab-Israeli conflicts, Brazil has traditionally assumed a position of guarded but not indifferent neutrality dictated both by the remoteness of the situation from Brazil's primary interests and the real potentials for domestic political repercussions should Brazil solidly back one party or the other. Such a supportive role would provoke protest from either the Jewish or the Arab immigrant organizations located in major cities. Neither would Brazil wish to jeopardize its growing trade and good relations with states on either side of the dispute, especially since the conflict politically affects Brazil's vital national interests only in general terms— as a danger to world peace in the event of a future escalation and Soviet-American confrontation. To demonstrate its continuing concern with the Mideast situation as well as its own neutrality, Brazil maintained an infantry battalion with the United Nations Emergency Force from the force's inception in 1956. Although the Foreign Ministry has been careful not to make its Middle Eastern policy a cause for internal controversy, Brazil has been active on several occasions in suggesting peaceful solutions. It usually supports direct Arab-Israeli negotiations, Arab recognition of Israel's legal right to existence, a just settlement of the refugee question by Israel, international status for Jerusalem, and a cessation of the regional arms race (necessitating great-power cooperation).

Since the June 1967 Arab-Israeli war, Brazil has further supported the withdrawal of Israeli troops from areas occupied during the hostilities, as a necessary precondition to fostering an atmosphere of conciliation in which successful bargaining may take place. During this crisis, Brazil presented to the Special Emergency Session of the United Nations General Assembly a peace formula incorporating the above points in addition to proposing a multilateral peace conference, under United Nations auspices, of all powers responsible for peace in the area. Presented in person by Foreign Minister Magalhães Pinto, this plan found some sup-

50. Brazilian-Israeli nuclear cooperation has disquieted some officials of the Arab League, who interpret it as embodying military objectives. See, for example, *Correio da Manhã*, 28 July 1968, p. 1.

port from other states, but the subsequent course of events and tensions precluded its implementation. Brazil's continued willingness to play a constructive role in the area was underlined by Foreign Minister Barboza in his visit to Cairo and Tel Aviv in early 1973. At that time he reiterated the Brazilian view that a just peace is possible only through compliance with Security Council Resolution 242.

India.—Although India and Brazil, by virtue of their resources, area, population, and potential, are among the most important of the developing nations, their antipodal positions on the globe and intervening distances have been factors until recently precluding the development of bilateral relations despite the significant cooperation which has taken place in the United Nations and its specialized forums such as the Eighteen-Power Committee on Disarmament and the UNCTAD. Brazil's embassy in New Delhi was established in October 1948, relations having previously been conducted at legation level. In the mid-1950s a career consulate was created in Bombay for the express purpose of carrying out an agreement with Lisbon to protect Portuguese interests in India in the absence of diplomatic relations between the latter two states. In conjunction with the embassy and a consulate in Calcutta, the Bombay consulate provided diplomatic and consular assistance for the Portuguese immigrants in India, estimated at 100,000.[51] From 1955 to 1960 this diplomatic mediation was one of the most important Brazilian activities in India.

Whereas, in 1959, Brazilian diplomatic personnel and staff in the New Delhi embassy numbered eight, in addition to four officials stationed at the Bombay and Calcutta consulates, by August 1968 the New Delhi staff had shrunk to seven and the only Brazilian consular service available outside the embassy was through an honorary post in Calcutta. During the same month, Itamaraty had an embassy staff of nine in Bangkok and eight in Taipei and Seoul, all capitals of less international status.[52] Thus India has not played as large a role in Brazilian diplomatic relations as smaller de-

51. Brasil, Ministério das Relações Exteriores, *Relatório* (1956), p. 55.
52. Figures taken from Brasil, Ministério das Relações Exteriores, "Lista do pessoal" (July 1959); and Ministério das Relações Exteriores, "Lista do pessoal no exterior" (August 1968).

veloping Asian states, whose ties to Brazil are actually more recent.

India maintains an embassy in Rio de Janeiro which serves as a listening post in Latin America, especially with regard to Peking's activities, and as a distribution point from which India can disseminate information explaining its position on important issues. Other official functions of the embassy are limited; for example, only fifteen to twenty visas are yearly granted to Brazilians. Most go to diplomats. Less than half a dozen Indian immigrant families live in Brazil, and few Indians (under one hundred per year) enter the country for business or tourist purposes. Significantly, all the printed material the embassy uses for public distribution is in English or Spanish, not Portuguese.[53]

Trade between Brazil and India has likewise been negligible, with the singular exception of the sale to India of nearly $7 million worth of Brazilian rice in 1966. This transaction, occasioned by the inability of India's traditional suppliers to furnish sufficient quantities of the grain, was accomplished with American help. Typically, commerce has been based on the exchange of Brazilian alcohol, carnauba wax, oils, and extracts for Indian shellac-making resins. Between 1956 and 1965 the value of exports to India dropped well under an annual average of $150,000. Since 1965, the prospects for increased commercial interchange have been heightened by mutual realization that in many ways the developing economies of the two countries are actually complementary, in both raw materials and industrial products. As seen in the conversations surrounding the 1964 tour of Brazil by an Indian commercial mission, India is interested in acquiring from Brazil a wide variety of manufactured goods, such as cargo ships, scales, tractors, cranes, pigments, and industrial machinery. In turn, the Brazilians have demonstrated a desire to import Indian cattle and other products once a regular trade flow is established. Initiating such flow, however, necessitates solution of the perennial problem of dependable transportation between the two nations.[54]

As a delayed result of the 1963 and 1964 exchange of trade missions, the first commercial treaty between the two coun-

53. Interview with Khalid Halim Siddiqi, 29 August 1968.
54. Brasil, Ministério das Relações Exteriores, *Relatório* (1964), p. 64.

tries was signed in New Delhi in February 1968, during the visit of Magalhães Pinto to the Second UNCTAD. Through this treaty and accompanying discussions, both governments pledged themselves to explore all feasible means to stimulate trade, stipulated the mutual concession of most-favored-nation privileges, and agreed to exchange technical information on common problems of economic development. One of the greatest remaining obstacles to trade, that of irregular maritime transportation, was to be removed by joint efforts to undertake new sea routes.

Indira Gandhi's September 1968 visit to Brazil, the first by any Indian head of government, yielded several tangible benefits. In a lengthy communique, Magalhães Pinto and Prime Minister Gandhi reaffirmed the opposition of their governments to a nuclear nonproliferation agreement which would hinder any developing nation from making full use of nuclear science and technology for peaceful programs or from conducting independent nuclear research for such programs. Both states had already assumed this position during their participation in the General Assembly debates on the subject. As if to underscore their common stance, the two leaders reached agreement on the essential content of a five-year nuclear cooperation pact regulating the exchange of technical information and scientists, as well as commerce in fissionable material. The pact became effective in March 1970. Brazil and India, possessing substantial reserves of thorium, are in a similar stage of atomic energy development. They are following the Canadian line of nuclear research, which makes reciprocal assistance feasible and, according to Brazilian diplomats, foreshadows a promising, mutually beneficial exchange program.[55]

A third treaty, signed during Gandhi's tour of the Foreign Ministry, promoted cultural, educational, and scientific exchanges, establishing a supervisory bi-national commission for this purpose. One outcome of this approach to increased relations was the early-1969 inauguration of a chair of Brazilian studies at the University of New Delhi, to be shared with the University of Bombay. Sponsored by the Brazilian embassy, the professorship is the first of its kind for Brazil in Asia. It may be interpreted, at least in part, as an attempt

55. Interview with Renato Mendonça, 11 November 1968.

to utilize the two countries' common link of former Portuguese colonization and the continued presence of many Portuguese-speaking Asians on Indian soil in Goa, Daman, and elsewhere. Whether the 1968 flurry of treaty-making produces fundamental change in the routine of Brazilian-Indian relations remains to be seen; perhaps the forces of distance, tradition, and economics still preclude it. The bases, however, have been set and interest evinced by both parties. For Brazil, it appears that the future of relations with India is contingent upon the success of its Asian policy—the systematic cultivation of ties with Asia in order to multiply markets for Brazilian exports and to diversify the sources of aid for economic development. It is within this framework that the rapprochement has been designed, in order to expand Brazil's commercial and scientific horizons and to make Brazil known in India.

5. Decolonization, Human Rights, and Brazilian Policy in Southern Africa

BRAZIL's policy toward Portugal, South Africa, and Rhodesia is explored against the background of Afro-Asian attempts to ostracize these states. This chapter illustrates Brazilian policy on colonialism, and it illuminates relations with these three countries as special cases within Brazil's general policy, cases highly suggestive of how the Brazilian government has assessed its interests in the continent facing it across the South Atlantic. Instead of emphasizing degrees of policy differences through time between Brazil and (1) certain Afro-Asian states, (2) radical or moderate groupings, or (3) caucuses as measured in such statistics as United Nations voting, this analysis aims at the bilateral relations between Brazil and the three governments in question. Special attention is paid to Portugal and South Africa. Afro-Asian antagonism toward these two regimes has been, with few significant exceptions, so unremittingly and uniformly intense that it is considered as a given group property for the purposes of this study. Brazil's policy, on the other hand, has frequently been replete with evidence of domestic doubt and vacillation, especially with regard to

Portuguese Africa (more salient domestically), but also with regard to the type of relations Brazil, as a nation professing true racial democracy, should pursue with South Africa, whose government practices the most extreme form of racism based on theories of racial incompatibility.

Brazilian Policy on Colonialism in the Postwar Decade

Brazil's initial disinterest after World War II in the problems of dependent peoples is evidenced by its failure to participate in the San Francisco Conference debates (in United Nations Committee II/4) on the documents which would become the core of Chapters XI, XII, and XIII of the United Nations charter. These portions of the charter regulate the trusteeship system and advance the thesis that colonial powers have certain stipulated responsibilities toward the inhabitants of their colonies. Paramount among their responsibilities are promotion of their colonies' well-being and preparation for their independence. Not having kept abreast of developments in the mandate system since Brazil had left the League of Nations, the Foreign Ministry did not anticipate the demand for independence soon to sweep the European colonies in Africa, Asia, and the Middle East.[1] It focused principally on inter-American affairs, as it had for the previous two decades. Like many Spanish American states, Brazil was reluctant to adopt an unambiguously consistent anticolonialist stance in international organizations because of the cultural attraction which the European colonial powers held for the Latin elite classes, the group Wagley terms the "metropolitan upper class."[2] This cultural attraction applied to Brazil to a greater extent than to many other American republics (such as Mexico, Guatemala, and Haiti). It gained additional weight through the exceptionally close relations between Rio de Janeiro and Washington existing since the days of Rio Branco. Brazil repeatedly seemed to follow Washington's lead in colonial matters, a stance not uncongenial to the metropolitan upper class, from which Brazil's diplomats were almost ex-

---

1. Brazilian Institute of International Relations, "Brazil and the United Nations," p. 232.
2. Charles Wagley, *The Latin American Tradition*, pp. 102–3.

clusively drawn before the 1946 installation of a broader-based recruitment and examination system. In opposition to the anticolonialism readily employed by the Communist bloc for purposes of discrediting the West, early Brazilian delegations to the United Nations regularly supported the colonial powers or abstained, even while they verbally advocated the rapid granting of independence to dependent territories as a matter of idealistic principle. To ease the strain between these two conflicting policies, Brazil typically defended the creation of an atmosphere of patient moderation and tolerance within which the administering powers themselves could best promote the eventual autonomy of colonial peoples provided for within the peaceful, legal framework of United Nations institutions. So carefully did Brazil avoid any language that could be considered prejudicial and offensive to its Western allies that to all appearances the Foreign Ministry considered anticolonialism mainly within the perspective of the Cold War struggle. In this frame of reference the national interest was clear—effective support for the West, with whom, after all, emotional ties were much stronger than those few links Brazil may have had with emergent Afro-Asian nations. Brazil still considered Afro-Asia more competitor than ally.[3] Brazil's own transition from colonial to independent status was both too remote in time and too dissimilar to that of Afro-Asia to provide any sense of solidarity.

Even when Cold War issues were not at stake, Brazil, by taking a strict juridical orientation, resisted intervention of international organizations into colonial disputes. Several such instances occurred within the inter-American system, separate from the East-West conflict in which Guatemala and Argentina (with overtones of self-interest) attempted to bring the status of British Honduras (Belize), the Falkland Islands (Islas Malvinas), and the Guianas under the surveillance of the Western Hemispheric regional organization. At the Ninth

---

3. Taking advantage of this attitudinal set and Brazil's Latinité, France frequently requested and usually received Brazilian support in its colonial difficulties in the United Nations, as it did that of other "moderate" Latin American states with Francophile leanings. Latin sympathies also produced Brazilian and general Latin American support for Italian interests in the disposition by the General Assembly of its former colonies after World War II.

International Conference of American States in Bogotá (1948), Guatemala introduced the topic "European Colonies in America." After its consideration of the question by a subcommittee, the conference declared the "just aspirations" of the American republics that the colonial status of these dependencies of extrahemispheric powers be ended. A draft resolution establishing an American Committee on Dependent Territories to find peaceful ways of decolonizing these areas and to report on their progress was approved, in spite of abstentions by the United States, the Dominican Republic, Chile, and Brazil.

João Neves da Fontoura, head of the Brazilian delegation, stated that an inter-American conference was not the "appropriate forum for debating a question that affects the interests of countries outside the continent," countries which had already solemnly assumed the obligation under the United Nations charter and machinery to prepare all dependent territories for self-government. Neither could the American states arrogate jurisdiction and condemnatory rights to themselves when international courts of justice had the function of deciding legal questions and the United Nations possessed adequate procedures for peaceful political solutions. A declaration to this effect was inserted by Brazil into the final act of the conference.[4]

Similarly, when the same anticolonial issue was raised at the March 1951 Consultative Meeting of Foreign Ministers in Washington, Brazil abstained from voting on the proposal as presented because it contained language which, according to the Brazilian delegate, might have been interpreted as hostile to several Western European powers and therefore become ammunition for Cold War propaganda. The draft, which dealt with the status of the aforementioned territories should the European administrator fall to communist imperialism, was also judged by the delegation to be redundant and in-

4. General coverage of the conference is found in Charles G. Fenwick, "The Ninth International Conference of American States"; and William Sanders, "Summary of the Conclusions of the Ninth International Conference of American States, Bogotá, Colombia, March 30–May 2, 1948." Brazilian views are given in Brazilian Institute of International Relations, "Brazil and the United Nations," pp. 65–70; and A. Camilo de Oliveira, "Linhas mestras da política exterior do Brasil," pp. 128–29.

opportune, but it was adopted in spite of American and Brazilian abstention.[5]

During the United Nations' first decade Brazil blended its traditional support of nonintervention in the domestic affairs of states with a conciliatory role directed to peaceful solutions and gradual emancipation. In the political conditions of the times, this stance meant, in practice, acceptance of interim compromises and acquiescence to the established powers and rights of the administering states. In 1947, for example, Brazil was a strong proponent of the position that Article 73(e) of the United Nations charter could not be interpreted to require obligatory transmission to the Ad Hoc Committee on Information from Non-Self-Governing Territories of any information by colonial powers about conditions within their colonies. Also, according to Brazil, this committee was not competent to analyze political (as opposed to social) information. With the colonial powers, Brazil argued that information transmission must be purely voluntary, a view not shared by many Latin American states.[6] Although Brazil later evolved under Vargas (1951-1954) to a position which favored stronger United Nations supervisory powers over administered territories, it continued to demonstrate an inclination to abstain when a particular colonial power was singled out by name in even a mildly condemnatory resolution. Brazil would instead advance conciliatory resolutions expressing hopes for and confidence in just and equitable settlements which would lead to greater freedom for the colonies and would be attained through pacific resort to mediation, arbitration, adjudication, or bilateral negotiations, in conformity with the principles outlined in the charter. Brazil's cautious approach reaffirmed United Nations competence in such matters, but also afforded Brazil the advantage of not antagonizing the major colonial powers (with which good relations were desired) by limiting the United Nations' competence to spheres which did not seriously interfere with their freedom of action. This was the implicit Brazilian rationale in the important questions of the independence of Morocco, Tunisia, and later Algeria: consideration

5. Brazilian Institute of International Relations, "Brazil and the United Nations," pp. 70–71.
6. John A. Houston, *Latin America in the United Nations*, pp. 170–71.

of concrete political power realities and interest took precedence over abstract principles of anticolonialism and self-determination. Although the latter were not by any means abandoned, they were pursued with considerably less than full vigor.[7]

Brazil, Portugal, and Portuguese Africa: The Controversial Triangle

When, in December 1955, Portugal was admitted to the United Nations as part of a package compromise involving fifteen other states, Brazil was one of Portugal's co-sponsors and most faithful allies. Cooperation with Portugal was assured by the sentimentality and affectivity long pervading Luso-Brazilian relations. Their shared romanticism evoked common historical, cultural, and linguistic ties to solidify (or perhaps justify) a common stand internationally. As described in 1957 by João Neves da Fontoura, foreign minister from January to July 1946 and from January 1951 to June 1953, "Our policy toward Portugal is not a 'policy.' It is a family affair. No one plays politics with his parents or siblings. He lives with them, in the intimacy of kinship and sentiment. In difficult times each one searches for support and counsel among his loved ones. Without rules. Without treaties. Without recompense. By virtue of kinship."[8] According to this interpretation, Brazil, as a faithful son, had a moral debt of unconditional support which it owed Portugal in return for Portugal's role in constructing the Brazilian civilization.

The legal groundwork enshrining this special relationship which has to date had great implications in Brazil's African policies was the Treaty of Friendship and Consultation, signed in Rio de Janeiro on 16 November 1953, ratified a year later, and promulgated by the Brazilian government in January 1955. Through this document both parties expressed their desire to "consecrate, in a solemn political instrument,

7. A good illustration of Brazil's relative isolation from most Latin American states and general coincidence with the United States on important trust, decolonization, and human rights votes is given by William G. Cornelius, in "The 'Latin American Bloc' in the United Nations."
8. "Por uma política luso-brasileira," *O Globo*, 10 June 1957, 2d ser., p. 13.

the principles which orient the Luso-Brazilian Community in the world." They attribute their desire to a realization of "the spiritual, moral, ethnic, and linguistic affinities that, after more than three centuries of common history, continue to tie the Brazilian Nation to the Portuguese Nation, from which results a most special situation for the reciprocal interests of the two peoples." The most important articles of the treaty were three:[9]

Article One

The High Contracting Parties, with the intention of reaffirming and consolidating the perfect friendship which exists between the two brotherly peoples, agree that, in the future, they will always consult each other on international problems of their obvious common interest.

Article Two

Each of the High Contracting Parties agrees to grant to the nationals of the other special treatment which will make them equal to its own nationals in everything which is not directly regulated contrariwise in the constitutional provisions of the two Nations, [equal] in the juridical, commercial, economic, financial, and cultural spheres, with the protection of the local authorities being as broad as that granted to its own nationals.

Article Eight

The High Contracting Parties pledge themselves to study, whenever opportune and necessary, the means of developing the progress, harmony, and prestige of the Luso-Brazilian Community in the world.

The treaty was to be in effect for ten years after its ratification, with renewal optional every ten years thereafter. It depended for its effectiveness upon the passage of complementary domestic legislation to expedite some of its provisions. The slowness of this legislation in appearing was a measure of the divided state of Brazilian opinion as to the relative advantages of "equal treatment." One consideration

---

9. The treaty's text may be found in Brasil, Ministério das Relações Exteriores, Divisão de Atos, Congressos e Conferências Internacionais, *Brasil-Portugal: Tratado de amizade e consulta.*

was the fact that Portuguese citizens and activities in Brazil far outweighed Brazilian citizens and activities in Portugal. A bi-national commission established in June 1957 was to coordinate the conclusions on treaty implementations reached by separate national committees.

The following joint declaration by the presidents of the two states in creating the commission gives an indication of the treaty's early role in foreign policy, an area in which enabling legislation was not necessary: "The Treaty of Friendship and Consultation has already had its practical and creative projection, causing a more fruitful and intimate collaboration of the two Governments in the field of foreign policy, continuing to tighten the traditional ties that unite them and the interdependent interests of the vast Portuguese-speaking world. Portugal and Brazil, in the consummation of a conception in which national ideals and interests find their place in the broader framework of common ideals and interests, are taking their position, hand in hand, in world politics."[10]

Despite any other manisfestations of anticolonialism which may have animated the governments of Café Filho (1954–1955) and Juscelino Kubitschek (1956–1961), their sympathy was solidly on the side of Portugal in its tribulations in the United Nations. Café Filho, in an official visit to Portugal in April 1955 to attempt to broaden the execution of the treaty to all Portuguese-speaking regions of the world, glorified the discoveries and civilizing mission of the Portuguese nation. At a banquet offered by Portuguese President Craveiro Lopes, he declared, "We have clear knowledge of all that we owe to Portugal, from the discovery of our country and its incorporation into the civilized world to the efforts and struggles of its national formation. . . . This is but a minor detail in comparison to a much wider debt, which is the debt of the human race itself to this country."[11] Alluding to questions raised in the General Assembly concerning the Portuguese territories in Africa, the Brazilian president explained: "The concern shown recently by Brazil when disquieting threats hovered over Portuguese territories was nothing but the spontaneous

10. *Tratados e actos internacionais, Brasil-Portugal*, pp. 250–51.
11. Brasil, Presidência da República, *Visita do Presidente João Café Filho a Portugal*, p. 67.

fulfillment of a fraternal duty, which should prevail not only in moments of rejoicing but equally in difficult times. . . . It is never out of place to call attention to the trait of generosity of the Portuguese, to bring about in all continents a labor of civilization which in practice has been much more useful and beneficial to others than to themselves."[12]

Referring to the treaty and what he termed the identical origins and aspirations of Portugal and Brazil, Kubitschek during an official visit to Brazil by Portuguese President Craveiro Lopes in 1957, observed the appropriateness of the unique solidarity provided for by the 1953 document: "We Portuguese and Brazilians have a single national soul and our desire of union is a nostalgia for the primordial union. Tying ourselves so strongly together on the international scene we are doing nothing more than reuniting and welding together the fragments of that same common soul which was dispersed in the astonishing epic of Portuguese expansion in the world."[13]

Effusive sentimentality, father-son relationship metaphors, idealization of Portugal's "glorious past," the unity of interests, and the concept of an immeasurable Brazilian debt toward Portugal were constants in Luso-Brazilian relations during the terms of Café Filho and Kubitschek. These were also investments which would pay off handsomely in Brazilian support in what was largely a unilateral obligation. For example, Portugal invoked the treaty to criticize Brazil privately whenever the latter failed to consult with Lisbon on "international problems of their obvious common interest." Such a situation arose in October 1957, when Brazil, without consulting Portugal, became co-sponsor of a General Assembly resolution creating an Economic Committee for Africa.

---

12. Ibid., p. 68. An illustration of the attitudinal set of Café Filho during this visit is his revelation years later in an interview that while visiting the Castelo de Guimarães, historic birthplace of Portugal, he was so overwhelmed emotionally by the experience that his personal physician accompanying the group saw it necessary to give him immediate treatment to ward off a possible heart attack. See "O ultramar é bastião avançado da comunidade," *O Mundo Português*, 23 June 1968, 2d sec., p. 1.

13. Américo Laeth de Magalhães, *Brasil-Portugal: Documentário da visita oficial ao Brasil do General Francisco Higino Craveiro Lopes, Presidente da República Portuguêsa (5–25 de junho de 1957)*, p. 153.

Portugal's Foreign Minister, Paulo Cunha, felt that such a committee would be harmful to Portuguese interests and made a complaint to the Brazilian ambassador. He based his complaint upon the treaty, even though it was not in full operation at the time.[14]

According to Horacio Láfer, Foreign Minister from August 1959 to January 1961, Kubitschek's clear instructions to Itamaraty were that in any case, and especially in difficult ones, Brazil should vote with Portugal in international organizations. In regard to controversial questions over Angola and Mozambique, Láfer himself felt that the best policy would be to second Portuguese decisions.[15] The irony of this state of affairs was that Portugal expected, and usually received, Brazil's involvement and assistance (votes, speeches, and whatever help it could muster in Latin America) whenever Portuguese Africa was discussed in the United Nations. But at the same time Salazar and his foreign ministers assiduously avoided any Brazilian involvement, presence, or influence in Portuguese Guinea, Angola, or Mozambique. Yet, Portugal never abandoned its set phrases about the "Portuguese-speaking world." Álvaro Lins, ambassador to Lisbon during most of the Kubitschek administration (from December 1956 to October 1959), was keenly aware of what he saw as Brazilian responsibilities and possibilities in the overseas territories and suggested to Itamaraty the desirability of promoting trade and cultural relations with these areas, but without stimulating or provoking their eventual drive toward independence. The many studies which the Brazilian embassy in Lisbon sent to the Foreign Ministry on the subject urged the government to prepare for an active role in the future of these colonies, which, reported Lins, would one day be independent Portuguese-speaking nations. If his advice on contact and trade was ignored by Itamaraty, the reaction of the Portuguese government was even more unfavorable.[16] The classified set of "Notas Interpretativas" drawn up in 1958 by the two governments to regulate the Treaty of Friendship and Consultation defined the treaty as taking in all of Brazil's territory but specifically excluded from the "community" the

14. Álvaro Lins, *Missão em Portugal*, pp. 8–9.
15. *O Globo*, 9 December 1961, special supplement on Portugal, p. 15.
16. Lins, pp. 272–79.

overseas territories of Portugal, a point which Lisbon made unmistakably clear in high-level diplomatic discussions.[17]

Despite this unequal yoke of obligations and privileges, the Brazilian delegation to the United Nations aided Portugal by subscribing to and defending the thesis of "overseas provinces" and by maintaining the discretionary and voluntary right of any administering power to yield or withhold information on the territories within its jurisdiction, under Article 73(e) of the charter. The latter point was somewhat of a reversal of the more anticolonialist stance of the second Vargas period—before Portugal was admitted to the United Nations and began to draw criticism. Most probably with an eye toward safeguarding Portugal's interests, although France's colonial problems certainly did not go unnoticed, Brazil voted and lobbied whenever possible in such a way as to have sensitive colonial issues declared substantive questions which would require a two-thirds vote for resolutions. Thus, Brazil deliberately hindered the efforts of the Afro-Asians to bring greater pressure or condemnation upon these colonial powers.[18] Such was the case when new United Nations members (especially Portugal) refused to transmit information about their non-self-governing territories. The problem was brought to the United Nations Fourth Committee by anticolonialist states in January 1957. The anticolonialists maintained that the General Assembly had clear responsibility and proper jurisdiction to determine which new members had an obligation to transmit reports. Ceylon, Greece, Liberia, Nepal, and Syria submitted a draft resolution to establish an ad hoc committee of the General Assembly for this purpose. Brazil, in completely rejecting the arguments of

17. Ibid., pp. 378–79. It is revealing to note that Lins, who finally broke with Kubitschek over what he considered the subservience of Brazilian policy to the wishes of the Salazar dictatorship, was replaced in 1959 as ambassador to Lisbon by Francisco Negrão de Lima, whose views were much less likely to offend the Portuguese government. Lins subsequently carried on an unsuccessful public campaign to discourage Kubitschek from paying an official visit to Lisbon in 1960 and then became an authorized spokesman for anti-Salazar Portuguese immigrants in Brazil.

18. The nucleus of the European self-image of the Brazilian metropolitan upper class was their cultural and historical links to Portugal and France, with whom they would much rather identify than any of the nations of Africa, Asia, or the Middle East.

the anticolonialist group, cited the Portuguese constitution as an authoritative source to determine the unity of all the national territory and favorably compared the situation in Portuguese Africa with the historical unity between Portugal and Brazil from 1808–1821. In short, Brazil defended Portugal as ably and in the same manner as did Portugal's own representative. Thus a two-pronged thesis was espoused: Regarding all identification of non-self-governing territories, the state responsible for the administration of its territory had the right to determine its constitutional status while the assembly was legally incompetent to do so (following practice since 1946). In the specific instance of Portugal, additional, unique factors were marshalled to show that ever since "Portugal took her civilization overseas," Portuguese territory had been "a cultural and psychological whole, a single unit" without discrimination as to race, color, religion, or social condition. The Brazilian representative concluded that his delegation could not find "any concrete reason for disagreeing with the Portuguese Government when it states that Portugal does not administer Non-Self-Governing Territories."[19]

Although the disparity between official characterizations of Brazil as an anticolonialist nation and Brazil's systematic support of positions which tended to postpone the end of colonialism could be satisfactorily maintained in the political atmosphere of the United Nations until 1958 or 1960, some delegates experienced misgivings about the continued viability of such ambivalence. They became especially concerned when subjected to rising pressure from African nationalism demonstrated in the April 1958 Pan-African Conference in Accra. They also anticipated admission of many new African members in the near future. An anticolonial consensus was making itself felt in the world organization. And in a wider range of cases the colonialist powers and their allies found themselves less capable of obtaining majorities to defend their interests.[20] Foreseeing the impending defeat of the overseas

19. United Nations, General Assembly, Eleventh Session, Fourth Committee, *Statement Made by the Representative of Brazil at the 617th Meeting of the Fourth Committee on 30 January 1957*, A/C.4/349, p. 6.
20. For an empirical treatment of this consensus, see Edward T. Rowe, "The Emerging Anti-Colonial Consensus in the United Nations."

provinces device as a means to keep the status of the Portuguese territories from becoming a subject of censure, a Brazilian senator serving as delegate to the Thirteenth General Assembly noted in his report to the Senate that a revision of the nation's policy on colonialism was imperative in order that Brazil adapt itself to clearly emerging trends: "The time has come for us to reconsider the middle of the road policy that always directed our action as we confronted situations generated by the nationalistic expansion of the African peoples. Without endorsing, of course, the extremism of the Arab-Asian group we can conciliate our course of action with the irrepressible dynamism of the political tendencies of the continent in the face of the obsolete and isolated conservative attitude of some administering powers. Otherwise we risk remaining isolated when other countries are reviewing their policies to fall into line with the reality that is daily being expressed in that organization."[21]

In August 1960, on the occasion of the celebrations marking the five-hundredth anniversary of the death of Prince Henry the Navigator, Kubitschek made an official visit to Portugal and signed six treaties designed to operationalize further the ideas of community enunciated by the Treaty of Friendship and Consultation. These treaties would regulate tourist exchange, passport visas, juridical assistance, diplomatic and consular representation, extradition, and questions pertaining to individuals holding citizenship in both states. The Brazilian president again, as always in similar ceremonies, emphasized the special character of Luso-Brazilian relations. He told Portuguese President Américo Tomás, "We have not merely diplomatic or cordial relations, but family ties. We are a unique case in the world." He also referred to a "solidarity which transcends material interests, which is even independent of our volition, which is stronger than our will—the solidarity of kinship, the solidarity of the cradle, of the first hours of development."[22]

Concrete ramifications of this primordial solidarity were seen later that year in the voting on the first General Assembly resolution which focused specifically upon the Portu-

21. *O Senador Cunha Mello na ONU*, p. 76.
22. *Revista brasileira de política internacional*, 3, No. 12 (December 1960): 136.

guese colonies. Although Brazil voted in favor of the historic Declaration on Independence for Colonial Countries and Peoples (Resolution 1,514) and in favor of Resolution 1,541, which enumerated principles to guide members in determining whether or not an obligation existed to transmit information on Non-Self-Governing Territories under Article 73(e), it voted against Resolution 1,542 of 15 December 1960. The latter resolution listed all Portuguese overseas possessions by name and declared that Portugal had the obligation to transmit information on them. In casting one of the six negative votes, Brazil isolated itself with Belgium, France, Portugal, Spain, and the Union of South Africa. Its delegation held that, since principles for determining obligations to transmit information had already been set forth and a Special Committee of Six existed to study such principles, it was inappropriate for the Committee on Information to discuss the transmission of information by Portugal and for the General Assembly to single out Portugal for noncompliance. The decision whether or not to submit information rested with the individual member state. This stand was clearly consistent with principles Brazil had espoused since Portugal's admission, but what was remarkable was Brazil's willingness to vote negatively when twelve Latin American states supported the resolution and five abstained, as did the United States and the United Kingdom.

Some Brazilians hoped for a stronger stand on Portugal when the outspokenly anticolonialist Quadros succeeded the Lusophile Kubitschek on 31 January 1961. In his public statements and ambitions concerning Africa, the new chief executive made clear his intentions of unambiguous anticolonialism, as in the following message to Congress: "We are a people of all races in which color, religion, and political affiliation are irrelevant and the individual stands on his personal worth. We do not accept any form or type of colonialism or imperialism. It can be affirmed with the most absolute sincerity that Brazil will strive so that all colonial peoples, we repeat, all, without exception, attain their independence in the shortest possible time and in conditions which best permit their stability and progress."[23] Kubitschek, by contrast, had

23. Jânio Quadros, *Mensagem ao Congresso Nacional*, p. 96.

trod much more lightly upon this issue, giving in his major policy addresses and programs merely cautious passing mention to anticolonialism of any style. It almost seemed as if anticolonialism were a trivial ephemera which merited only Brazil's passive observation and its de jure recognition of new states.

Quadros consciously sought to use an anticolonial posture as an ideological instrument to increase Brazilian prestige among African nations for cooperation in development. But his plans to vote independently on matters affecting Angola and to follow African events without consultation with Lisbon clashed with strong pro-Portuguese opposition in most politically important sectors of Brazilian society, the large Portuguese immigrant organizations, and the Foreign Ministry itself. For the first time, Brazilian support for an increasingly isolated Portugal was openly questioned. The result of this severe divergence of opinion was that Brazil sometimes abstained and sometimes voted against rather than with Portugal from 1961 to 1964. This pattern led Salazar's regime to devise various expedients to attempt to recover the lost vote.

The first test of Quadros' philosophy and resolve came in early 1961 as the Security Council and General Assembly discussed the outbreak of nationalist rebellion in Angola. After the divided council failed to act on the draft resolution initially introduced by Liberia, the matter was referred to the General Assembly with Brazilian approval. However, Brazil did not immediately state its position on the problem, basing its actual vote, in the phrasing of the Foreign Ministry, on the "*duty* of concluding the conversations with Portugal according to the Treaty of Friendship and Consultation" (emphasis added).[24] These conversations were accomplished via Foreign Minister Arinos' visit to Lisbon en route back to Brazil from the independence celebrations in Senegal. In the official interpretation of Brazil, made public on 14 April, these Lisbon conversations left the Brazilian government "entirely free to accompany the development of the African situation, according to its firm anti-colonial and anti-discriminatory policy, outspokenly favorable to the self-determination of all peo-

24. *O Globo*, 30 March 1961, p. 9.

ples."[25] In the General Assembly vote of 20 April, Resolution 1,603 (XV) passed 73 to 2, with 9 abstentions. It called upon the Portuguese government "to consider urgently" measures to bring independence to Angola in accordance with Resolution 1,514 and created a subcommittee of five members to conduct inquiries on Angola. Although Brazil supported the first part of the resolution, it attempted unsuccessfully to convince the thirty-six Afro-Asian sponsors to modify or eliminate the second part. Brazilian officials found the second portion "inoperative, excessive, and conducive to useless complications, as in the cases of the commissions on Hungary and Southwest Africa."[26] As the sponsoring group remained intractable, Brazil abstained on what could be considered either as a technical point or as a desire to protect Portugal's freedom of action in Angola.

The following month Francisco Negrão de Lima, ambassador to Lisbon, visited Angola at the invitation of the Portuguese authorities and publicly uttered only praise for what had been accomplished there. Although his final report to Itamaraty remained veiled in secrecy, his well-known pro-Portuguese partisanship led to some Brazilian criticism of his probable lack of objectivity in assessing the situation as it pertained to the national interest. Nevertheless, in December 1961 Brazil supported two resolutions of the General Assembly, the first recommending United Nations assistance for Angolan refugees in the Republic of the Congo and the second condemning Portugal's noncompliance in the transmission of information and its refusal to cooperate with the Committee on Information. The second resolution also established a special committee of seven members to investigate conditions in the territories and formulate recommendations to the assembly.[27] Although Brazil now agreed to the concept of an investigatory committee, its delegation stated that the word "deplored" was preferable to "condemned" to describe Portugal's noncompliance.

25. Brasil, Ministério das Relações Exteriores, *Relatório* (1961), p. 69.
26. Ibid., p. 70.
27. General Assembly, Resolution 1671 (XVI) passed by 67 votes to 0, with 11 abstentions; and Resolution 1699 (XVI) passed by 90 to 3, with 2 abstentions.

The year 1962 marked a watershed of sorts in Brazilian policy on Portuguese Africa. Itamaraty under President Goulart and Minister San Tiago Dantas sent out orders, dating from Quadros, to advance gradually with a firmer anticolonialist line. The Foreign Ministry wanted to avoid any attrition of Brazil's image in Afro-Asia because of its hesitancy in taking a clearer stand when Portugal, in African interpretation, was left as the only example of unrelenting, white, foreign-imposed colonialism. Even while appreciating and understanding Brazil's unique position, most Afro-Asian states expected an evolution in this stance and observed that many moderate states appeared to base their statements in general debate on the tenor of the Brazilian delegation's presentation.[28] To some extent, then, the Brazilian position was pivotal in setting the tone of debate if not in the outcome of the votes.

The classic definition of the Foreign Ministry's position at this time was carefully phrased by Chief Delegate Afonso Arinos in January 1962. As he opened the General Assembly plenary debate on Angola, he attributed Brazil's position to two factors: (1) Brazil's "most special" historical and cultural ties to Portugal; and (2) its traditional anticolonialism evolving from racial brotherhood, geographic position, economic interests, and a conviction that anticolonialism was, with disarmament, one of the two great problems of the century. Classifying the situation in Angola as worsening and dangerous to the maintenance of world peace, Arinos warned that the military solution proposed by some would not solve the impasse. He prophesied a peaceful outcome should Portugal recognize the right of the Angolans to self-determination and prepare the administrative and legislative reforms requisite to the granting of self-government. He urged Portugal itself to "assume the direction of the movement for the liberty of Angola" and to "accept the natural march of history." In this area Brazil, according to Arinos, felt a definite responsibility to assist Portugal in the pacific resolution of her colonial conflicts, to assure the survival of Portuguese language and culture in Africa and harmonious relations

---

28. Interview with a former Brazilian delegate (Antonio Houaiss) to the United Nations Fourth Committee, 29 October 1968.

within the Portuguese-speaking world; relations could only be strained by prolonged armed struggle.[29]

Routine in its call for compromise and moderation, this important policy statement differed sharply from previous ones in that the friendship with Portugal (*laços especialíssimos*) was no longer construed to require either tacit or explicit support for Portuguese colonialism. Brazilian defense of independence for the territories was said to be designed to protect the enlightened long-run interests of Portugal, even if Lisbon should choose not to acknowledge the fact. Desirous of maintaining friendship with Portugal, yet defending the independence of Portuguese Africa, to which Lisbon did not concede the remotest probability, Brazil was running the risk of alienating both Portugal and Black Africa. This clearly announced position greatly disturbed Lisbon and pro-Portuguese elements in Brazil, but equal Afro-Asian obstinacy precluded Brazil's assumption of its coveted role as moderator. Indicative of the political climate of the Sixteenth Assembly was the failure to gain general acceptance of a Brazilian idea aimed at seeking a conciliatory rather than a mutually inflammatory formula via a noncondemnatory resolution. Such a resolution would have asserted that no state need feel its sovereignty infringed in allowing on its soil an investigating committee duly established under the charter by the General Assembly. The resolution would also have urged Portugal to cooperate with the Subcommittee on the Situation in Angola and would have expressed hopes that Portugal would take adequate measures to grant the same independence to Angola that other European states had granted to their non-self-governing African territories.[30]

29. The speech, which was given widespread domestic publicity, is reproduced in San Tiago Dantas, *Política externa independente*, pp. 195–200.
30. Consistent with its long-established blanket policy against the use of force as a means to settle territorial disputes, Brazil protested the December 1961 Indian occupation of Goa, Daman, and Diu, a position shared by few Afro-Asian states, less concerned with legal questions and more with matters of principle relating to Western colonial enclaves entrenched for centuries. To emphasize Brazilian solidarity with Portugal in this matter, the official protest was delivered to U Thant by the head of the Brazilian delegation in the company of Portuguese Foreign Minister Franco Nogueira. Under Kubitschek, Itamaraty had generally accepted the Portuguese interpretation of

Brazil supported the actual draft resolution as it came before the assembly (although it was considerably broader and stronger in coverage than the preferred Brazilian version), because it did not "condemn" Portugal. Rather, it "deplored" that country's lack of cooperation and "deprecated" its repressive measures while reaffirming the "inalienable right of the Angolan people to self-determination and independence" and while urging Portugal to institute reforms leading to independence. At the same time it requested all member states to refrain from lending Portugal any assistance which might be used to suppress the Angolans.[31] The record on Portuguese Africa during the remaining years of Goulart's presidency reveals a notable and curious ambivalence. The delegation abstained on all the important resolutions in the General Assembly but cast votes against Portugal twice in the Security Council. It always spoke in favor of independence for the territories but on occasion resorted to abstention on procedural grounds to avoid open condemnation of Portugal. Such painful inconsistency was a function not only of changing figures in the Foreign Ministry and the United Nations but also of the great domestic resistance encountered whenever a vote contrary to Portugal was cast for the supposedly gratuitous purpose of appealing to the anticolonialist bloc. The latter issue of contention was in reality an international ramification of the domestic political struggle between conservatives and developmental nationalists. Neither could gain the upper hand in what had rapidly become the number-one issue of the Afro-Asian policy. As a consequence, the Foreign Ministry was the focus of powerful cross pressures.

An example par excellance of the lengths to which this conflict was carried within the executive branch itself has been documented by historian José Honório Rodrigues, who reveals the discrepancies existing between two separate printings of the 1963 presidential message to Congress. The wording of the first printing, in reaffirming Brazil's anticolonialism, stated, "We have recognized and will continue to recognize

---

conflict with India over these territories as well as protected Portuguese interests in India after Portugal and India had severed relations, so the 1961 protest conformed to past practice.

31. General Assembly Resolution 1,742 (XVI), 30 January 1962, adopted 99 to 2, with 1 abstention.

the right to independence of all colonial peoples and the obligation of colonial and administrative powers to accelerate the preparations for independence, *including that of Angola and the other overseas territories of Portugal as well as South West Africa"* (emphasis added).[32] The second version casually omitted the portions of this sentence relating to Portuguese Africa and South West Africa, reportedly at the behest of Foreign Minister Hermes Lima, who wanted to avoid offending the Portuguese and the vocal Portuguese sympathizers in Brazil. This pressure group, according to Honório Rodrigues, was responsible for substantial modification in Brazil's United Nations position on Angola after 1961. It marshalled well-coordinated domestic opposition to any votes or remarks antagonistic to the African aims of the Salazar regime.[33]

As if to further accent the internal divisions over policy, the most unequivocal stand against Portuguese colonialism ever taken by Brazil was assumed in the presence of the Portuguese Foreign Minister in July 1963 in the United Nations Security Council. The stand led to a nadir in relations between the two countries. Representative Carvalho Silos, while still recommending avoidance of drastic measures which would serve merely to antagonize Portugal and preclude conciliation, spoke clearly in favor of the independence of the territories. Brazil no longer accepted them as overseas provinces and therefore as beyond the jurisdiction of the United Nations. Although Carvalho Silos reaffirmed the responsibility felt by Brazil in the matter and placed the services of its diplomacy at Lisbon's disposal to expedite a peaceful evolutionary granting of self-determination, the Brazilian representative went so far as to warn that his country would be forced to harden its policy should Portugal fail to reconsider its actions in Africa.[34] Following up this declaration, Brazil voted to favor Resolution S/5,380, which stated that Portuguese policies represented a threat to peace and security in Africa and called upon Portugal to take steps to end the colonial wars and transfer power to freely elected representatives with a granting of independence. The resolution also re-

32. José Honório Rodrigues, *Brasil e Africa: Outro horizonte*, 2: 398.
33. Interview with José Honório Rodrigues, 17 September 1968.
34. United Nations, Security Council, Eighteenth Year, 1,043rd Meeting, 24 July 1963, *Official Records*, S/PV.1,043, pp. 2–5.

quested all states to refrain from offering the Portuguese government any assistance, arms, or military equipment which could be·used to pursue colonial wars.

The Security Council speech was applauded by those who, like José Honório Rodrigues, felt that Brazil could not "approach Africa arm in arm with Salazar" and that it could cooperate fully with independent Portuguese-speaking nations on the opposite shores of the South Atlantic.[35] Although there were some sympathizers with Holden Roberto's Union of the Angolan People (UPA) and Mário de Andrade's People's Movement for the Liberation of Angola (MPLA), they were rather few and were restricted largely to the intellectual class of journalists, professors, and authors. They energetically denounced tacit complicity with the Portuguese as constituting submission to "sentimental blackmail" through a Lusitanian community into which Brazil would enter belatedly "as a dupe just to pay for the broken china."[36] To this small group, failure to support the Angolan liberation movements was tantamount to a betrayal of all the ethnic and biological elements which were absorbed from Angolan Negroes, who had helped give Brazil its unique racial and cultural cast. This failure was also considered a fatal stumbling block to desirable growth of Brazilian prestige in Africa.[37]

Brazilian books and magazines circulating comparatively freely in Angola gave the Portuguese-speaking Africans an opportunity to become acquainted with Brazil. But curiously, either because of lack of interest or the conspiracy of silence which the anticolonialists attributed to pro-Portuguese groups, no similar literature from or about Portuguese Africa found a readership in Brazil. Even at the height of Goulart's independent foreign policy little information about Portuguese Africa and the conflicts there was published in Brazil. The items which did appear usually were either noncommittal wire releases or they adhered to the Portuguese line. The

35. Rodrigues, p. 367.
36. Jorge Amado, "Conversa com Buanga Fêlê, também conhecido como Mário de Andrade, chefe da luta de Angola," p. 29.
37. Even after Eduardo Mondlane formed the Front for the Liberation of Mozambique (FRELIMO) in 1962 and launched armed struggle the following year, Angola remained for Brazilians by far the most salient of the Portuguese African territories because of its greater proximity to Brazil in both geographic and cultural senses.

most notable exceptions were campaigns undertaken by the staid *Estado de São Paulo* and by the populist *Última Hora* of Rio de Janeiro to publicize the nature of the liberation struggle and assist liberation leaders in finding the support they were hoping for in Brazil.[38]

From 1961 to March 1964, a group of exiled young Angolan students in São Paulo, several with scholarships from the Foreign Ministry, formed the nucleus of the resistance movement in Brazil. They organized under the name of the "Afro-Brazilian Movement for the Liberation of Angola" (MABLA) and collaborated with journalists, professors, students, and intellectuals. In correspondence with Mário de Andrade, the leaders of MABLA proposed to counteract the strong pro-Portuguese propaganda (this promptly labeled them as Communist) and to establish a climate of public opinion conducive to the exertion of Brazilian suasion upon Lisbon to expedite the independence of Guinea, Angola, and Mozambique. Laboring under a double burden, the sparsely equipped organization was forced to contend not only with diffuse pro-Portuguese sentiment and ignorance about conditions in the territories but also with the growing inclination of their ideological Brazilian associates to combine the African and Cuban problems into one. This trend Mário de Andrade judged counterproductive to the movement. The principal sources of effective cooperation came from a prominent São Paulo daily, the Foreign Ministry under San Tiago Dantas, and interested African embassies in Rio de Janeiro, but they proved insufficient to impel the group beyond the status of a mere exile movement exerting little influence on the politically relevant sectors of public opinion.[39]

If certain nationalist activists were encouraged by the hardening of Brazilian policy toward Portugal during the last year of Goulart's regime, other influential and more traditionally oriented politicians were dismayed by the turn of events, which they considered one more irresponsible devia-

---

38. A publishing house noted for leftist ideological and developmental nationalist studies released a collected volume of poems and stories written by black Portuguese-speaking Africans. It enjoyed only narrow circulation. See João Alves das Neves, ed., *Poetas e contistas africanos de expressão portuguêsa*. Several of the works of Mario de Andrade were published in the short-lived magazine *Paratodos*.

39. Interview with Paulo dos Santos Matoso Neto, 20 June 1968.

tion from established patterns in national political style. Typical of such reaction was the report presented to the senate by the delegation of observers from that body to the Eighteenth Session of the United Nations General Assembly. The report criticized the recent evolution of policy (and particularly the Security Council vote of July) as harmful to the national interest and a retreat based merely upon doubtful political considerations. According to the delegation, these political considerations did not adequately take into account such factors as Brazil's special relationship with Portugal, the place of Portuguese Africa in national security, the advantages Portugal could afford in expanding exports to Europe, and the tenacity of the Africans in protecting their own economic privileges in Europe against Latin American penetration.[40]

The 1964 revolution was generally regarded by the Lusophiles as a triumph over what they called the Afro-Asian group in the Foreign Ministry, which had antagonized Portugal and sabotaged the Luso-Brazilian community ever since the early days of Quadros' presidency. The actions of the military government bore out this expectation. The more vocal Itamaraty anticolonialists were quietly removed from positions of power and the chief Brazilian delegate to the First UNCTAD in Geneva was called home to explain the position of his delegation. Most pointedly, the Brazilian delegate was questioned about the rationale behind Brazilian accompaniment of several African delegations which left the conference hall after Portugal requested the floor. Under the name of "The Military-Police Inquiry into the Angolan Group" and reputedly with supervision from agents of Salazar's International Police for Defense of the State (PIDE), intelligence officers of the Secret Service of the Brazilian Navy (CENIMAR) imprisoned and interrogated MABLA activists and other African students because of their participation in a proliberation movement. Several African embassies had to intervene to secure the release of their affected nationals. The results of this investigation were delivered in documentary

40. Antônio Carlos Konder Reis, *Missão na ONU: Relatório apresentado pela delegação de observadores parlamentares do Senado a XVIIIª Assembléia Geral da Organização das Nações Unidas*, p. 15.

form to the Supreme Military Tribunal for evaluation.[41] From the first days of the revolutionary government, Foreign Minister Vasco Leitão da Cunha declared that Brazil's policy would be one of defense of Portuguese interests. And, after four months of new regime, he counted the improvement of relations with "beloved Portugal" as one of the most important accomplishments of the Foreign Ministry under his direction.[42] In the United Nations Brazil clarified that it would begin to vote with Portugal on questions concerning Portugal's African possessions.

In a graduation address at the diplomatic corps' Rio Branco Institute on 31 July 1964, President Castello Branco, for the first time officially, touched upon a topic long discussed in private circles. He suggested that a possible solution to the national dilemma of anticolonialist sentiment clashing with special ties to Portugal might be found in the "gradual formation of an Afro-Luso-Brazilian Community, in which the Brazilian presence would strengthen the system economically."[43] This conception had been championed for several years by Gilberto Freyre, a fellow Northeasterner, as "a federation with common citizenship and a number of other common rights and responsibilities."[44] During Goulart's regime, however, the Brazilian government was reluctant to consider such a plan publicly for ideological reasons. Portugal also hesitated to allow Brazilian penetration into its overseas provinces, although former Foreign Minister San Tiago Dantas revealed, in commenting on Castello Branco's speech, that such a triangular community had in fact been the subject of earlier "very interesting conversations" between the two states in 1962. He indicated that Brazil had then taken the position that this integration could occur only after Portuguese Africa had gained its independence.[45]

The new political configuration in Brazil, coupled with greater international resistance to Portuguese colonialism,

41. Márcio Moreira Alves, *Tortura e torturados*, pp. 187–90.
42. Brasil, Ministério das Relações Exteriores, *Itamaraty*, 1, No. 9 (30 July 1964): 240–41.
43. Brasil, Ministério das Relações Exteriores, Departamento Cultural e de Informações, *Textos e declarações sôbre política externa (de abril de 1964 a abril de 1965)*, p. 12.
44. Gilberto Freyre, *New World in the Tropics*, p. 183.
45. *Jornal do Brasil*, 5 August 1964, p. 8.

not to mention the outbreak of fighting in Mozambique, produced by the end of 1964 a set of circumstances in which Brazil dropped its insistence on the prerequisite of independence (stressing instead the dangers of "premature disengagement" and "new imperialisms"). Portugal, too, began to ponder seriously the merits of closer association with Brazil in maintaining itself as an African power after 400 years of attempts to keep Brazil out of its African possessions. A transformation in the basic tenor of Luso-Brazilian relations was becoming discernible. President Castello Branco expressed the belief of his government that Portugal was giving birth to new Brazils in southern Africa: "Regarding the Portuguese policy in the overseas [provinces], Brazil, although confirming its position on the issue of self-determination, expresses its conviction that Portugal will be able to resolve its problems in the spirit of its historical traditions, traditions which directed the formation of the Brazilian national soul and gave shape to the type of multiracial society dominant in Brazil. The confidence of Brazil in the civilizing mission of Portugal therefore derives from the consideration of concrete facts, proven by sociology and by history."[46]

On 5 August 1965, two months after a productive official visit to Brazil, Portuguese Foreign Minister Alberto Franco Nogueira formally proposed in a Lisbon news conference the expansion of the Treaty of Friendship and Consultation to encompass all of Portugal's overseas territories. He suggested eventual integration of the two nations into a huge Luso-Brazilian community which would afford Brazil free ports, markets, and resources around the world, should the necessary treaties be negotiated and ratified.[47] This reversal of position, garnished with the usual rhetoric, contained two points upon which serious discord would arise. The first, in the guise of reciprocity in delineating common borders, stipulated, "When we place without restrictions all that we are and have at the disposition of Brazil, we assume that Brazil will also accept without restrictions all we are and have."

46. Brasil, Ministério das Relações Exteriores, Departamento Cultural e de Informações, *Textos e declarações sôbre política externa* (*de abril de 1964 a abril de 1965*), p. 35.
47. Franco Nogueira's interview is reproduced in "A idéia da comunidade luso-brasileira," *Jornal do Brasil*, 15 August 1965, special sec., p. 4.

This precondition and a reference to "the whole Portuguese nation" indicated that Brazil was being requested to stamp its approval without reservations on Portuguese colonialism in Africa by becoming part of it. The second consideration, all the more ominous because of its imprecise formulation, centered on what Franco Nogueira cryptically called "common external action for the guarantee and defense of the territorial, cultural, and moral estate that belongs to both [nations]." This phrase, in the context of further explanations, implied an eventual military alliance as the ultimate desideratum. Portuguese insistence that the community was primarily political in nature did little to quell the apprehensions that, should the concept develop further, Brazil might find itself morally implicated or physically involved in Portugal's colonial wars and by association in Portuguese dealings with South Africa.[48] After the offer became known, higher officials in the Foreign Ministry and the Army as well as leaders in Congress were prone to praise the advantages of the plan in Brazil's emerging global economic strategy. But to others, misgivings about the unforeseen political and military ramifications of what could become a Pandora's box dictated more scepticism and cautious circumspection.

Brazil's impetus to action came after the November 1965 visit to Portugal by the President of the National Bank for Economic Development (BNDE). He was given a tour of Angola and Mozambique at the unanticipated invitation of the Salazar government and returned home with hopes to

48. During Franco Nogueira's trip to Brazil in June 1965, this community concept was discussed in confidential meetings with officials of the Castello Branco government. Although it is difficult to establish the date when both parties considered the undertaking feasible, it appears that discreet Portuguese soundings began soon after the foreign policy course of the revolutionary government became known and that the leadership of the revolution was ideologically predisposed to the general principle. The more troublesome question of a military alliance was another matter, for although there was a modicum of interchange between the armed services of the two countries, it did not yet extend beyond the occasional exchange of visits and decorations or the attendance of officers in technical schools in the other nation. The Portuguese military, however, welcomed any assistance it could receive in Africa and looked favorably on an alliance with Brazil. See, for example, the suggestive feeler addressed to the Brazilian military shortly after the revolution by the chief of the general staff of the Portuguese Navy: Vice-Admiral Armando de Roboredo, "Aspectos militares da comunidade luso-brasileira."

revise commercial agreements in order to initiate a promising triangular trade which would facilitate Brazil's penetration into the markets of the European Free Trade Association (EFTA) and of southern Africa. Publicizing what he saw as Portuguese achievements in the metropolis and in Africa, Garrido Torres reasoned that through the formation of an intercontinental political and economic community Brazil could (1) strengthen the ideal of racial tolerance which was threatened in Africa; (2) obtain a guaranteed market for manufactured exports; and (3) enhance national security. His viewpoint corresponded closely to those of Foreign Minister Juracy Magalhães, Pio Correia (Secretary-General of the Foreign Ministry), and Donatelo Grieco (Associate Secretary-General for Western European Affairs). In conjunction with Hélio Scarabotolo of the Ministry of Justice, they were the prime movers in the events which led to the start in May 1966 of negotiations in Rio de Janeiro with the General Directors of Political and Economic Affairs of the Portuguese Foreign Ministry.

Signed in Lisbon on 7 September 1966 (Brazil's Independence Day), the consequent treaties provided for a wide range of cooperation in various fields, supplanted all previous treaties in those areas, and were hailed as a logical continuation of the process which had also led to the 1953 signature of the Treaty of Friendship and Consultation. A cultural agreement regulated educational, scientific, and artistic exchange (including the granting of scholarships and fellowships), with the objective of reinforcing and integrating common cultural values. A bi-national economic commission to stimulate trade was created by the commercial pact. This pact also permitted the establishment of free ports in the territory of either state, encouraged the formation of joint ventures by Brazilian and Portuguese entrepreneurs, and sanctioned trade fairs or expositions for promotional purposes. A Basic Agreement on Technical Cooperation covered the exchange of students, specialists, and information in the sciences according to programs to be elaborated by the two governments at a later date.

Even before this set of documents was approved by the Brazilian Congress, suspicions were voiced about the still undefined intentions of the government concerning Angola and Mozambique, identified in the phraseology as an integral part of Portugal. A series of apparently interrelated incidents lent credence to the contention that, official denials to the contrary, Brazil was becoming engaged in those territories. In September and October a high-level mission visited Angola and Mozambique as part of an interministerial project started five months earlier to sound out prospects for the placement of exports in southern Africa. Rather than returning directly to Brazil, the group stopped in Lisbon for consultations with the Brazilian embassy concerning their impressions of Portuguese Africa, last visited by the Brazilian ambassador in 1965. In United Nations debates the Brazilian delegation avoided as much as possible any discussions of colonialism. It voted against a General Assembly resolution which strongly condemned Portuguese policy in its territories, requested all states "to take all the necessary measures to prevent the sale or supply of arms and military equipment to the Government of Portugal," and appealed to the World Bank and the International Monetary Fund to refrain from granting any financial or technical assistance to Portugal as long as the colonies should be maintained.[49]

In January 1967 a diplomatic crisis was precipitated when the naval officers' customary training cruise on the *Custódio de Melo* scheduled a week's stopover in Angola but no visit to an independent African nation despite the Ghanaian ambassador's repeated invitations to visit Ghana instead of Angola.[50] Rumored secret military pacts with Portugal in exchange for copper and petroleum concessions in Angola, the tone of statements on Portuguese Africa made by President-elect Costa e Silva in Lisbon, and general governmental ambivalence on the subject produced concern on the part of the ambassadors from Algeria, Ghana, and Senegal and the chargé d'affaires of the United Arab Republic. These ambassadors

---

49. General Assembly Resolution 2,184 (XXI) passed on 12 December 1966, by a vote of 70 to 13, with 22 abstentions. In casting a negative vote, Brazil sided with Australia, Austria, Belgium, Canada, Luxembourg, the Netherlands, New Zealand, Portugal, South Africa, Spain, United Kingdom, and the United States. Significantly, in his statement opening the general debate of the General Assembly's twenty-first session (on 22 September 1966), Juracy Magalhães did not even allude to the issue of colonialism.
50. H. Jon Rosenbaum, "Brazil among the Nations," pp. 539–40.

went to the Foreign Ministry as a group to request a definition of the official position on colonialism and Portuguese Africa. Unsatisfied by the reply received and of the belief that the *Custódio de Melo* episode portended a shift from covert to overt support of Portugal, they, in an unconventional gambit to generate a wave of public reaction favorable to their purposes, distributed to the press a memorandum on their inquiry.[51] Obviously irritated, Foreign Minister Magalhães refused to comment on the ambassadorial note because "it abandons all the normal rules of communication between governments." He added that there was no basis for preoccupation about the state of Brazilian relations with Africa, because Itamaraty was showing that continent great interest and attention.[52] Magalhães' response failed to dispel the doubts entertained by the ambassadors and held, in fact, by the governments of several other African nations since the signing of the Lisbon accords and continuing Brazilian research into trade possibilities with Angola and Mozambique. The political implications of Brazil's setting up trade with Angola and Mozambique could not be disregarded, especially when understood in relation to the opinion prevalent in the Foreign Ministry that the rebellions faced by Portugal represented agitation fomented by and supported from neighboring states rather than an authentic indigenous self-determination movement.

The Costa e Silva government inaugurated in mid-March brought a new configuration of personalities and policies founded on a somewhat different set of assumptions about international politics than that held by key officials in the previous administration. This policy alteration extended to the relations with Portugal. In contrast to their predecessors, Foreign Minister Magalhães Pinto and Secretary-General Sérgio Corrêa da Costa were sceptical about the effects of the treaties on the national interest, an uncertainty which manifested itself in a lengthy postponement in ratification after

51. *Correio da Manhã*, 7 January 1967, p. 2. The rumor which sparked fears of military collaboration originated with an unconfirmed report that Brazil was prepared to serve as an intermediary for the sale of combat aircraft by West Germany to Portugal for use in Angola.
52. *Correio da Manhã*, 10 January 1967, p. 3.

the agreements had been approved by the Congress in July. Itamaraty, newly engaged in an expansion of trade and communication with Afro-Asian states, was now more sensitive to the effects of the Portuguese policy on its image among the states with which it was planning to negotiate in the Second UNCTAD and in other United Nations agencies. Brazil had planned to elaborate a common economic stance vis-à-vis the developed states. Hence the problem was no longer simple, for it was necessary to weigh the benefits accruing from the projected cooperation with Portugal against those expected should Brazil attain leadership among developing states in New Delhi (as was hoped). At that moment the consequences of each course of action were still unclear. Several important officials in the Foreign Ministry felt that a political approximation with Portugal at that inopportune time would seriously endanger the opportunities for economic collaboration with anticolonialist governments. These same officials were also concerned about the extent to which, if the whole set of treaties became operative and were invoked, Brazil would be under pressure to comply with a possible future request from Lisbon for troops or war material to be used in Africa, a concern voiced by the 1966 mission to Angola and Mozambique.

Diplomatic tensions heightened and dissension came to public notice during the October 1967 visit of Franco Nogueira for the annual meeting of foreign ministers envisioned within the Lisbon agreements. Nogueira returned to the Portuguese capital disappointed by the change in Brazilian political climate. He had been told politely but firmly that the Costa e Silva government, while not favoring the use of violence in the decolonization process, considered that the ideal solution in the case of the overseas provinces would be an eventual plebiscite to allow the inhabitants to determine their future political status in much the same manner as France had finally managed the disposition of the Algerian question. He also learned that preparations for such granting of self-determination were recommended to be undertaken immediately. The Portuguese foreign minister had, to all appearances, been desirous of continued support in keeping the colonies under control, including perhaps certain types of military aid. Both governments, under fire from the Brazilian press, soon thereafter issued statements denying the existence of secret military clauses in the treaties. Increased pressure both for and against ratification bore down, nevertheless, upon Itamaraty as a result of doubts raised by the quasi-public airing of national differences coming after several years of relative harmony at the official level. The sense of the talks was conveyed by the careful wording of the joint communiqué. The dispatch spoke of a mutual desire to intensify relations in the fields of culture, science, technology, and commerce, but discreetly avoided any mention of political positions (which had been habitually included in past communiqués).[53]

Barely a week after Costa e Silva gave his approval by executive decree to the Basic Agreement on Technical Cooperation (one of the least controversial of the treaties), on 18 January 1968, Foreign Ministry discord again rose to the surface with a news "leak" that a firmer policy toward Portugal was being formulated to protect national interests against the concession of excessive advantages to Portugal, or to the Portuguese in Brazil, via the commercial treaty. According to the same source, a policy brief advising greater opposition to Portugal's African policies was being drawn up by high-level diplomats to guide Costa e Silva in reorienting his position on the colonies question.[54] This restructuring of policy was denied in an interview granted to a large, pro-Portuguese daily by Corrêa da Costa (said by many to be one of the most active in opposition). Corrêa da Costa also announced the imminent ratification of the remaining treaties. Ratification, in fact, took place on 21 March.[55] The prolonged indecision and the nearly successful campaign of the anticolonialists, carried on with unusual publicity, ended with the reaffirmation of traditional Luso-Brazilian solidarity. But this occurred only after internal resistance so reminiscent of the Quadros-Goulart years that some pro-Portuguese Brazilians were prompted to wonder if the revolution's purges had actually passed over Itamaraty and the "Afro-Asian" group of younger diplomats which they blamed for the delay. In

53. *Jornal do Brasil*, 12 October 1967, p. 1.
54. *Jornal do Brasil*, 26 January 1968, p. 7.
55. *O Globo*, 5 February 1968, p. 3. Corrêa da Costa, absent from the ratification ceremonies, was sent to London as ambassador in June.

the end, however, the attraction of Portugal and the Luso-Brazilian concept overcame any propensity to deal with Afro-Asia in any way contrary to Portuguese interests. The participation of Brazil in Portugal's colonial wars, however, was precluded, according to government sources.

No small part in the decision to ratify was played by the attractiveness, for Brazil's commercial expansion and economic development programs, of the proffered concessions and privileges in Angola and Mozambique. These colonies were to serve as markets for manufactures, sources of supply (for low-paraffin-content petroleum, copper, phosphates, uranium, etc.), entrepôts for the important South African market (among others), and an area for foreign investment.[56] The discovery of Angola's high-quality petroleum deposits opened a substitute source for this commodity. Petroleum had formerly been exported almost exclusively from the politically unstable Middle East at the cost of highly unfavorable balances of trade with the oil-producing states, which purchased little in return. An additional coveted energy source was made available by another simultaneous ratification, that of the Cooperation Agreement on Nuclear Energy for Peaceful Purposes, signed in June 1965. Through this agreement, Portugal, a major uranium producer, offered (at Brazilian request) to supply Brazil with substantial quantities of the element without any notification of or consultation with the International Atomic Energy Commission. Portugal did so because of what Nogueira termed "the intimacy of the relations between the two countries."[57] Embarking on an energy program which stressed nuclear power development, yet possessing domestically only reserves of relatively low-yield thorium, the Costa e Silva government saw nuclear cooperation with Portugal as a means to secure both fuel and technology regardless of any future measures adopted by the

---

56. In 1966 and 1967, Brazil's exports to South Africa were nearly double those to Portugal, which has been a very minor trading partner with a yearly average of only $4.5 million in imports from Brazil between 1960 and 1967. Exports to Angola and Mozambique in 1966 and 1967 totaled $1.17 million, composed largely of agricultural products but with a significant component of manufactures. Brazil has a well-equipped consulate-general in Lourenço Marques and a consulate in Luanda, but none in independent Black Africa.

57. *O Mundo Português*, 14 August 1968, p. 4.

nuclear powers under the Non-Proliferation Treaty (opposed by both Brazil and Portugal). Compared to these many pragmatic and tangible advantages, any conceivable detriment to economic relations with anticolonialist Afro-Asian states caused by closer ties with Portugal would seem of little import. Citing the cases of the United States, France, and Great Britain, Foreign Ministry economic officials now privately refuted as a chimera any correlation between Brazil's position in the United Nations on Portuguese questions and the penetration of its goods into Afro-Asian markets.

The occasion of the celebrations commemorating the five-hundredth anniversary of the birth of Pedro Álvares Cabral, Brazil's discoverer, was chosen by Costa e Silva, in the words of Geraldo Eulálio, Associate Secretary-General for Western European Affairs, as an opportunity "to give a complete demonstration of our affection and friendship for the Mother Country."[58] The effusive festivities and adulations were carried out in Portugal with the participation of the Brazilian delegation of three ministers (Foreign Relations, Air Force, and Navy), numerous diplomats, journalists, and academicians. Accompanying the Brazilian delegation was a flotilla of four destroyers with over 1,000 crewmen and nearly 100 officers, commanded by Rear Admiral Coelho Lobo, a Portuguese descendant of strong pro-Portuguese sympathies. He had also commanded the controversial voyage to Angola in 1967 and favored strong ties between the Portuguese and Brazilian navies to make them "owners of the whole South Atlantic" by virtue of bases in Brazil, Portuguese Guinea, and Angola.[59] A joint parade of Marines from the two countries marched past the monument to Cabral. The military ministers attended the unveiling of a monument to soldiers killed in combat in the overseas provinces. They also invited the Portuguese Secretary of the Air Force to visit Brazil and made arrangements for regular exchange flights between the two air forces as a beginning to intensified contacts. Referring to the success and cordiality of the conversations concerning the execution of the Lisbon treaties, Magalhães Pinto revealed with satisfaction upon his return, "We have practically no

---

58. *O Mundo Português*, 21 July 1968, p. 11.
59. See his interview in *O Mundo Português*, 12 June 1968, p. 4.

problems with Portugal on the bilateral level and have a good understanding with respect to common international problems."[60]

Various indications signaled a growing interest in Angola and Mozambique, one of the most symbolic being the journey in June via Lisbon of a specially selected Brazilian national soccer team to engage in competition against a team representing Portugal to inaugurate the Salazar Stadium in Lourenço Marques, Mozambique. The political connotations of this location were calculated as were those of the four-day layover of the school ship *Custódio de Melo* in the same port seven weeks later. Simultaneously the Bank of Brazil was studying the opening of branches in Lisbon and Luanda, Angola.[61] In May 1968 the Brazilian Lloyd Lines began a regular sea route to Luanda and Lourenço Marques as part of a comprehensive plan to encourage trade with Afro-Asia. Four months thereafter the president of Petrobrás announced in a press interview the possibility that his company might invest capital in petroleum prospecting and drilling in Angola in order to save domestic reserves and at the same time produce refined petroleum derivatives for the international market.[62]

An ever growing number of influential Brazilians are traveling to Portuguese Africa and returning with impressions that the region is indeed racially unique and incomparable to countries affected by Black nationalism or white racist minority rule. More are beginning to believe that Guinea, Angola, and Mozambique can adequately be described only by a theory which posits "four Africas": Arab, Black, White-minority, and Portuguese. Many of these observers are struck by what they interpret as a lack of independent nationalistic conscience among the tribes and marked economic and social progress. These traits, when combined with the presence of Portuguese culture and a life-style Brazilians see as somewhat reminiscent of their own nation's earlier history, almost invariably lead to either a moderate or a pro-Portuguese position. The Salazar government, by sponsoring tours for well-chosen individuals (sympathetic politicians, journalists, and

60. *Jornal do Brasil*, 7 July 1968, p. 4.
61. *O Mundo Português*, 7 July 1968, p. 8.
62. *O Globo*, 24 September 1968, p. 17.

businessmen), made effective use of this affinity reaction subsequent to its 1965 offer to expand the community to include the territories. Several of the individuals so favored have become the most ardent supporters of closer ties and of the thesis that Brazil also has something at stake in the survival of the common language, customs, and culture in Africa.[63] Since that time more Brazilians have been going on their own initiative for such purposes as journalistic reporting, agricultural study, or commerce, all facilitated and encouraged by the community concept and likely to serve as reinforcement for future approximation.

In international forums Brazil gave additional proof of a more vigorous defense of Portugal's colonial policies, putting Brazil in the awkward position of habitually reaffirming its "traditionally anti-colonialist stand," yet either voting with Portugal or failing to condemn the conditions in the only remaining colonies. In the International Conference on Human Rights in Tehran (22 April–13 May 1968), Brazil was the only state to vote against a draft resolution passed in the First Committee to condemn all colonial regimes, and particularly Portugal, for continued refusal to implement General Assembly Resolution No. 1514 (XV) on the termination of colonialism. Brazil also voted against the committee's support for "firm determination of liberation movements of peoples in their struggles for freedom and independence" and against its recommendations to the conference "to appeal to all states and organizations to give political, moral, and material assistance to peoples struggling for freedom and independence."[64] In the plenary session Brazil abstained on the whole of this resolution (Draft Resolution VII) but voted against Preambular Paragraphs Five and Six, which referred

63. See, for example, the interviews of Senator Vasconcelos Torres and Deputy Cunha Bueno, who subsequently became active spokesmen for the community concept in Brazil: "A África portuguêsa vista por um senador brasileiro," *Boletim geral do ultramar*, No. 490 (April 1966): 210–11; and "Declarações do deputado brasileiro Dr. Cunha Bueno, ao regressar da visita a Angola e Moçambique," *Boletim geral do ultramar*, No. 492 (June 1966): 276–78.

64. United Nations, General Assembly, *International Conference on Human Rights, Tehran, April 22–May 13, 1968*, First Committee, Provisional Summary Record of the Eleventh Meeting, May 8, 1968, at 10:30 AM, A/CONF.32/C.1/SR.11. Draft Resolution A/CONF.32/C.1/L.15 passed in the First Committee by a vote of 52 to 1, with 20 abstentions.

to the "legitimate armed struggle being waged by the populations under Portuguese domination," and against Operative Paragraph Three, which expressed support for liberation movements.[65] Brazil's position contrasted quite sharply with that of the developing Afro-Asian states, only one of which (South Vietnam) abstained on the resolution as a whole. Brazil adamantly refused to denounce Portugal or condone the use of force in the pro-independence movements. Summing up Brazil's participation in the conference for a Rio de Janeiro newspaper, Ciro de Freitas Vale, head of the delegation, succinctly stated this: "Brazil was totally on the side of Portugal, that is to say, opposing everything that was aimed at the Portuguese nation. While others abstained, we took a position compatible with our traditions, our fidelity to the kindred Motherland, and the special instructions we received from Foreign Minister Magalhães Pinto."[66]

With the September 1968 stroke of Prime Minister Oliveira Salazar and the ascension into his place of Marcelo Caetano, Magalhães Pinto went to Lisbon for conversations with the new administration and a visit to the ailing former head of government. He arrived amid speculations that he would take advantage of this opportunity to hint that Brazil would look favorably upon a change in Portuguese policy to lessen tensions in the overseas territories. Although he spoke with Caetano for two hours, Magalhães Pinto denied having suggested any policy modification because "it is not up to the Brazilian government to interfere." He added, however, that it was obvious that Portugal was determined to maintain the status quo. As far as Luso-Brazilian relations were concerned, the talks were auspicious and indicative of continuing cordial relations.[67]

On 29 November 1968 Brazil suffered the greatest isolation it ever experienced in the General Assembly when colonial

65. United Nations, General Assembly, *International Conference on Human Rights, Tehran, April 22–May 13, 1968*, Provisional Summary Record of the Twenty-Fourth Meeting, May 11, 1968, at 3:30 P.M., A/CONF.32/SR.24. Draft Resolution VII was approved by a vote of 54 to 0, with 25 abstentions. Preambular Paragraphs Five and Six were approved by a vote of 42 to 1, with 27 abstaining, and Operative Paragraph Three was approved by 53 to 5, with 21 abstentions.
66. *O Mundo Português*, 2 June 1968, p. 1.
67. *O Mundo Português*, 13 October 1968, p. 2.

matters were voted upon. It sided with Portugal and South Africa to cast one of the three votes against Resolution No. 2,395 (XXIII) which among other things (1) condemned Portugal's failure to grant independence to its territories; (2) appealed to all states to grant the inhabitants of these territories "the moral and material assistance necessary for the restoration of their inalienable rights"; (3) reiterated an appeal to all states to cease granting to Portugal any assistance which helps it to prosecute the colonial war; and (4) deplored the foreign financial activities obstructing the territories' self-determination.[68] Brazil's willingness to isolate itself in this manner from even the Latin American states (only Ecuador abstained) derived in part from the orientation taken since the Lisbon accords. More than this, as a long-range tendency, Brazil's isolation results from its reluctance since 1964 to change position in the face of a mounting anticolonial consensus which has focused on Portugal, the first and the last of the colonial powers, and has finally pressured all other Western states into at least abstaining regularly. For Brazil the decision whether to abstain or vote in the negative is uniquely difficult; this time it was deemed more desirable to support Portugal and suffer Afro-Asian criticism than to abstain on a technical or substantive point and avoid the criticism. The official rationale for this vote was that it placed Brazil in a better position to persuade Portugal to compromise at some future date, an aim which justified the attrition of the national image.

The final year of Costa e Silva's administration saw greater cooperation with Portugal in spite of the cool official reaction to Prime Minister Caetano's public appeal during an important July 1969 visit to Brazil. He exhorted Brazilians to lend decisive and overt assistance to keep the Portuguese-speaking world intact. The response chosen was the pattern of limited political and military involvement to avoid either endorsing Portuguese colonialism or condemning Portugal.

By choosing Professor Gama e Silva as his ambassador to Portugal, President Médici selected a well-known defender of Luso-Brazilianism and a former minister of justice active in

68. General Assembly Resolution 2,395 (XXIII), approved by 96 votes to 3, with 13 abstentions.

extending the rights of Portuguese residents. The intentions of the new government were also shown by the 17 October 1969 addition of Article 199 to the Constitution. It states that Portuguese nationals in Brazil may enjoy the same rights as natives if Portuguese law extends reciprocity. Similar preferences had already been applied to the approximately 1.5 million resident Portuguese nationals in, for example, the rights to practice law, to purchase rural property, to remain in Brazil permanently or become citizens without a professional classification, and to reside in Brazil for only one year prior to eligibility for naturalization. In mid-1970 Foreign Minister Gibson Barbosa visited Lisbon for three days on a special mission. His trip extended understandings reached during Caetano's visit.

A series of negotiations and legal adjustments in both countries culminated in the signature in September 1971 and the ratification ceremony in March 1972 of the Convention on Equality of Rights and Duties. This definitive legal instrument to consolidate the community is based on Article 199 of the Brazilian and Article 7 of the Portuguese constitutions. A unique document, it establishes equal rights and duties for citizens of each state in the other, thus obliterating any juridical distinction between the citizenships; even the rights to vote and hold public office are included.

To provide the proper celebration, both nations declared 1972, the one hundred fiftieth anniversary of Brazilian independence, as the "Year of the Luso-Brazilian Community." In a symbolic gesture, President Thomaz arrived in Rio on 22 April, the "Day of the Community," with the remains of Emperor Dom Pedro I, hero of national independence. The emperor's body was to lie in state in various Brazilian communities, then be reinterred at the spot where the emperor had proclaimed independence. Also on 22 April, Médici declared in Brazil the validity of the convention (as did Caetano in Portugal). He signed a communiqué with Thomaz pledging further cooperation in many fields. The system of consultation specified for international matters by the 1953 treaty was also, through common agreement, to be amplified.

From the perspective of Brazilian interests, the convention certainly was not negotiated solely to gain access to Portuguese Africa, for there is strong sentiment for closer relations with metropolitan Portugal. Brazilians hope to gain not only easier entry into EFTA and eventually into EEC markets through Portugal but also mutual assistance in economic and technical aid and political positions (for example, Brazil's claim to 200 miles of territorial waters, to which Portugal subscribes). The convention and its adjuncts will have considerable significance for Brazilian policy in Africa, however, for although the "overseas provinces" are not mentioned in the treaty, both parties consider them an integral part of Portugal. Numerous signs of Brazilian interest in the "overseas provinces," and particularly in Angola, are apparent. The Portuguese, in turn, anxiously await the political and economic boost which Brazilian presence and interest may provide. But they have shown concern that should the larger and more dynamic Brazil become heavily involved they might lose some freedom of decision. This is probably why Portugal waited so long to make the present arrangements.

Since Brazilians can now legally operate in Portuguese Africa on the same footing as the Portuguese, business opportunities have brightened considerably. Joint ventures or direct investments are being encouraged along the lines of the contemplated installation in Angola of a Brazilian fish cannery which will be supplied by an offshore fleet. The president of the Bank of Brazil visited Angola, Mozambique, and South Africa in early 1972, giving rise to more discussion of a Bank of Brazil agency in Luanda; one has been opened in Lisbon. Plans are advancing to establish a joint private investment bank, open to outsiders, for transactions in southern Africa. Transportation by air was facilitated when Varig in mid-1970 undertook weekly flights to Luanda and Johannesburg. Additional sea routes are to be initiated from Brazil to handle travel increases resulting from trade missions (like the 1972 trade mission from Pernambuco to southern Africa) and from trade fairs (like one to be held in Mozambique with likely participation from the Luso-Brazilian Businessmen's Committee). As Portuguese goods will enjoy custom-free zones in Rio and São Paulo, Brazilian goods will have similar privileges in Lisbon, Angola, and Mozambique. The latter two will serve as bases for commerce with Black Africa and South Africa as well. Petrobrás is to explore for petroleum in Angola, and other raw materials are to be exploited. Brazil's aspirations as a sea power will be aided both by advantages across the South Atlantic and by Portugal's offer to purchase from Brazilian shipyards vessels used to ply community trade. Africans wary of a Brazilian–Portuguese–South African entente will likely balk at such Brazilian expansion.[69]

In addition to the attractive economic aspects, cultural considerations stimulate the community's growth. Brazilian intellectuals and diplomats, in furthering Brazil's image abroad, have long felt frustration at the obscurity of their native language. Although it presently counts well over 120 million native speakers (more than the number enjoyed by French), it is practically unknown outside Brazil, Portugal, and the Portuguese colonies. Elsewhere it passes for a fractured dialect of Spanish. The resultant sense of cultural isolation explains in part why most Brazilians seriously contemplating future Brazilian presence in Africa have been intrigued by the existence of a similar culture in Portuguese Guinea, Angola, and Mozambique as well as by the fact that, ranked by number of speakers, Portuguese is the third European language on that continent.[70] Progress in closer relations with Portugal has been hindered by mixed reaction to unyielding Portuguese colonialism, one of the greatest obstacles to a full-fledged Portuguese-speaking commonwealth as far as Brazilians are concerned. A most difficult psychological situation has thus been thrust upon Brazil, an approach-avoidance reaction in which the undeniable attractiveness of these territories for self-projection invites action, but the controversial and nearly universally condemned colonial wars are a repellent factor and counsel prudence. In the interim, with the future status of the territories in doubt, the Foreign Ministry faces a painful choice: how much involvement best serves national interests? Complete aloofness has been ruled out since the ratification of the 1966 treaties and the 1972 convention. Portuguese military superiority and the

69. "Brazil: Side Door into Africa," *Latin America*, 6, No. 27 (7 July 1972): 209–10.
70. On cultural similarities between Brazil and Angola, see René Ribeiro, "Estudo comparativo dos problemas de vida em duas culturas afins: Angola-Brasil."

failure of a strong African nationalism to emerge prolong the awkward problem, as both Lisbon and liberation leaders appeal for Brazilian understanding and assistance in the struggle. Further complications result from the determination of white Portuguese African residents to continue the counterinsurgency even if Lisbon's efforts should falter for financial reasons. This white backlash leaves open a door for South African intervention. South Africa might thus be able to consolidate white supremacy and safeguard its own regime.

Senegalese President Leopold Senghor suggested in his September 1964 visit to Rio de Janeiro that the most constructive solution to the deadlock would be the concession of a period of transitional home rule before independence. Such a transitional period might prevent the type of relapse suffered by the Congo. He further suggested that the preparatory transitional period be carried out within the framework of a community relationship, with Brazilian participation.[71] Brazilian and African diplomats regard Senghor's plan as a feasible alternative only if some unlikely flexibility should be introduced into Portuguese policy, allowing Brazil to serve (1) as mediator between Lisbon and Black Africa; (2) as a nonsuspect associate in training the territories for self-government and development; or (3) as the principal component of a United Nations trusteeship administration. Regardless of their ideologies, proponents of a more vigorous African diplomacy are unanimous that Brazil only stands to lose should Portuguese language, culture, and religion disappear from Africa through postindependence repudiation, political chaos, or racist foreign intervention. The differences in opinion arise over the questions of how this culture can best be preserved in the interests of all the inhabitants and of how Brazil's moral responsibilities can be met. What would otherwise be agreement has broken on the rock of Portugal's obduracy. In spite of this, Brazilians feel the need to pursue some kind of involvement now rather than waiting indeterminately. They realize that with the probable independence of the territories Brazil could become the major influence in Portuguese-speaking Africa and the chief pillar of a huge

71. Instituto Brasileiro de Estudos Afro-Asiáticos, *Senghor em diálogo*, p. 64.

community based on three continents, a tempting opportunity for an aspiring world power.

Although up to this point Brazil's policy toward Portuguese Africa has been explained as a function of a varying mixture of affectivity and national interest consideration, a final domestic factor emerges—the existence of a large, well-organized colony of Portuguese immigrants and first-generation descendants centered in Rio de Janeiro, São Paulo, Recife, and Belem. The group contains influential members so numerous and well placed that a pro-Portuguese journalist once aptly described it to a new Portuguese ambassador as "a nation inside another nation."[72] Conceptually the colony fits into the picture as an important linkage group whose activities and privileges, combined with certain attitudinal characteristics of Brazilian society, place it in a position different from that of a mere pressure group; it is rather, as Karl Deutsch defines the term "linkage group," a "group with links to the domestic system and with some particular links to the international or foreign input."[73] The emotional, financial, and political links to both Brazil and Portugal which it possesses make the colony uniquely able to be a significant shaping force in the formulation of Brazil's policy toward Angola and Mozambique. This factor, although not determinant, strongly reinforces the predisposition of the foreign policy elite to be responsive to Portuguese, not African, demands on the colonialism issue.

The domestic environment within which the colony exercises its political role is one of diffuse but palpable goodwill, based upon an idealization of Portugal's part in the creation of Brazilian national unity and culture.[74] This image in the popular mind was transferred onto the Salazar government. A Rio de Janeiro newspaper working with Marplan conducted in September 1968 a citywide sample survey of public opinion about the Salazar government. It showed results highly favorable to Salazar. To the question "In your opinion, is the Oliveira Salazar government a dictatorship or not?" 54 percent replied that it was, 26 percent that it was not, and 20

72. *O Globo*, 3 April 1968, 2d sec., p. 2.
73. Karl W. Deutsch, "External Influences of the Internal Behavior of States," p. 12.
74. In Brasília there is a "Monument to the Portuguese Immigrant."

percent did not know. To secure an overall evaluation the survey asked, "As you see it, has the Salazar government been good or bad for Portugal?" A total of 68 percent responded "good," 8 percent "average," and only 6 percent "bad," while 18 percent had no opinion, meaning that those with a favorable image of Salazar outnumbered those with an unfavorable image by over 12 to 1.[75]

The formal national organization of the colony is coordinated at the top by the Superior Council of the Colony of the Federation of Portuguese and Luso-Brazilian Associations. In February 1968 it had enrolled 183 clubs and institutions, most of which were differentiated on the basis of the Portuguese region from which the members came and the Brazilian region in which they lived.[76] The statutes of the Conselho Superior state its purpose (Article 3) as the stimulation of the spirit of "Portuguesism" of the colony by "taking steps by all means so that the Portuguese residing in Brazil maintain all their bonds to the Motherland" and as "exalting Portugal and Brazil through their historical roots, with the objective of establishing a force to contribute decisively to the creation of a Luso-Brazilian Community."[77] The membership being scattered, there are state councils where agglomerations of immigrants are found, but according to Article 2 of the statutes, the headquarters must always be in the same city as the Portuguese embassy, an important provision approved by the Brazilian authorities. The pro-Salazar elements (strongest in Rio) long exercised the leadership of this and all major subordinate organizations and exerted pressure to exclude Salazar's critics from membership, in order to maintain ideological purity.[78] Publicly and officially the council and the federation, as innocuous immigrant organizations, take no part in Brazilian politics but confine their attention strictly to the colony's internal matters such as social services and preservation of regional folklore. In reality, these bodies actively support policies suggested by the Lisbon government

---

75. *Jornal do Brasil*, 22 September 1968, p. 22. N = 310. This newspaper was not considered to be heavily committed on either side of the Portuguese question, but members of the management were regaled with trips to Portugal and medals.
76. *A Voz de Portugal*, 25 February 1968, 2d sec., p. 6.
77. *O Mundo Português*, 15 May 1966, 2d sec., p. 8.
78. Interview with Fernando Quiroga, 17 October 1968.

and criticize anyone who so much as questions those policies. They refuse to even admit to debate the future status of Portuguese Africa. Among the immigrants a sense of attachment to Portugal (and not incidentally ipso facto to its government) is fostered by appealing to homesickness (*saudosismo*), family ties, and nationalism. Colony leaders propagandize not only through the associations but also via weekly newspapers such as *O Mundo Português* and *A Voz de Portugal* (both subscribe to the Portuguese government–controlled National News Agency) and radio stations such as Radio Veracruz in Rio. Several prestigious newspapers and magazines (including *O Globo*, *O Cruzeiro*, and *Manchete*) have been won over by the colony. They take strongly pro-Portuguese and procommunity stands, defending as well the Lusitanian presence in Africa.[79]

The colony works on an informal basis through an intricate network of personal contacts with the many Brazilian businessmen, authors, professors, bankers, military officers, legislators, and diplomats sympathetic to the community. It thus gains access to political and financial decision makers as well as to publishable pro-Portuguese interviews.[80] At crucial junctures, public opinion campaigns have been launched with notable success, as during the following episodes: Goulart's 1963 attempt to restrict the quota-free immigration of Portuguese, the controversial 1967 statements of African ambassadors, the delay in ratification of the 1966 Lisbon treaties, and the 1969 visits of Caetano to Portuguese Africa and Brazil. Important colony leaders approach the Foreign Ministry itself, invoking the inevitable "traditional bonds," in order to register requests or complaints and ask for statements of position from the foreign minister. The colony press often publishes such statements, which serve to focus more than

---

79. Theophilo Andrade, director of *O Cruzeiro*, was the first Brazilian journalist to be granted a formal interview by the new prime minister, Marcelo Caetano, and was actively involved in promoting the projection of Brazil into Africa through Angola. See Theophilo Andrade, "Visita a Marcelo Caetano."

80. Several important Brazilian spokesmen for the community ideal are not Portuguese descendants, and the most outspokenly pro-Portuguese journalist in Brazil is a Brazilian, Alves Pinheiro (editor of *O Mundo Português* and former chief editor of *O Globo*). His editorial opinions are indistinguishable from those of the colony leaders for whom his paper serves as a mouthpiece.

normal attention upon policy toward Portugal.[81] Against this effective propaganda and in this climate of public opinion, the minority democratic opposition-in-exile has had very little success; their few newspapers suffer from limited circulation and financial problems, while the widely circulated colony press discredits them as traitors, renegades, moral vermin, and worse. The colony press equates loyalty to Portugal with absolute loyalty to Salazarist principles (including the integrity of the empire). This multifaceted set of tactics serves to generate more diffuse support for Portuguese policy among immigrants and native Brazilians and makes a policy change on Portuguese Africa more difficult and politically risky than it would be if the issue were not so salient and volatile domestically. It is, moreover, played up during election campaigns in areas of Portuguese concentration and above all in Rio. The colony presently serves to amplify and re-echo Portuguese propaganda in Brazil, at times taking on the features of an arm of Lisbon's foreign policy.

The colony's linkage to the foreign input is particularly important. At the 19 April 1968 inauguration of the new members of the council, Federation President Leal Rodrigues observed that the council had never failed to support the Portuguese ambassador. He called upon the colony to set as its principal goal presentation to the national public of more information about Portuguese Africa. Replying, Portuguese Ambassador José Manuel Fragoso, who presided over the session and inaugurated the new councilmen, underlined the necessity of unity and conciliation of personal quarrels within the colony as well as an "intimate connection" between the council and the embassy for ready defense of the "superior interests of the Fatherland." He added for clarification, "It happens that at certain times the embassy can and should be in a better position to point out what these superior interests are," a relationship he euphemistically characterized as

81. Rodrigo Leal Rodrigues, president of the federation, addressed a letter to Magalhães Pinto to express the displeasure of the colony over the visit of Indira Gandhi and traced this "grief" and "sadness" to India's 1961 seizure of Goa. This is not a surprising communication if it is recalled that the Portuguese government openly criticized Pope Paul VI's 1965 visit to India and boycotted it in the press for the same reason. See, "Indira Ghandi foi uma visita indesejável aos portugueses," *O Mundo Português*, 29 September 1968, 2d sec., p. 3.

"collaboration, understanding, confidence" rather than service.[82] Congratulating the new directors, the ambassador wished them success in their duties. He pledged that, "in the execution of these tasks, these most high tasks of patriotic concerns, you will not lack the support of Portugal, of its government, and of its representatives in Brazil."[83] The established system of mutual consultation and assistance has been the basis for colony-embassy relations. For example, a financial subsidy of more than $130,000 was granted over a five-year period by the Portuguese government to Rio's Real Gabinete Português de Leitura, a colony-run cultural center and library well respected among Brazilian scholars and engaging in the expansion of Luso-Brazilian relations on an educational plane.[84] Coordinated efforts such as these have had a tangible but hard to measure effect on foreign-policy makers by generating domestic pressures favorable to Portugal, in a manner not unlike the way American Jewish organizations work for United States support for Israel at both public opinion and governmental levels.

Human Rights, Nonintervention, and Trade in Relations with South Africa: The Attraction of Opposites?

Brazil's international affirmation of its professed creed of racial equality has led it to initiate several declarations in favor of human rights and against racial discrimination. Brazil participated in the drafting of the Universal Declaration of Human Rights in 1948 (brought to vote with a speech by the Brazilian delegate). More recently, Brazil has played a role in the International Convention on the Elimination of All Forms of Racial Discrimination (1965). It was the first nation to sign that agreement. Brazil's characteristic self-assurance and high moral tone on such racial matters appeared in Foreign Minister Juracy Magalhães address opening the general debate of the General Assembly's twenty-first session. Referring to the 1965 convention, he made these points: "Within the boundaries of Brazil, indeed, small need would be felt for such a document, since Brazil has long been an outstanding, and in fact I would be tempted to say

82. *O Mundo Português*, 28 April 1968, 2d sec., p. 10.
83. Ibid.
84. *A Voz de Portugal*, 2 June 1968, 2d sec., p. 1.

the foremost, example of a true racial democracy, where many races live and labour together and freely mix, without fear or favour, without hate or discrimination. Our hospitable land has long been open to men of all races and creeds; no one questions, or cares, what may have been a man's birthplace, or that of his forebears; all enjoy equal rights, and all are equally proud of being part of one great nation. While the new Convention is, therefore, superfluous insofar as Brazil is concerned, we nonetheless welcome it as a useful pointer to other countries placed in less favourable circumstances. And I would hereby take this opportunity to suggest that racial tolerance should be exercised by all races towards other races: to have been sinned against is no valid reason for sinning against others. May the Brazilian example, and the moderation without effort, easy tolerance and mutual respect in our racial relations be followed by all multiracial nations."[85]

Although Brazil was among the first nations to decry South African apartheid as contrary to Articles 1 and 55 of the United Nations charter and although it has continued to denounce this extreme form of racial separation, its noninterventionist stand (independent of changes in domestic regimes) has consistently been invoked to prevent any retaliation beyond an embargo on military equipment. General mandatory sanctions are, in the Brazilian view, an inappropriate method of handling the situation. Brazilians believe that such sanctions are as counter-productive as the direct military intervention now requested by most African members. And they feel that placing sanctions may call into question United Nations authority, because many powerful member states would certainly refuse to institute sanctions or condone invasion by either guerrilla or regular forces. Not regarding the situation itself as an imminently serious threat to international peace and security, Brazil has favored the creation through education of an anti-apartheid world opinion climate to force revision of the white regime's program. It has therefore opposed all attempts to eject South Africa from world organizations, to break diplomatic and trade relations, and to sever land and sea routes. Brazil is thus try-

85. Brasil, Ministério das Relações Exteriores, *A política exterior da revolução brasileira*, 2: no page numbers designated.

ing to maintain clear communication channels between South Africa and the rest of the globe and to keep open the possibilities for peaceful endogenous political change stimulated by exogenous opinion. This plan would not be effective in an atmosphere of isolation. On resolutions contradicting this philosophy Brazil has either (1) abstained or (2) voted in favor, while stating its reservations about objectionable paragraphs. Brazil usually objects to precisely those points most favored by the Afro-Asian majority.

On South African control of South West Africa, the Brazilian thesis has been that the League of Nations mandate was transferred to the United Nations, with all obligations still binding, and that any change in the territory's international status can legally take place only through the world body. Because this question is clearly international and falls within United Nations jurisdiction, Brazil has either co-sponsored or supported draft resolutions to resist the extension of apartheid into South West Africa, to transfer administration of that territory to the United Nations, and to establish a council to administer South West Africa until it attains independence. Thus Brazil strikes a pose similar to that of most Afro-Asian states, a position strengthened by the International Court of Justice's June 1971 ruling that continued South African presence in Namibia would be illegal.

In bilateral relations with Pretoria, however, Brazil has aroused African suspicions since Quadros' days, by simultaneously trying to further cordial relations with both Black Africa and South Africa. Even during the height of the independent foreign policy, South Africa's economic potential attracted Brazilian attention and that territory garnered over three-quarters of Brazil's exports to sub-Saharan Africa. Although in 1962 the Senate was able to stall for a time the nomination of a minister plenipotentiary to head the legation in Pretoria, the Foreign Ministry was letting it be known without fanfare that, in its interpretation, universal relations and trade really meant precisely that. The Foreign Ministry disregarded uneasiness in the United States over Brazil's relations with the Soviet Union and criticism from Africans over its relations with South Africa. The consensus was expressed by the editorial staff of an important economic journal which, in surveying national interests in Africa, advised moral support for the African bloc but counseled opposition to sanctions which would be ineffective, prejudicial to United Nations prestige, and injurious to a favorable and growing trade relationship.[86]

The Castello Branco government, somewhat less reluctant to incur African displeasure, sought new ways to increase trade, drawn by the possibility of large manufactures sales and an extremely favorable trade balance. Between 1964 and 1966, exports to South Africa increased by over 25 percent. The year 1966 highlighted several ironies in Brazilian policy. South African Foreign Minister Hildgard Müller and Minister of Economic Affairs H. Kotzemberg arrived in Rio to discuss trade expansion with officials of Itamaraty barely one month before the start of the United Nations Human Rights Seminar on Apartheid in Brasília. The symposium was both largely organized and hosted by Brazil. Although in December Brazil voted in favor of General Assembly Resolution 2,202 A (XXI), which, among other things, appealed to all states to "discourage immediately the establishment of closer economic and financial relations with South Africa," its own growing trade had qualified it as the Latin American state which exported the most to that same republic. Brazil led by 62 percent the combined total of Argentina and Mexico, its closest rivals,[87] a statistic not unnoticed by the ardent opponents of apartheid. In October a Brazilian trade mission returned from a fact-finding tour in South Africa related to the July discussions with Müller and Kotzemberg. The special group's report was frankly optimistic about prospects for greater commerce, an opinion contrasting with the modest outlook seen for the Negro republics on its itinerary.[88]

Acting upon these recommendations, the Foreign Ministry arranged for participation in the 1967 Rand Easter Show in Johannesburg, where with its investment of $110,000, Brazil obtained orders for over $3 million worth of merchandise, much of this in manufactured goods such as lathes. The

86. "A África e os interêsses do Brasil."
87. United Nations, Department of Economic and Social Affairs, Statistical Office, *Yearbook of International Trade Statistics, 1966*, p. 720.
88. Brasil, Ministério das Relações Exteriores, *Relatório* (1966), pp. 70–71.

rented space for the 1968 show was doubled; in three days orders totaling nearly $3 million were received for lathes alone (an item not manufactured in South Africa), in addition to other machinery for heavy and light industry.[89] Interest in the new market rapidly grew to such an extent that in the 1970 Johannesburg International Exposition forty Brazilian enterprises from seven states displayed their products for importers from South Africa, Rhodesia, Angola, Mozambique, South West Africa, and other areas. Various surveys of the market potentials for Brazilian-made products revealed excellent demand for garage equipment, hydraulic motors and lifts, machinery for plastic and textile industries, hospital supplies and equipment, bicycles, bathroom fixtures, and mining equipment. Brazilian industrialists also anticipated the addition of railroad equipment, ocean freighters, chemicals, and pharmaceuticals as part of the new trade expansion spurred by the recently begun Lloyd Lines shipping route to major South African ports and by other incentives of the Brazilian government, including the opening of a trade section in the Pretoria legation.[90] In contrast, trade had been characterized by the exchange of Brazilian raw materials (cotton, coffee, wood, sugar, etc.) for South African minerals.

To improve their balance of trade with Brazil (running at 14 to 1 in their disfavor), the South Africans opened a commercial office in Rio de Janeiro in late 1967. They wanted to discover complementary trade possibilities so that Brazil could regularly import other South African products, not just small quantities of gold and asbestos. For this purpose, the South African government set up a $5 million revolving credit fund in the Brazilian National Bank for Economic Development. It applies the credit to Brazilian purchases of capital goods and services. Under this program South African officials expect only a limited trade in consumer goods but excellent growth in primary and capital sectors. The program is also to encompass such technological cooperation as South African mineral prospecting and mine establishment for Brazilian companies. South African commercial officials feel that, although spontaneous contacts from Brazilian businessmen are few and of little import, the weight of the political ques-

89. Personal interview with J. N. van Schalkwyk, 29 August 1968.
90. *Brazil International Report*, February 1968, p. 2.

tion of apartheid has not posed an obstacle in business dealings with Brazilians even though Pretoria's official racial policy is clearly diametrically opposed to the Brazilian ideal.

South Africa has been using Brazil's enthusiasm for greater trade in manufactures to gain penetration into South America. An economically feasible and politically controversial attraction between racial opposites, it is hoped by Pretoria, may allow South Africa to diversify its sources of supply, improve its image in Latin America, further differentiate the politics of apartheid and the economics of international trade, and counteract the trend toward its complete isolation. As the first step in a publicity campaign, the South African Ministry of Information in 1968 invited two Brazilian journalists. Theirs was the first official trip of any South American reporters. A popular news magazine published with rich illustration their six-day tour. The article reflected the South African policy line. It included not even the slightest criticism of apartheid, which was explained by quotations taken from an official publication and conversations with white supporters of the system, who stressed the higher living standards thereby assured the Bantus. Not a single hint was given of the controversial aspects of apartheid or United Nations action on the issue in what was to that time the most inclusive presentation of South Africa to the general Brazilian public, occasional newspaper reports and editorials notwithstanding.[91]

On 23 February 1969 a weekly flight of South African Airways from Johannesburg to New York via Rio de Janeiro was begun after months of planning, in spite of a request from the United Nations Special Committee on the Policies of Apartheid of the Government of South Africa urging Brazil and the United States to reconsider establishing the flight. Replying that a total boycott of South Africa would benefit only the racists and fail to alleviate the condition of the oppressed, Brazil sent on the inaugural flight a high-level delegation, including Minister of Commerce and Industry Edmundo Macedo and Minister of Planning Hélio Beltrão. The

91. "O país do Doutor Barnard," *Manchete*, No. 844 (22 June 1968): 116–30. This magazine also publishes reports on Portuguese Africa which corroborate Lisbon's points of view and favorably compare the overseas territories with Brazil.

delegation was to discuss trade with South African officials and businessmen, who were certain to be entering Brazil in greater numbers because of the new route. About the same time, Magalhães Pinto had talks in Brazil with South African Foreign Minister Müller. The talks led to rumors of a political-military anti-Soviet South Atlantic defense pact between the two states and including several others of the Southern Hemisphere. This report caused considerable embarrassment to the Brazilian government. Under African censure, Brazil denied ever considering such a treaty and sent a note to this effect to the president of the United Nations Special Committee on Apartheid. Even this episode and the resulting vocal Afro-Asian criticism did not diminish Brazilian ambitions to cooperate economically with South Africa. However, in order to prove its good intentions toward Afro-Asian interests (even if not to demonstrate its consistency), Brazil that November co-sponsored United Nations General Assembly Resolution 2,506B (XXIV). This resolution, like the usual condemnations of South Africa, requested member states to prohibit economic and financial dealings with South Africa by interests under their jurisdiction, to cut off air and sea routes from their territory to South Africa, and to dissuade the main trading partners of that country from cooperating with the government and foreign companies registered under it.

Such awkward stances result from Brazil's desire to increase trade with South Africa without antagonizing Black Africa. This most difficult balancing act has occasioned splits within the government between agencies (including the Finance Ministry) which wish to completely ignore political implications because of the low value of trade with Black Africa and those (principally the Foreign Ministry) which desire relations with South Africa to be carried out within the context of the entire continental situation. The latter philosophy has prevailed, but whether it can be made convincing to those strongly opposing apartheid is questionable. Taking a long-term view, Brazilians expect economic interests and "realism" to take preference over "ideology" among the other African states. When that occurs, their policy of courting both camps will pay off, however incongruous that policy may now appear. As indicators, they point to efforts by about fifteen African states, led by the Ivory Coast, to coexist with

South Africa despite racial-political divergencies, to maintain dialogue, and perhaps to influence the regime to ease the harsher aspects of apartheid.

In reality, relations with South Africa have been cultivated more within the context of southern Africa than bilaterally. The Luso-Brazilian community will intentionally provide much opportunity for Brazil to deal with South Africa, as well as with Mozambique and Angola, since routes of Brazilian trade missions, air linkages, and steamer lines to Mozambique and Angola always include South Africa on the trip. Brazil may well be more economically interested in South Africa as a target area via the Luso-Brazilian community than in Angola and Mozambique; $32.6 million in export trade went to South Africa in 1969–1970, while only $1.9 million was exported to the much poorer territories. In Mozambique and Angola, future possibilities are seriously limited, and these colonies depend on South Africa. The Bank of Brazil is already contemplating opening an agency in South Africa. Future relations will show, as in the case of Portuguese Africa, that concrete and substantial advantages have taken precedence over political or racial considerations remote to Brazilians, however real and proximate they may be to the Afro-Asian experience.

Rhodesia

As the Rhodesian case involves more than strictly internal considerations with the unilateral declaration of independence, Brazilian policy (like that of many Western states) has been somewhat more favorable to the Afro-Asian viewpoint than its policy on South Africa and Portuguese Africa would indicate, even if the policy has not taken a form fully congenial to the demands of the anticolonialist bloc. Brazil's dealings with Rhodesia have always been minimal, hence no loss was suffered by not recognizing the Ian Smith regime or by refraining from opening a consulate already authorized in Salisbury. While condemning with most United Nations members the repression of the Negro majority, Brazil refuses to agree with most Afro-Asian states and numerous Latin nations that international force or support for liberation movements is the only effective solution. It abstains as well from singling out Great Britain as responsible for the onset and prolongation of the problem and from chastizing Portugal and South Africa for rendering sustenance to the white-dominated government.

Even while holding in principle that a total embargo of nonmilitary goods only produces hardships for the whole population rather than being an instrument for the eventual realization of political reform, the Brazilian government issued decrees to implement within the national territory provisions of the mandatory general economic sanctions declared by the Security Council in Resolutions 232 and 253 (1966 and 1968). Perhaps Rhodesia's relative lack of economic importance for Brazil has made Brazil's compliance with the sanctions less painful and the consistency between its words and deeds easier to achieve than in its relations with South Africa. Total exports to Rhodesia from 1964 to 1967 inclusive were only $118,000 as compared to $41.1 million for those to South Africa. Until mandatory comprehensive sanctions were declared, Brazilian exporters were disposed to improve upon this figure without regard for politics or moral theories, but under present conditions Foreign Ministry plans have been at least temporarily shelved. In South Africa and the Portuguese colonies Brazil has given ample demonstration of its ability to discount as immaterial any Afro-Asian protests over closer relations, but the Security Council's unanimous comprehensive sanctions verdict of 29 May 1968 posed an obstacle between Brazil and Rhodesia which Brazil would not circumvent.

6. Economic Conflict and Cooperation with Afro-Aisa

ALTHOUGH Brazil's anticolonialism has proved less than fervent, on the issue of economic development Brazil has exhibited a higher degree of consistency. And because of its recurrent ambitions to emerge as a spokesman or leader of the underdeveloped states, Brazil has been cooperating with Afro-Asian countries to attempt a united front vis-à-vis the developed states in order to create an international climate conducive to development through organizations such as GATT, UNCTAD, and the International Coffee Agreement. Much of the multilateral contact between Brazil and the developing nations outside the Western Hemisphere has occurred in conferences and negotiations about agricultural exports or about problems of economic development. These topics weighed heavily in Quadros' overtures to Africa and still form the core of Itamaraty's dealings with those regions. Development has remained the prime concern within Brazilian foreign policy since it (1) emerged as a dominant theme under Kubitschek, (2) was elevated as one of the 3D's by Goulart, (3) was transformed in Costa e Silva's diplomacy of prosperity, and (4) was continued in Médici's export promotion policies. In conjunction with most Afro-Asian states, Brazil has vocally advocated not only reversing the unfavorable terms of trade suffered by producers of raw materials, but also stabilizing international prices of agricultural commodities, increasing the amount of bilateral and multilateral financial aid available on soft terms, creating a United Nations Capital Fund and an Agency for Industrial Development, and internationalizing the right to resources on or under the seabed to benefit less-developed countries. It has also promoted nuclear disarmament to insure world security and to release resources which could be better employed in reducing the growing gap between the metaphorical North and South.

The general coincidence of Afro-Asian–Brazilian positions on these broad issues as these nations confront the industrialized states may obscure the numerous ways in which Brazilian interests actually run counter to those of most Afro-Asian states when finer points are discussed and compromises sought. Beyond agreeing on principles as vague as the "collective economic security" proposed by Brazil in the General Assembly, Afro-Asia and Brazil begin to conflict. The mixture of conflict and cooperation in Brazil's relations with Afro-Asia arises from divergent interests inherent both in the nations' competition in the same or similar agricultural exports and in Brazil's status as an economy with strong areas of industrialization and considerable future potential not possessed by the majority of the Afro-Asian states. These differences persist and reappear in spite of the common group interests subsumed under the epithet "Third World," often taken to include Latin America.

Greater appreciation of some of the economic conflicts of interest may be gained by briefly examining Brazil's participation in the UNCTAD and by comparing with Brazil's positions those assumed by other members of the caucus "Group of 77" developing states. A comparison of policies and interests in international negotiations concerning coffee and cocoa illustrates agreements and differences which have characterized Brazilian interaction with Afro-Asia in the more narrowly restricted agricultural issues for which Brazil has demonstrated a serious concern.

Brazil and UNCTAD

Having consistently supported greater intervention by the United Nations into the flow of capital and technology to developing nations, Brazil was sympathetic toward the concept of establishing a permanent forum to deal with trade as the chief instrument to promote development. As one of four Latin American participants in the June 1962 Cairo Conference on Problems of Economic Development, Brazil played a central role in the events which led up to the First UNCTAD. The UNCTAD was convened by the Economic and Social Council of the United Nations through Resolution 917 (XXXIV) of 3 August 1962. In the preliminary meetings held by the thirty-two-nation Preparatory Committee, Brazil helped construct a common united front with the United Arab Republic, India, Nigeria, Ghana, Indonesia, and Algeria. It thereby gained prestige among important developing states and imbued its economic goals with a neutralist political cast. As preparations for the First UNCTAD progressed, Brazil (considered by some to be among the countries predestined for leadership) became a principal articulator and moderator in the drafting by seventy-five developing countries of a joint declaration. The declaration, presented to the General Assembly on 11 November 1963, expressed the developing countries' recommendations and expectations for the forthcoming Geneva talks. This collaboration was accomplished over some internal resistance within the Foreign Ministry from officials who were reluctant to oppose so frontally the United States, the nation's chief creditor. The officials feared that deviation from the traditional low-key relations of the previous half-century would discourage the United States from renegotiating and refinancing Brazil's external debt, especially since Brazil's economic position was weakening. Additional uneasiness was felt by this predominantly East-West–oriented group because the Soviet Union initially used the UNCTAD idea to attack the Kennedy Round, which Washington favored over the Geneva plans.

The *política externa independente* forces in national diplomacy, however, were aiming for precisely such a decisive confrontation with Washington in particular, and the industrialized states in general. These forces hoped that Brazil, lacking the capability to bargain bilaterally with the United

States from a position of economic and political power, could take advantage of the pseudo-parliamentary politics of the General Assembly to gain greater economic independence or concessions from the United States. Thus, in the General Assembly Brazil could mobilize the Afro-Asian states in a multilateral drive against the entrenched privileges of the North. The Brazilian goal before the Geneva conference and during its first week was to appeal to the Afro-Asians to support Brazilian actions which would certainly evoke American disapproval. The optimum outcome in the opinions of some diplomats who doubted the efficacy of any business-as-usual, GATT-type negotiations would have been complete polarization between North and South. These diplomats wanted at least an abrupt breakoff in the middle of the conference, precipitated by a walkout of the Group of 77. They wanted a new radicalized hard-line unity of the developing states under Brazilian leadership, with headquarters to be set up in Brasília if possible. But, if Brazilian leadership were not feasible, they would settle for sponsorship by a more radical Afro-Asian member. Success in such a long-shot endeavor, besides changing the face of world commerce, was expected to have repercussions propitious to thoroughgoing domestic reforms.

Brazil's task during meetings in São Paulo, Brasília, and Alta Gracia (Argentina) was to establish and express Latin unity through a Special Latin American Coordination Commission (CECLA). Brazil would thus resist American efforts to broaden economic discussions to evolve a regional platform for all members of the OAS. The United States' plan would have tended to inhibit an independent Latin stance at UNCTAD. (The United States took a negative position on UNCTAD from the start.) The impression was not lost on Washington when, at a ministerial-level gathering of the Inter-American Economic and Social Council in São Paulo, João Goulart neglected to mention the Alliance for Progress and concentrated instead on the imperative to treat the root of the development problem rather than place faith in palliatives. Goulart implicitly emphasized Latin cohesiveness over bilateral hemispheric cooperation with the Colossus of the North.

Brazil's design in Geneva was to link the Latin and Afro-Asian blocs, but this was prevented by Brazil's 31 March revolution. A brusque and immediate mid-course shift in Brazilian policy occurred after the first week of the UNCTAD. The shift effectively removed Brazil from spokesman ranks for which the Goulart regime had been aiming. And it restricted Brazil's cooperation with Afro-Asia for ideological motives, because the revolutionary government repudiated what it termed the "neutralist" cast of the previous government. For this reason Brazil's participation at the conference itself turned out to be considerably less radical than planned, although opposition from inside the new regime was sufficient to deter a complete about-face.

To evaluate Brazil's position at the First UNCTAD and compare it with the positions of other developing states, a voting study was carried out using all of the nominal roll call votes in which abstentions or negative votes were recorded, a total of thirty-eight roll calls. Since all of the measures were sponsored by developing states and favored their interests, numerical values were assigned each vote as follows: yea (+2), absent (0), abstain (−1), and nay (−2). All states which were absent on more than four votes (i.e., about 10 percent of the total number of votes) were omitted to minimize error through distortion. A voting score was thus obtained for each participant, with the maximum possible range running from +76 to −76; the higher the score, the greater the state's agreement with the theses of the Group of 77.[1]

Actual scores ranged from a "perfect" 76 (obtained by thirty-six states) to the United States' −52. To allow comparison of regional scores with Brazil's, the means and medians were computed for each region as geographically defined earlier. In each region the Afro-Asian states which cannot be classified as developing on the basis of their scores (Japan, Australia, New Zealand, and South Africa) and those developing states which had scores deviating widely from

1. The votes computed were the following:
General Principles: 1–12, 14, and 15.
Special Principles: 1, 4, 5, 7–9, and 11–13.
Annexes: A. III. 1, A. III. 6, A. IV. 4, A. IV. 6, A. IV. 7, A. IV. 8, A. IV. 9, A. IV. 15, A. IV. 19, A. IV. 23, A. IV. 25, A. VI. 2, A. VI. 3, A. VI. 4, and A. VI. 5.
The countries omitted from analysis by the four-vote absence guideline were Albania, Burundi, Congo (Brazzaville), Costa Rica, Cyprus, Dahomey, El Salvador, Ivory Coast, and South Vietnam.

their group's mean (Nationalist China, Thailand, and Turkey) were omitted from regional consideration. The results are presented in tabular form in Table 16 and indicate both the high degree of cohesion and the marked agreement on issues displayed by Afro-Asian states. The mean for all of developing Afro-Asia, with the three deviants excepted, fell at 74.3. In sharp contrast stood Brazil with a score of 61,

TABLE 16. Regional Scores on Issues before the First UNCTAD

Region	Number of states	Mean score	Median score
Middle East	14	75.7	74.4
Asia	12	74.3	73.3
Africa	22	73.5	75.0
Latin America	19	69.7	69.6
Communist bloc[a]	11	62.1	58.8

a. Includes Cuba.

lower than any other Latin American state and all Afro-Asian developing states except the deviants Turkey (56), Thailand (53), and Nationalist China (45). The latter three nations are not neutralist but American allies, with Turkey actually being the highest-scoring member of the Organization for Economic Cooperation and Development (OECD).

Entering the UNCTAD with ambitions of leading the developing states, Brazil finished the conference trailing behind other developing nations. Because of the revolutionary government's reservations, Brazil abstained on at least five crucial votes. The votes concerned tariff barriers against primary products, stabilization of commodity prices, new preferential general nonreciprocal concessions from developed to developing countries, elimination of the regional vertical tariff preferences "enjoyed by certain developing countries in certain developed countries," and adoption of special measures to favor the least-developed states. These reservations can be explained most generically by the conciliatory attitude toward the West in general and the United States, France, and West Germany in particular which the new government donned in order to mend relations after the frictions caused by Brazil's two previous regimes. Nevertheless, as significant as Brazil's fringe position in the Group of 77 may have been, its separation from the major developed states was even clearer and more pronounced. Brazil's 13.3-point deviation from the Afro-Asian mean or its 8.7-point deviation from the Latin American mean seem small when paired with its deviations from the scores of individual OECD states. For example, Brazil varied 113 points from the United States, 86 points from Great Britain, 80 points from West Germany, 69 points from Japan, and 57 points from France. Thus, the 1964 Geneva conference, which dramatically documented the magnitude of the North-South split also saw Brazil take an economic position which, although more "South" than "North," made difficult Brazil's neat classification into either group.

On the eve of the Second UNCTAD (in 1968) Brazil's reappraisal of its relations with Afro-Asia was under way. Foreign policy officials were psychologically more disposed toward close cooperation than they had been during the earlier days of the revolution when the restrictive formula was "cultural and political fidelity to the Western democratic system" and good relations with Washington were of the highest priority. The Costa e Silva government in its more nationalistic spirit was less hesitant to cross Washington but was still careful to divest economic developmental problems of ideological implications by approaching each issue pragmatically as if it were an overriding global problem amenable to a technical solution free of Cold War political overtones. Accordingly, in a speech to the General Assembly on 21 September 1967 Magalhães Pinto felt obliged to issue a political disclaimer concerning Brazil's role as a member of the Group of 77. He stated: "In the concerted action undertaken by UNCTAD there is no place for ideological motivation, which would vitiate its meaning. The seventy-seven nations, united by common interests, make up a group for the attainment of clearly defined and specific goals, exclusively linked to the promotion of economic development. It is strictly in this sense and in full awareness of our responsibilities that Brazil participates in the group."[2]

Not all political sectors, however, evidently felt that such a reliable "safe" distinction could be kept. Even though the

---

2. United Nations, General Assembly, Twenty-Second Session, *Provisional Verbatim Record of the Fifteen Hundred and Sixty-second Plenary Meeting, Thursday, 21 September 1967*, p. 8.

Brazilian diplomat Azeredo da Silveira had been elected president of the Group of 77's coordinating committee organized to prepare the October 1967 ministerial-level Algiers conference and even though Magalhães Pinto had planned to attend the Algiers meeting, at which the Group of 77 planned to prepare a unified front, the National Security Council insisted successfully that Magalhães Pinto not attend the Algiers conference.

When considered from an economic perspective, Brazil's 1968 position in New Delhi overlapped and supplemented its 1964 position in Geneva. Magalhães Pinto, the first speaker representing one of the 77 in the plenary conference, roundly condemned the developed states for their resistance to UNCTAD. He criticized not only their systematic refusal to put into practice the recommendations of the First UNCTAD by making concessions on the basis of already completed technical studies but also their apparent unconcern over problems to peace posed by the poverty experienced by two-thirds of the world's population. Brazil went to New Delhi with high hopes, the third largest delegation (surpassed only by Japan and India), and with instructions from the foreign minister to place the blame for any failure of the conference squarely upon the industrialized states should they continue a rigid line with no willingness to grant concessions. Elected president of the Group of 77 for the conference's final and decisive phase (succeeding representatives of the Philippines and the Ivory Coast), head of the Brazilian delegation Azeredo da Silveira aggressively attempted to maintain a viable concensus among the group around the minimum program agreed upon in Algiers. His own delegation believed that a total and generally acknowledged failure would be preferable to acceptance of half-measures which would do little more than perpetuate the disagreeable status quo.[3] When the recal-

3. In an unusual retroactive declaration, the Brazilian delegation announced at the seventy-seventh plenary meeting of the Second UNCTAD that Brazil was withdrawing its reservations on General Principles Seven, Eight, and Fifteen approved by the First UNCTAD so that it could go on record (somewhat belatedly) as fully supporting all the Principles enunciated in UNCTAD's first session. In reversing the votes of the Castello Branco government, Costa e Silva's administration was putting itself on consistent footing congenial to Brazil's more assertive role in the Second UNCTAD and its interaction with

citrance of OECD members as well as schisms inside the Group of 77 foreclosed significant progress, Azeredo da Silveira in an impassioned condemnatory speech in plenary session and in a press interview declared that the Second UNCTAD's miserable outcome for the developing states was due to the developed nations' refusal to face the problem seriously. He added that, given this seemingly perennial attitude, the Group of 77 would do well to create a permanent organization of developing countries to be the counterpart of the OECD.[4]

Far from demonstrating unanimity of goals and purpose between Brazil and Afro-Asia, the Second, like the First, UNCTAD revealed that as one of the "relatively developed" of the developing countries Brazil has a set of interests which only partially coincides with those of the "typical" Afro-Asian state. Nevertheless, all of the Group of 77, including Brazil, had the avowed purpose of translating into reality the recommendations of the First UNCTAD. The "all-or-nothing" thesis which envisioned full and united institutional political pressure to solve at one fell swoop the complete range of problems plaguing the Group of 77 found little support among Afro-Asians. As a group, Afro-Asians showed an inclination to be amenable to less ambitious piecemeal gains whenever detailed proposals were being discussed. Their willingness to compromise further weakened the South's already precarious cohesion. At the conference, African states were ill-disposed to taking part in a wide-ranging effort to push for across-the-board solutions or to condemn the European states. They did not wish to risk the preferences which they already enjoyed from European states in order to merely advocate that these

Afro-Asian states in defense of precisely those principles on which the Castello Branco government had abstained.

4. Although this chain of postrevolutionary events is strikingly similar to that planned for by some Foreign Ministry leaders under Goulart, several Brazilian news publications did not neglect to point out that Brazil's hard-line international position in these issues and nuclear development was not paralleled by credible internal measures in the conduct of economic and financial policy. Several such sources, alluding to Rui Barbosa's flamboyant but ineffectual oratorical performances at the Second Hague Convention (1907), suggested that shunning the "Eagle of the Hague complex" and more realistically entering into bilateral negotiations rather than self-defeating revolutionary multilateral proclamations might produce more of substance for the nation. See the editorial in the *Jornal do Brasil*, 3 October 1968.

European Common Market or Commonwealth-based advantages be either abolished or spread to encompass all their competitors in Latin America and Asia. Several Afro-Asian delegates (including India's), claiming to belong to the majority sentiment, offered rebuttals to Silveira's pessimistic conclusions about the conference. This move left Brazil rather set apart, even from some Latin American states. The division became so pronounced within meetings of the Group of 77 that Silveira made it clear that he was prepared to resign as president of the group should the conciliatory pacifist viewpoint prevail and should the Group of 77 then fail to censure the North and proclaim the breakdown of the negotiations. Brazil came away from the conference embittered by what its diplomats termed Afro-Asian "capitulationism" which thwarted the Foreign Ministry's plans for the Group of 77 and, according to Brazilians, masked the unwillingness of the North to negotiate effective solutions for international economic inequities.

Following the trade expansion in manufactures theme of the Costa e Silva government, Brazil was the nation most vocal in proposing a new system of general nonreciprocal and nondiscriminatory preferences on the part of all developed countries for any manufactured and semimanufactured exports originating in developing countries (a "new international division of labor"). Two resolutions adopted by the Second Conference affirmed this trade principle. Resolution 21(II) unanimously established the general validity of the principle and set up a committee to study its implementation. Resolution 25(II) (over opposition by the developed states) called for an investigation of the restrictive business practices adopted by private enterprises of developed countries. The creation of a universal preference system is one of Brazil's main objectives in UNCTAD, for, along with India and Argentina, Brazil stands to benefit most from its operationalization. As early as 1963 Brazil ranked second among all developing states in value of manufactures exported; it had nearly one-eighth of the total manufactures exports of developing countries to its credit.[5] Nor has Brazil overlooked the probable consequences of such a general system on the

5. John Pincus, *Trade, Aid, and Development: The Rich and Poor Nations*, pp. 184–85.

Europe-Africa vertical preference arrangement. It hopes to use a global nondiscriminatory system as a wedge to eliminate the discriminatory preferences which European manufactures enjoy in Africa. Then its own manufactures will have greater access to African markets.

To most Afro-Asian states, at a much more primitive industrial level, the manufactures preference issue as seen by Brazil either does not demand great emphasis or is irrelevant to their own economic realities. It was to the least-developed Afro-Asian nations that the OECD members deliberately tried to appeal in the Second Committee by offering concessions in the low-value manufactured products they exported while excluding from consideration a list of higher-value manufactures which interested the most-developed among the Group of 77 (Brazil included). This tactic almost successfully endangered the Group of 77's common front. The Africans (and some Asian and Middle Eastern states) remained unconvinced of the merits of Brazil's general scheme when their own present status was considered. They were more in favor of merely expounding the Brazilian idea as a general principle and less concerned about establishing a special committee to study its implementation, although the latter was finally agreed upon.

Other divergences derived from Brazil's semi-industrial condition, including a resistance to the arguments of the least-developed states that they should receive special treatment throughout UNCTAD's sphere of competence because of their lower per capita income and more limited possibilities for industrialization. This conflict presents the other face of the manufactures preference issue. Having one of the larger merchant marine fleets among the Group of 77, Brazil is notably more sensitive to questions bearing upon the distribution of freight tonnage between exporter and importer nations, freight rates, and other items of "invisible trade." Brazil is also quite sensitive to any measures taken to encourage the development of national merchant marines in developing nations, since it plans both to build up its own fleet and to export vessels to buyers throughout the world. It concedes high priority to activities in the UNCTAD's Committee on Shipping. Along the same lines, Brazil is more convinced than most Afro-Asian states that the UNCTAD should be empowered to stimulate the growth of trade among underdeveloped states of different geographic regions, which would complement the Foreign Ministry's recent commercial ventures into Afro-Asia.

These differences in industrial progress aside, the fact that Brazil still depends heavily on the export of raw materials means that Brazilian diplomats will have to spend much time in efforts to stabilize the international price structure in coffee, cocoa, cotton, and sugar. Each of these products entails competition with Afro-Asian producers. To illustrate the chief agricultural rivalries, I must examine the two commodities over which the greatest friction with sub-Saharan Africa has arisen—coffee and cocoa.

Coffee

As the historically dominant producer of coffee, the most important agricultural commodity in world trade, Brazil has a vested interest in maintaining price stability for this source of nearly 30 percent of its export earnings in 1971 (even higher figures, 35 percent to 55 percent, have been registered in recent previous years). Since Brazil supplied an estimated 85 percent of the world's coffee at the turn of the century, unilateral retention policy (valorization) measures proved capable of exerting satisfactory leverage on the international price structure at least until great crop increases and decline in demand during the Depression combined to yield an excess-supply crisis. World War II further aggravated this crisis. After the war, generally favorable market conditions followed for a decade until the huge crop of 1957–1958 made it clear that, because of a general rise in production worldwide (accompanied by a decline in the power of Brazil's semimonopoly), supply would soon begin to outrun demand. In 1957, at the urging of Brazil and Colombia, seven Latin American producers signed an export quota agreement. It was expanded a year later to become a regional pact among fifteen Latin nations. A producers' agreement including most African exporters and counting on the cooperation of çolonial powers was reached in 1959 and renewed yearly until succeeded by the International Coffee Agreement between exporters and importers. The first International Coffee Agreement came into force on 1 October 1962 for a period of five years.

Among International Coffee Agreement producers, the basic cleavage of interests is found between Latin America, as a region where arabicas and mild coffees are grown, and Africa, where the harsher robustas predominate. The latter variety has cut deeply into the Latin share of the market. Brazil, traditionally the spokesman for Latin interests, was the supplier of 56 percent of the world's green coffee exports in 1949, a year in which Africa's contribution by weight amounted to only 13 percent. A substitution involving increased blending of the cheaper robustas with arabicas in instant coffee, as well as the better quality control initiated by Africans during the 1950s, threatened by 1966 to reverse the relationship and put Brazil on the defensive. The Africans had by then captured 31 percent of the market, while Brazil's percentage had gradually dwindled to slightly less than one-third.[6] The acceleration of this trend, in conjunction with imminent price downturns, had stimulated Brazil to become the chief sponsor of an international agreement and to make great efforts in 1959 and 1960 to persuade the Africans to join the agreement. The already-existing multilateral channels were thus augmented by Brazil's new bilateral communication to the Inter-African Coffee Organization. Bilateral talks were initiated with the July 1961 signature of the "Declaration of Rio de Janeiro." This declaration provided for discussions on product commercialization, production control, and the strengthening of the agricultural sectors of the signatories' economies. It had prepared the way for the International Coffee Agreement.

During the life of the International Coffee Agreement (as renewed in 1968), several points remained in dispute between Brazil and the African coffee producers, chiefly the Ivory Coast, Uganda, Malagasy Republic, Cameroon, Zaire, Kenya, and Tanzania.[7] Some of these countries have been displeased that a Brazilian has been serving as executive director of the agreement's council since its inception. First,

---

6. Pan American Coffee Bureau, *Annual Coffee Statistics, 1966*, pp. A-14 and A-15.

7. Ethiopia's case is unique. As a producer of mostly unwashed arabicas, it is outside European Commonwealth and Common Market preference systems, so its interests coincide more nearly with those of Brazil than do those of the other countries.

João de Oliveira Santos served (1963–1968) and then Alexandre Beltrão (previously with the New York office of the Brazilian Coffee Institute and president of the Pan American Coffee Bureau). The Africans fear that a Brazilian in this central position will merely reinforce his country's dominance and point of view in the market negotiations.

Recent market conditions have been characterized by a near-balance between total quota allocations and world import requirements. Most producers handle a surplus, because world coffee consumption grows by only 2 to 3 percent per year. In these circumstances, jockeying for annual quota adjustments has been vigorous. A slowness in the expansion of demand has usually made an almost zero-sum game of the adjustment procedures. Each state has been aware that a permanent expansion of its allowance will result in at least a partial reduction of the allowance of another country and vice-versa. Quota assignments are also related to price fluctuations. As the market price of a certain variety of coffee moves upward in comparison to any of the others, the producer becomes eligible for a temporary quota increase on the basis of selective gains. Both of these stipulations result in annual quota competition between Brazilian arabicas and African robustas. The African push for higher quotas on the basis of its greatly increased production and future potential, Africa's relative incapacity to store large quantities for extended periods, and the upswing of the price of robustas in relation to that of Brazilian Santos 4, all heighten the competition. Ever since the signing of the agreement, the Africans have been edging up on Brazil in percentage of the world's green coffee exported. This gain, although not as spectacular as that of the 1950–1961 period, has led Africans to demand that Brazil yield some of its quota since it remains the single largest benefactor of price stabilization. The selectivity system of temporary quota increases has benefitted the Africans more than the Brazilians, so the former wish to translate their temporary gains into permanent increases. Brazil has resisted this and has tried to hold its advantage dating from the original quota allotments based on world ratio relationships of 1961 sales. Upon this ratio the International Coffee Agreement had been formed, giving Brazil 39.5 percent of the total and Africa 20 percent. But these figures no longer reflect production or export reality (now more favorable to the Africans). Through the terms of the agreement, then, Brazil has been capable to some extent of stemming the African onrush but incapable of stopping it entirely. On the one hand, Brazil was required by the 1968 agreement to reduce its quota by 1.9 percent. On the other hand, in negotiations during August 1969, Brazil was successful, in a coalition with Colombian and Central American producers, in weakening the selectivity system as it had benefitted the Africans. But it had met stiff opposition from Africans and from consumers.

Brazilian officials believe that much of the increase in consumption of African robustas has resulted from nonquota, unrecorded sales of a clandestine nature, including the so-called "tourist coffee" (coffee re-exported to the intended destination from a third country under false pretenses). They have been calling for stricter controls and checks within the agreement in order to halt circumvention by what Executive-Director Beltrão estimated at a million sacks between October 1967 and October 1968. Even higher figures have been estimated for the previous years.[8] Brazil is also strongly in favor of stabilizing the market near the export ratios of the early 1970s by instituting all the effective controls possible on production and by stimulating economic diversification through the Diversification Fund—long a Brazilian goal. The Diversification Fund would in reality affect Africa more than Brazil, because Brazil has been following successful programs of production control (eradication and diversification) unilaterally with more emphasis and persistence than have the Africans. This policy, combined with minimum export price programs, actually contributed to the decline of Brazil's relative position in total sacks exported. If counterbalanced by equal African efforts, however, it would tend to strengthen African economies, curb worsening global overproduction, and, not incidentally, help Brazil keep its dominant position somewhat more easily. In return for African cooperation, Brazil, and probably Colombia, might have to yield a small part of their quotas. Brazil, along with other Latin American members, is anxious to receive greater assurances from the Africans that

8. *O Jornal*, 13 September 1968, p. 5.

they will abide strictly by the letter of agreement. Brazilian officials have criticized them privately in strong terms for what they interpret as failure to do so.

A perennial cause for disagreements between Brazilian and African coffee producers since 1957 has been the tariff discrimination system. Under the Treaty of Rome and the Yaounde Convention, European Common Market nations allow duty-free access of coffee to their domestic markets from the associated states of the Ivory Coast, Cameroon, Togo, Central African Republic, Malagasy Republic, Chad, Dahomey, Senegal, Congo (Brazzaville), Zaire, Mali, Mauritania, Niger, Nigeria, Upper Volta, Ruanda, Burundi, Somalia, and, since 1968, Kenya, Uganda, and Tanzania. This group encompasses well over 90 percent of the African coffee producers. Brazilian and other Latin American coffee producers, on the other hand, must pay varying ad valorem duties of up to 9.6 percent before their coffee can enter the European Common Market. Supported by other Latin American states, by Portugal (in defense of its Angolan interests), and by Ethiopia, Brazil has led the fight in denouncing the European-African association as harmful to nonassociated producers, distorting to world price levels, destructive of international competition, and a mockery of UNCTAD principles. Brazil maintains, basing its reasoning on OAS studies, that abolition of the tariff barrier would place the Latin coffees on more nearly equal entrance terms with the Africans. Consequently, an increase in sales volume and in revenue would occur, directly resulting from the lowered price of Latin coffee in the European Common Market. Brazil has also attacked the tariff as restrictive of expanded world coffee consumption. It made this point a plank in its 1968 campaign against world "underconsumption" of coffee and utilized, as it had previously, Article 47 of the International Coffee Agreement ("Removal of Obstacles to Consumption") to call for elimination of import barriers.

The Africans accepted the Brazilian Coffee Institute's thesis that a stabilized production-consumption relationship should be attained by raising consumption as high as possible in old and new markets rather than by merely lowering production. They were not ready to go along with Brazil in condemning the European tariff as a principal cause of "underconsumption." Nor would they support the amendment to Article 47 presented by Brazil during the 1968 renegotiation of the agreement. Brazil's amendment would have demanded that importers refrain from creating new commercial barriers against coffee and reduce present barriers against the commodity in order to increase consumption. The European Common Market as usual ignored these Latin protests and went even further in a discriminatory direction in 1968 by including the three above-mentioned English-speaking East African states in the European preferential arrangement. The tariff question thus became one of the major obstacles in the negotiations for pact renewal. In the end, the agreement was extended for another five years without Brazil, Africa, or the Common Market changing policy, even though the Common Market nations agreed in principle to a gradual lowering of tariffs.[9]

The second and more serious dispute upon which renewal of the agreement almost foundered was that between Brazil and the United States over Brazil's rapidly growing exports of soluble (instant) coffee to the United States. By 1967, only its third year on the United States market, yearly sales of soluble coffee reached $23.3 million.[10] Brazil turned to exporting soluble coffee as a means of using its low-quality, otherwise non-exportable beans to compete with the African robusta incursion into the American trade. It saw as well a unique opportunity to build up a profitable industry based on an abundant raw material. Brazil also increased and stabilized its exchange earnings because of the added economic value and use of an otherwise largely wasted inferior product

9. The limited validity of the common Brazilian affirmation that the tariff discrimination heavily favors the Africans is demonstrated by the fact that, according to official French statistics, Brazilian participation in French coffee imports climbed from 16 percent in 1967 to 23.8 percent in 1969 while the African suppliers' percentage fell. In the case of coffee, at least, promotion campaigns and quality-differential stress have proved effective in making inroads into Africa's most important market and the Common Market country with the highest tariff (9.6%). Conversely, during the same period, African robustas gained at the expense of Brazilian coffees in the United States market, where tariffs are not a consideration.

10. Only a brief outline of this significant and bitter dispute can be given here. The best sources for further analysis are Arthur J. Cordell, "The Brazilian Soluble Coffee Problem: A Review"; and William G. Tyler, "A política norte-americana e o impasse do café solúvel."

—the low-quality beans lost most of their disagreeable taste characteristics in the soluble-making process. Brazil gained an additional benefit because under the agreement soluble coffee exports, while figuring as part of a member's quota, are not subject to price controls as are sales of green coffee. Brazil was finally able to enter the American market with an instant coffee selling at a lower price per pound than that produced by American plants using the usual higher-quality, higher-price green coffee.

Despite profits made by American regional brand and private-label roasters utilizing the Brazilian solubles in their blends, the larger companies (roasters and green-coffee importers) filed complaints with the United States State Department. They alleged (1) that Brazil was engaging in unfair trade practices and was circumventing the agreement by in effect subsidizing the soluble industry (exempt from export taxes which fell upon green coffee); and (2) that Brazil was thereby undercutting the American industry and placing it in very unfavorable competitive circumstances. Reacting to strong pressures, the State Department contacted the Brazilian government on the problem. Bilateral talks were begun in late 1966, but no agreement was reached. At the urging of the American coffee trade and against Brazilian wishes, the matter was dragged into the International Coffee Agreement, thereby raising the stakes.

The United States soon began pressuring Brazil to create an export tax on its own soluble coffee so that its soluble exports would enter the United States market on an equal footing with American-produced solubles of Brazilian origin. This demand was a step beyond conventional protectionism, because, in forcing Brazil itself to levy the duty, the United States used its power position as the largest Brazilian customer and avoided the stigma of placing the duty itself. When Brazil showed great reluctance to accept this solution, the United States laid out the options: either the new agreement with the above terms or no agreement and untaxed soluble. This unpleasant choice was what Washington (and the large coffee concerns) hoped would make Brazil yield.

Brazil considered the soluble coffee conflict an important test of the resistance of the United States, and developed countries generally, to manufactured exports originating in developing countries. Given the blatant techniques employed by the Americans, the soluble coffee controversy became a nationalist issue. According to Minister of Industry and Commerce Macedo Soares, Brazilian diplomats were prepared to go as far as nonrenewal of the agreement in order to protect national interests.[11]

Because it gravely endangered the International Coffee Agreement and because the American position was seconded by most major importers, the deadlock definitely influenced Brazilian-African coffee relations. Although Brazil appealed to the Africans for support on the grounds that African industrialization of agricultural products would also be prejudiced if the American challenge went uncontested and similar pressures appeared in other commodities, it found itself isolated. The Africans' low-level industrialization made the problem irrelevant to them. Concrete short-run interests dictated African attention to the agreement's renewal, rather than concentration on what was in African opinion not a matter of principle but a side-issue of a monetary value insufficient to justify the inherent risks. With most Latin producers of a similar mind, particularly Guatemala and Colombia, Brazil was unable to muster significant producer support; the United States readily found support among consumers.

Brazil's willingness to endanger the pact in order to defend the soluble coffee industry was not well received by the Africans, many of whom depend more on coffee for exchange receipts than does Brazil. The specter of the pact's demise might well have served to arouse latent African discomfiture in the knowledge that, although Africa is gaining in world sales, Brazil retained a powerful ultimate advantage. Despite its recent drastic reduction in excess productive capacity, Brazil at the time maintained about one full year of the world's coffee supply in exportable stocks. In the absence of an agreement, this supply could have been used in a price war, or for outright dumping as a devastating retaliatory measure.

Even with the drastic production falloff, Brazil is still in a much better position to influence prices unilaterally; it is the single supplier of over one-quarter of the world's

11. *Jornal do Commércio*, 29 March 1968, p. 5.

total coffee exports. The several African nations are comparatively helpless with their relatively less-diversified economies. Should a pre-1963 type of producers' arrangement again become necessary, Brazil would be furnished with a considerably more potent arsenal of economic weapons than would the Africans, who need not be reminded of the fact. Thus in the soluble coffee affair, while the Brazilians privately criticized the Africans as capitulationists and desirous of concluding an agreement at any price, to the Africans the Brazilians were irresponsible and rash for rocking the international trade boat so wildly for a minor issue.

The differences in economic development between Brazil and Africa kept the conflict from widening to the consumer-producer dimension. Through it all the Africans were well aware that any disadvantage thrown onto the Brazilian soluble coffee in the American market would lead the smaller roasters to include less Brazilian soluble coffee and more African robusta in their instant and freeze-dried blends, which were gaining favor with the American coffee drinker. Should Brazil have been forced to impose its own duty on soluble exports to any destination, the African robusta producers would actually have been the chief benefactors in markets throughout the world.

Faced with a very real American threat and lacking any effective backing among producers, to save the pact Brazil conceded the inclusion in the new agreement of a special Article 44. This article forbids any member from exporting soluble or processed coffee under any more favorable conditions than those enjoyed by the green coffee, for which the agreement was originally designed. Passing back to the bilateral level, the dispute was resolved by additional American pressure—in the form of a Senate amendment to the legislation authorizing United States participation in the International Coffee Agreement. The amendment stipulates that the United States must withdraw from the agreement should any discriminatory action be taken against American coffee interests. To avoid taking any internal steps to provoke drastically lessened sales of its soluble coffee in all foreign markets, Brazil, in March 1969, announced that it would levy an export tax of 13 cents per pound on the soluble coffee shipped to the United States. This solution was accepted by the State Department, and it remained in force until succeeded by another agreement in April 1971.

Cocoa

Contrary to the massive role played by its coffee, a source of nearly $1 billion annually in foreign exchange, Brazil's cocoa exports (originating largely from Bahia state) have remained around $100 to $130 million in recent years, or approximately 5 to 6 percent of the country's total export value. This figure has been sufficient to keep Brazil in third place among cocoa producers, following Ghana and Nigeria, with the Ivory Coast a close fourth, even though Brazil's share of total world production by weight dropped from 20.8 percent in 1957–1958 to 12.9 percent in 1966–1967 while West Africa's rose from 57.2 percent to 71.4 percent. Expressed in terms of interest in the market, Ghana, Nigeria, and the Ivory Coast combined produced during the early and mid-1960s from 4.1 to 8.7 times as many tons of raw cocoa yearly as Brazil. Cocoa and its derivatives averaged 69 percent, 18 percent, and 19 percent of their total recent export value, respectively.[12] As with coffee, the fundamental split among cocoa producers is between Brazil and Africa. But with cocoa, Africa is by far in the dominant position. Brazilian cocoa takes a minority status domestically and internationally. Rather than diminishing its economic conflict with Africa, Brazil's inferior position has actually heightened the conflict because of the quite different stakes involved for the two producer sides during negotiations for a world cocoa agreement. Such negotiations have been unsuccessful since their origins in 1956 because of the three-way wrangle among Africa, Brazil, and the major consumers—the United States, West Germany, the Netherlands, the United Kingdom, and France.

Within the Cocoa Producers Alliance (COPAL), the conflicts between Brazil and West African members—Ghana, Nigeria, Ivory Coast, Cameroon, and Togo—have most frequently occurred over price, quotas, and European Common Market and Commonwealth tariff preference systems. Sometimes these factors have created as much of a hindrance to the negotiation of a pact as have group disagreements with con-

12. "World Production of Raw Cocoa."

sumers. The Brazilians have usually held out for higher minimum prices per pound than have the Africans. They have more consistently expressed the view that the consumer states should finance the buffer stock which helps balance supply and demand, a demand the consumers reject. The Brazilians carried the price issue to such an extreme that the June 1969 talks which had crystallized around the general acceptance of a package deal providing for a price range of 20 to 29 cents came to a precipitous and unexpected close when Brazil suddenly introduced and stood firm upon a proposal for a range of 25 to 34 cents. This proposal met with prompt consumer rejection. Although this was the clearest instance of Brazilian inflexibility on price (and at a time when prices were at a ten-year high), previous negotiations had been hampered by the same problem which had already earned for Brazil the criticism of consumers and West Africans alike.

Brazil considers itself as somewhat of a future challenger to the Africans on the market. Through the Executive Commission for the Economic and Rural Recovery of Cocoa Agriculture (CEPLAC) the national government has been pursuing a program to encourage the growth of cocoa exports. Accordingly, in discussing quota-determination systems, Brazil has tried to defend procedures which favor itself as a producer whose production temporarily fell during the mid-1960s but who expects to glean a rising share of the world market in the 1970s. In more general terms, Brazil has defended initial quota determinations covering averages over longer periods of past production than the Africans would suggest. Brazil thus brings into play earlier harvests when its own production was relatively higher. At the same time (and especially since the late 1960s), the country has favored a flexible system of future readjustment of quotas geared to recent production and reconsideration of criteria. It would rather not bind all producers to old ratios. Brazil essentially planned to extract the maximum feasible advantage from previous, more favorable crop years while avoiding any future stabilization of the market which would be unfavorable to its interests as a contender. The Ivory Coast, also anticipating a greater share of the market, has agreed with Brazil, but established producers such as Ghana and Cameroon feel that this thesis would speed the undercutting of their position. Brazil is trying to make certain that a future cocoa agreement does not retard growth of its share in the cocoa market as the International Coffee Agreement has tended to retard the Africans' in coffee.

Through producers' agreements (begun as a result of Brazil's suggestion) Brazil has been successful to date in being able to negotiate rights to export most of its cocoa crops, occasionally at notable African expense. For example, in the 1964–1965 and 1965–1966 seasons, the methods used to arrive at basic export quotas clearly favored countries whose production was falling. This situation led President Houphouet-Boigny of the Ivory Coast to remark, "We are struggling to get more justice in this quota system, for it is not possible that a country like ours can stock four-sevenths of its production when certain countries like Brazil have only had to stock a third or two-fifths of their production."[13] The Ivory Coast, whose cocoa contributes nearly one-fifth of the gross export revenue, found itself stocking a greater percentage of its production than did Brazil, an only slightly larger producer to whom cocoa is of marginal importance. To make matters worse, cocoa is difficult to stockpile in tropical zones, and Brazil has greater storage facilities. Among the Africans, only Ghana has a sizeable capacity. Even the fact that the Brazilian Temporão variety of bean has a different harvest cycle from the African types caused complications and conflicts of interest in the crop estimations necessary to assign quotas or even decide the dates to bracket quota years. The years were eventually set at 1 October–30 September.

As in the coffee negotiations, Brazil regularly has attacked preferences granted to associated states of the European Common Market and the British Commonwealth as discriminatory and restrictive of the expansion of world consumption. In comparison to Africa, Brazil exports much more of its cocoa and derivatives to the United States (42.3 percent in 1970) and much less to the Common Market (8.4 percent in 1970). The expansion of demand is generally conceded to be more promising in the latter, and Brazil would like to regain a greater share of its cocoa trade than the 1 percent it had in 1965 (in 1958 it had 12 percent). Brazil blames the rapid decline upon the tariff barriers, but the Africans attrib-

13. "Cocoa Group in Geneva—New Ivory Coast Prices."

ute it to other causes. Supported by the United States and Ecuador and claiming to be motivated by a desire to reverse the trend toward regional preferences which violate the spirit of UNCTAD resolutions, Brazil, at the 1967 United Nations Cocoa Conference, split the producing countries severely during negotiations. It presented, without previous consultation with other COPAL members, an amendment to eliminate or suspend preferential tariff arrangements. Combined with the producer-consumer dimension of the conflict, this insistence was sufficient to preclude possibilities for agreement.

In rather heated tones the West Africans retorted by accusing Brazil of lack of good faith in suddenly introducing a gratuitous amendment on a sensitive question at a late stage in a conference about a single commodity. They felt trade preference as a broad field could best be treated privately within COPAL or the Group of 77 and should not be deliberately used as an obstruction to threaten agreement. The Ivory Coast accused Brazil of reneging on previous agreements mutually arrived at during the Algiers Conference which had been called to settle the preference question as a whole before taking up individual commodities. But Ghana, the world's largest cocoa producer, for which prices are a domestic political issue, was even more candid. It declared that it could not countenance "some delegations," for which cocoa was not of vital interest, reducing the labors of the conference to an "academic exercise."[14]

Episodes such as this have been useful for several Brazilian objectives not directly related to an immediate cocoa pact. Brazil is obsessively determined to destroy the discriminatory European Common Market tariffs by whatever multilateral means necessary. Stalling the cocoa talks is one method of pressuring the Africans, because cocoa is not so vital that Brazil cannot afford to use cocoa as an integral part of a general strategy to extract concessions from African competitors regarding their special economic relations with Europe. Such concessions would also apply to coffee, which is of

14. United Nations, United Nations Conference on Trade and Development, United Nations Cocoa Conference, 1967, Executive Committee, *Summary Records of the First to Thirteenth Meetings Held at the Palais des Nations, Geneva, from 29 November to 19 December, 1967*, p. 102.

transcendent importance to Brazilians. This plan could be successful if the associated states are split internally, even though the Ivory Coast is the only major producer of both coffee and cocoa among them. As with price ranges, Brazil can afford to ask for more, barter, and then wait for the Africans to come around because they are harder-pressed to get an agreement. In torpedoing the talks of December 1967 and June 1969, Brazil may also have been allowing itself time to advance its cocoa output before initial quotas were fixed. Then it could enter at a higher quota level. Against this opposition Africans privately threatened to retaliate in kind in the International Coffee Agreement—to reverse the tactic where Brazil was most vulnerable. But the effectiveness of this plan would have been questionable since the coffee market is so greatly dominated by a single seller and a single consumer, unlike the more diversified cocoa market. Also of dubious viability as a means to escape what the Africans see as Brazilian obstructionism would be a suggested alternative agreement encompassing only West Africa and the consuming countries or even a Common Market–based agreement which would not include the market variables represented by the United States and Brazil.

Of much more consequence to Brazil than to the Africans have been the consumers' attempts to prevent any producer from granting special price treatment to exports of cocoa products (such as instant cocoa or cocoa butter) in order to sell them below going world prices. Such a demand is uncomfortably closely related to the soluble coffee question, which left Brazil isolated in the International Coffee Agreement and which Brazil resists in cocoa as a matter of principle and precedent. In West Africa only Ghana has a cocoa-processing industry of promising capacity for cocoa butter, powder, chocolates, and animal feed. But even Ghana was not as concerned with the matter as Brazil. Ghana needed much more to attain a price-stabilization scheme for raw cocoa than to hold out over what was for it an extraneous and hypothetical problem. For Brazil the basic ground rules of the cocoa agreement cannot be separated from its stands on coffee and are, in fact, planned to reinforce those stands. This tendency is made plausible by American cocoa policies, which are similar to those it holds on the soluble coffee issue. For example, the

United States refuses to cover instant cocoa within the ambit of the agreement so that it can more readily apply strong unilateral measures as it deems expedient. Strains within the Cocoa Alliance, then, are produced not only because of divergent, internally determined national interests but also by the fact that for Brazil the principal consumer frame of reference is represented by the United States, while for the West Africans it is Western Europe.

7. Afro-Asia in the Global Context of Brazilian Foreign Relations

ALTHOUGH they are now acquiring a logic of their own, Brazilian relations with Africa, Asia, and the Middle East have been heavily conditioned by the interaction patterns Brazil had established with her longtime economic and political allies. The gradual extension of its diplomacy and trade into Afro-Asia and its increasing contact with Afro-Asian representatives through United Nations agencies have wrought changes in Brazil's Afro-Asian policy. But the main body of Brazilian foreign relations must serve as a backdrop to the narrower scope of the Afro-Asian policy. A multi-dimensional approach takes into account Brazil's conflicting interests and priorities as major Brazilian–Afro-Asian issues are examined in the central context of Brazilian relations with Latin America, the United States, and Western Europe.

Brazil's multifarious interactions with other states may be conceptualized as occurring or being mediated through sets of international multiple-group affiliations or cross-cutting memberships defined by common economic, political, and cultural interests. Such affiliations tend to reinforce each other on some international issues and clash on others, creating dilemmas and cross-pressures for foreign policy decision makers. This occurs much as multiple-group memberships of individuals can produce tensions or conflicts of interest within their various groups or within their own attitude structure.[1] The diversity of Brazil's international behavior and the legacy of its history place it in five groups which are relevant to this study because of the implications they engender for relations with Africa, Asia, and the Middle East. Each membership, while roughly delimiting Brazilian interests in regard to certain issue areas, also involves internal conflict with other group members because of divergent interests since Brazil differs somewhat from the mean characteristics of each group. Likewise, each membership implies solidarities that may conflict with solidarities arising from one or more of the other memberships.

The most established of all the memberships, imposed by geography, culture, and history, is Brazil's status as a Latin American nation. Brazil plays a major role by virtue of the skill of its diplomacy, the enormity of its territorial extension, and the magnitude of its population. It accommodates within its borders 47.3 percent of the area of the South American continent and over half of its population. In international forums Brazil has traditionally been one of the spokesmen for the Latin bloc and in the opinion of some observers may, within several decades, rival United States' dominance on the South American continent. All Brazilian governments in recent times have stressed the high priority granted to Latin America in national diplomacy, but Brazil's growing inclination has been to regard its Latin American activity not merely as an end in itself but also as a means to greater prestige outside the hemisphere and particularly in Afro-Asia. Counterbalanced with this ambition of using Latin America as a springboard to a worldwide role is the necessity Brazilians feel to safeguard the national image intraregionally by vocally defending Latin interests against African interests, as in commodity conferences on coffee and cocoa. Aside from the broader scope of its international aspirations and ultimate capabilities, Brazil has experienced conflicts of interest with Latin American states within the OAS and LAFTA. The con-

1. For an elaboration of this theory at the individual and group levels, see, inter alia, David B. Truman, *The Governmental Process*.

flicts reflect differences in economic development and ideology, buttressed by Brazil's long association with American policy and a prevalent national attitude depicting the country as significantly different from Spanish America. These differences set Brazil's perspectives somewhat apart from the Spanish American norm and contribute to its occasionally deviant behavior.

Evolving out of its Latin American affiliation—with expansion to the hemispheric level—is Brazil's participation in the inter-American subsystem, including OAS membership and bilateral relations with the United States. Within this set of interactions we can place the traditional alliance with Washington, which gave to some of the foreign policy elite an image of world politics resembling that of the Americans. The American view extended most importantly into Brazil's evaluation of Cold War matters and even into its perceptions of Afro-Asia. The United States also greatly influenced Brazil's economic and political policy toward other nations.

Of greater consequence for relations with Afro-Asia is Brazil's strong self-identification as a member of the Western ethnic, cultural, and political community. Its Western identification derives from historical antecedents as well as from the pro-European cultural affinities of Brazil's upper classes. They found greater prestige in emulating American and European styles than in developing uniquely national tastes or outlooks. The operationalization of this amorphous sentiment created a decided impediment to closer Brazilian relations with Afro-Asians. It also led to Brazil's acceptance of the ideological pro-Western interpretation of its role in the Cold War and of the primacy of the East-West conflict as the dimension of world tension within which the parameters of foreign policy had to be constructed. It led to suspicion of neutralism (seen as tending to favor international communism) and tacit support for Western colonialist powers as they came under attack from Afro-Asian members of the United Nations.

The erosion of this attitude set has been very gradual. Even during the years of the "independent foreign policy" the vast majority of Brazilian intellectuals preferred to "aspire upward" internationally by emphasizing the nation's background as a European offshoot. Most Brazilians did not value the cultural or ethnic contributions of Africa, as do Haitians. Although most pronounced as public policy during the Castello Branco regime, Western affiliation has been a persistent variable in relations with Afro-Asia since the independence of the new states and has been noted by African representatives in Brazil. On the other hand, Brazil, although it has been unable to sympathize fully with the emotions of négritude and anticolonialism, has not fallen victim to white chauvinism, for its contemporary racial composition is neither typical of the Western nations nor similar to that of tropical Africa.

Nor is Brazil a typical Western nation in terms of political or economic development. Its characteristic political style and per capita income clearly classify it as a developing state. A primarily agricultural but rapidly industrializing state, it has many economic interests in conflict with those developed members of the industrialized Western grouping which are institutionalized economically in OECD and militarily in NATO. Within this "developing-group" membership, now most concretized in the Group of 77, Brazil has found common cause with Afro-Asian states, attacking developmental problems and mediating between NATO and Warsaw pact spokesmen as a nonaligned member of the Eighteen-Nation Committee on Disarmament (now comprised of twenty-six nations), which has been meeting in Geneva since 1962. On the other hand, while promoted by common interests vis-à-vis the developed states and by a Brazilian desire to expand trade in manufactures, cooperation with Afro-Asian states has been restricted, as demonstrated in chapter 6, by a competition in agricultural exports, divergent views on tariff preferences, and the general consideration that Brazil is more economically developed than most Afro-Asian states and so possesses a different range of concerns on questions of international economic policy.

Brazil's isolation from Afro-Asian support because of its relatively well-developed condition is effectively illustrated by the politics surrounding the signature of the Nuclear Non-Proliferation Treaty. An advocate of nuclear arms limitation, a member of the Eighteen-Nation Disarmament Conference, and a leader in the negotiations leading to the Treaty of Tlatelolco (which prohibited the proliferation of nuclear weapons into Latin America), Brazil refused to sign the non-proliferation treaty. Brazilians criticized the treaty as an imposition by the sponsoring nuclear states on the non-nuclear powers because it did not provide for any real sacrifices on the part of the former in return for the responsibilities and obligations undertaken by the latter. Further, according to Brazil, the treaty contained no clear commitment by the nuclear powers to press for further measures to reduce their own arsenals, but it did throw restrictions upon the peaceful uses of atomic energy by non-nuclear states, particularly in the field of explosions for peaceful purposes. Brazil initially tried to persuade other developing states that the treaty was a piece of "technological neo-colonialism" and presented the matter as a danger to the right of industrializing states to develop their own independent technology. Since few non-nuclear states agreed, Brazil abandoned its argument in early 1968 and, partly in response to American requests, subsequently ceased its lobbying efforts. Not only did the hoped-for Afro-Asian opposition practically melt by the time the General Assembly voted on the treaty in June 1968, but the African bloc also indicated its readiness to exchange votes in favor of the treaty for Western approval of the liberation of South West Africa from South Africa's control. Although such a tradeoff never actually materialized, the reversal of priorities was unmistakable: the nuclear question which Brazil considered a vital interest was for the Africans quite secondary while the opposite was true in regard to the issue of South West Africa. Only two African states voted negatively on the resolution. Sixteen Afro-Asian bloc members abstained. To most of the Afro-Asians, halting proliferation was more important than safeguarding a supposed right that was beyond their means to exercise.

Finally, Brazil's relations with Afro-Asia are influenced by its membership in the Luso-Brazilian community—Brazil, Portugal, and the latter's overseas territories. For Brazil, however, this growing affiliation has been a two-edged sword. While recently providing inroads into Portuguese-speaking Africa and promising Brazil a more important international role, the Luso-Brazilian community has provided Brazil with embarrassing moments. It has subjected Brazil to Afro-Asian criticism for what appears to be Brazilian complicity in the last outstanding examples of colonialism. Brazilian officials have tried to determine what type of policy would best suit national interests in the only other Portuguese-speaking parts of the developing world. At the same time, they have tried to avoid loss of face before the anti-colonial states in Afro-Asia.

These cross-cutting international memberships have resulted in heavy cross-pressures on Brazil, and have especially influenced its Afro-Asian policy. The multiple and overlapping memberships it possesses in disparate groups are only partially inclusive, so they produce recurrent contradictory demands, overlapping conflicts, and resultant indecision. The indecision may appear to be uncertainty or vacillation, particularly in low-saliency regions such as Afro-Asia. There (with the possible exception of Portuguese Africa) the remoteness of the issues from the attentive public, combined with Itamaraty's traditional secrecy, give foreign policy elites wide latitude for choice as far as domestic pressures are concerned. What may appear to be incoherence is explained by the fact that Brazil is not fully committed to any one membership, nor is it polarized by only highly congruent memberships. Thus, in 1966 Brazil almost simultaneously received the South African foreign minister and the Minister of Economic Affairs in Rio de Janeiro and sponsored the United Nations Seminar on Apartheid in Brasília. In 1968 it opened new embassies in sub-Saharan Africa while standing alone to defend Portugal's colonial policy at the United Nations Conference on Human Rights in Tehran. The net long-term effect of such heterogeneous cross-cutting affiliations has been to moderate the Brazilian position on most issues and to inhibit Brazilian adherence to a rigid, doctrinaire polar position on any single issue. The most outstanding exception, over which Brazil almost completely isolated itself, has been the Nuclear Non-Proliferation Treaty. Brazil, part "Western" and part "non-Western," part developed and part underdeveloped, was therefore unable in the light of the full range of its own interests to give complete solidarity to the Afro-Asian interpretation of the ultimate consequences of even the widely accepted "Disarmament, Development, Decolonization" slogan which the Brazilian delegation itself had articulated. Brazil preferred to oppose the treaty, differ with Afro-Asian members of the 77 on important economic points, and tacitly defend Portuguese colonialism.

Brazilian economic and political interests converge with and diverge from those upon which the Afro-Asian bloc has struck a consensus in much more subtle and complicated ways than the mere grouping of Brazil with Afro-Asia as a "developing," "Southern," or "Third World" state would lead one to assume. However, the ideology of the government in Brasília at any given time may modify that convergence or divergence slightly by emphasizing the set of interests implicit in one membership as opposed to another or by pursuing different versions of the national interest within any one membership. Viewed in this manner it is not surprising that the crisis of identification, the new emerging balance of countervailing membership pressures, should have been so severe from 1961 to 1964. Brazil was then beginning actively to expand contacts with Afro-Asia and Iron Curtain nations, while reappraising its relations with traditional associates in the light of its new global ambitions, rising nationalism, and internal demands for development. Far from being immune to this reappraisal, the developmentalists' so-called Afro-Asian policy was largely a result of it. At the same time, Brazil's Afro-Asian leanings were not strong enough to free Brazil from the constraints imposed by its four other memberships. Hence Brazil hesitated and contradicted and reversed itself because of its misjudgments about Afro-Asian reality and because of the resistance it encountered through its other memberships and from those who judged events in terms of Brazil's more salient memberships.

In conjunction with the higher saliency given to Latin America, the United States, and Western Europe by the weight of historical affiliations, other factors merge to relegate Afro-Asia to an inferior plane in Brazilian diplomacy and trade. The first set of limiting factors is economic; aid for development and trade for foreign exchange reserves must come largely from the industrialized states—Japan included. Developing Afro-Asia's role in the present rapid trade expansion, even in manufactures, will remain much less important in comparison. Accordingly, whatever diplomatic and commercial effort Brazil can muster for trade expansion will most economically be directed toward the markets with the greatest inherent probability of successful return. This is not to say that Afro-Asian–directed commercial activity has not grown or will not grow. Precisely the opposite has been the case, and with good success during the Costa e Silva and Médici governments. It is merely to affirm, on the other hand, that the benefits to be garnered from the Afro-Asian economic policy are long-run benefits. These benefits will be realized and further developed as Brazil takes on global interests, but, for the short run, they will be treated as merely supplementary to the greater promotional effort invested in the larger traditional markets. The reciprocal is also true for the Afro-Asian states: Brazil's power of economic or political attraction for them is quite limited relative to that of the developed metropolitan areas. In this respect Brazil lacks the internal capacity for a powerful Afro-Asian policy. Its policy is restricted to meager or token representation in several areas because of the nagging question of economic priorities.[2]

On the political, economic, and cultural levels, Brazil can nevertheless be expected to expand its representation in Afro-Asia and its interaction with these regions because a global diplomacy is an integral part of Brazil's self-image as a future power, a vision which the younger Foreign Ministry officials, the "hard-line" elements of the military, and informed public opinion have taken quite seriously. The domestic political situation can not be entirely discounted, however, for some leftists still tend to identify the Afro-Asian bloc with the "international proletariat" while the traditionalist, national security–conscious right still has qualms about the ideologies the leftist bloc espouses and about the anti-Western positions it takes. Both of these attitudes are overreactions related to erroneous assessments by the "independent foreign policy" theorists, who anticipated an overwhelming Afro-Asian response to the slightest Brazilian advance, and by the leading officials of the 1964 revolution, who feared ideological contamination from Afro-Asia. The reality proved to be something else, but a sense of "leftness" still pervades an aggressive, active diplomacy in Afro-Asia in the minds of

2. Among developing states of different geographical regions, low saliency is not a problem characteristic just of Brazil's relations with Afro-Asia. For descriptions of the low levels of bilateral relations between Africa and members of the Asian caucusing group which occurred despite well-known cooperation at the United Nations, see Fred R. von der Mehden, "Southeast Asian Relations with Africa"; and Richard L. Park, "Indian-African Relations."

traditionally oriented politicians and statesmen. The rising nationalism evident in recent foreign policy, the intensification of the North-South conflict, and the strictly economic nature of the post-1964 approach to Afro-Asia have served to attenuate somewhat the doubts of this group. A final settlement of the independence question in the Portuguese colonies would also be likely to have a stabilizing effect as well by removing one of Brazil's principal handicaps among the Black Africans.

The present militarily supported regime of Garrastazú Médici follows the Superior War College slogan of "Security and Development." In practice this slogan has meant a varying mixture of conscious attention to the Western community (especially the United States) for national security, on the one hand, and simultaneous collaboration with developing countries (including those of Afro-Asia) to reach common stands on developmental problems, on the other. Although not a foregone conclusion, we may hypothesize that some future, more leftist-nationalist, and perhaps civilian government might de-emphasize the security aspect and widen Brazil's multilateral political cooperation with other developing states. Then Brazil might find itself in an objectively more-accepted position, from which it could compete for leadership and enhance its image both domestically and abroad.[3]

A recapitulation of current Brazilian goals in or vis-à-vis Afro-Asia can be drawn up as follows, with no priorities implied:

    1. Increase in trade relations, involving preferably the exchange of manufactured products for raw materials to be used in Brazil's new industries; otherwise the general expansion of all types of sales to new markets.
    2. Defense of national economic interests in competition in primary commodities, notably coffee, cocoa, sugar, and cotton, including persuasion for African

---

3. Basing their conclusions on ideological evaluations of the domestic accomplishments of the Costa e Silva government, many of the proponents of the 1961–1964 rapprochement with Afro-Asia openly doubted the sincerity of the 1967–1968 overtures to those same areas via UNCTAD. They characterized the shift in policy as mere "window dressing" for the sake of appearances, unsupported by elite attitudes which would make real political cooperation viable.

states associated with the Common Market to either yield or universalize their tariff preferences there.

3. Encouragement of solidarity among developing countries to negotiate as a group with the developed states for the reversal of unfavorable terms of trade and other economic concessions sought by the Group of 77.

4. Preservation of Portuguese language and culture in Africa to serve as a facilitator for a future Brazilian presence on that continent, under the supposition that the Portuguese territories will eventually achieve independence and that Brazil, while not meddling in Lisbon's internal affairs, should do everything possible to make this emancipation relatively painless and of a nature to ensure the continuation of Portuguese language and culture rather than alienation from them on the part of the Africans.

5. Enhancement of national prestige as a leader among developing states, a rising middle power with a worldwide diplomatic network, utilizing the projected image of a pacific, multiracial, rapidly industrializing tropical civilization.

6. Exchange of technical knowledge in fields such as nuclear power, tropical medicine, tropical agriculture and cattle raising, civil aviation, architecture, and road building.

Some of these objectives may require time for full realization and new ones may be added or substituted, but at present, at least the above have emerged from the statements and actions of policy makers. The exact form the Afro-Asian policy will assume in the future is difficult to determine because Brazil, historically speaking, is just beginning to emerge as an actor in international relations. It has not yet elected a definite, clear course of action. Much depends upon how Brazilians evaluate the national interests in Afro-Asia as separate from or related to Brazil's older Latin American, Western Hemisphere, Western community, and Luso-Brazilian community memberships and priorities. For this reason, Brazil's Afro-Asian policy serves as a useful case study of the priority conflicts arising when a large developing nation tries to redefine and recast its international role. It is a difficult task to weigh the attraction of traditional behavior patterns against the expected benefits to be gained from an alternative course of action.

This study also reveals the problems hindering closer relations among developing states as a group, and especially among developing states of different geographical regions. It casts doubt on the operational validity of the term "Third World" beyond rather narrow economic limits prescribed by the particular national interest of each developing state. In the absence of military or national security considerations, the economic factor appears to be the most important in relations among developing states. It usually diverts the developing states' attentions away from each other and toward the richer nations for trade and aid purposes—measured in the flow of trade and diplomatic personnel.

Some critics of national foreign policy have suggested that Brazilian diplomacy's traditional bent for compromise solutions, "muddling through," and institutional, juridical means for solving international problems has been a hindrance to the achievement of its goals. Paradoxically, given the presently conflicting nature and priority levels of Brazil's interests in Afro-Asia, that pragmatic balancing act is quite understandable and may eventually prove to be Brazil's strongest point.

Bibliography

Books, Manuscripts, and Reports

Ahmed, M. Samir. *The Neutrals and the Test Ban Negotiations: An Analysis of the Non-Aligned States' Efforts between 1962–63.* New York: Carnegie Endowment for International Peace, 1967.
Alencastre, Amílcar. *O Brasil, a África, e o futuro.* Rio de Janeiro: Editôra Laemmert, 1969.
Archer, Maria. *Terras onde se fala português.* São Paulo: Editôra da Casa do Estudante do Brasil, 1957.
Arinos de Melo Franco, Afonso. *Planalto.* Rio de Janeiro: José Olympio, 1968.
Azevêdo, Thales de. *Cultura e situação racial no Brasil.* Rio de Janeiro: Editôra Civilização Brasileira, 1966.
Bailey, Norman A. *Latin America in World Politics.* New York: Walker and Company, 1967.
Bailey, Sydney D. *The General Assembly of the United Nations: A Study of Procedure and Practice.* Rev. ed. New York: Frederick A. Praeger, 1964.
Bastide, Roger. *Les religions africaines au Brésil.* Paris: Presses Universitaires de France, 1960.
Berle, Adolf A., Jr. *Tides of Crisis.* New York: Reynal and Company, 1957.
Bezerra de Menezes, Adolpho Justo. *Ásia, África, e a política independente do Brasil.* Rio de Janeiro: Zahar Editôra, 1961.
―――. *O Brasil e o mundo ásio-africano.* Rio de Janeiro: Irmãos Pongetti, 1956.
―――. *Subdesenvolvimento e política internacional.* Rio de Janeiro: Edições GRD, 1963.
Bonilla Frank. "A National Ideology for Development: Brazil." In

Expectant Peoples, edited by Kalman H. Silvert. New York: Random House, 1963.
Brams, Steven J. "Flow and Form in the International System." Ph.D. dissertation, Northwestern University, 1966.
"Brazil: Modernization, Independence, and Great-Power Status." In *Nationalism in Contemporary Latin America*, by Arthur P. Whitaker and David C. Jordan. New York: Free Press, 1966.
Brazilian Institute of International Relations. "Brazil and the United Nations." Rio de Janeiro, 1957. Mimeographed.
Burns, E. Bradford. *Nationalism in Brazil*. New York: Frederick A. Praeger, 1968.
———. *The Unwritten Alliance: Rio Branco and Brazilian-American Relations*. New York: Columbia University Press, 1966.
Cabral, Castilho. *Tempos de Jânio e outros tempos*. Rio de Janeiro: Editôra Civilização Brasileira, 1962.
Carneiro, Édison. *Ladinos e crioulos: Estudos sôbre o negro no Brasil*. Rio de Janeiro: Editôra Civilização Brasileira, 1964.
Carvalho, Carlos Miguel Delgado de. *África: Geografia social, econômica e política*. Rio de Janeiro: Instituto Brasileiro de Geografia e Estatística, 1963.
———. *História diplomática do Brasil*. São Paulo: Companhia Editôra Nacional, 1959.
Cascudo, Luís da Cámara. *Made in Africa*. Rio de Janeiro: Editôra Civilização Brasileira, 1965.
Castro, Moacir Werneck de. *Dois caminhos da revolução africana*. Rio de Janeiro: Instituto Brasileiro de Estudos Afro-Asiáticos, 1962.
Castro, Paulo de. *Terceira fôrca*. Rio de Janeiro: Editôra Fundo de Cultura, S.A., 1958.
Chacon, Varmireh. *Qual a política externa conveniente ao Brasil?* Rio de Janeiro: Editôra Civilização Brasileira, 1963.
———. *A revolução no trópico*. Rio de Janeiro: Instituto Brasileiro de Estudos Afro-Asiáticos, 1962.
"Colóquio sôbre as relações entre os países da América Latina e da África, September 24–30, 1963." Rio de Janeiro: UNESCO and Instituto Brasileira da Educação, Ciência, e Cultura. Mimeographed.
Comissão de Recenseamento da Colônia Japonêsa. *The Japanese Immigrant in Brazil*. Tokyo: University of Tokyo Press, 1964.
Confederação Nacional do Comércio and Associação Nacional dos Exportadores de Produtos Industriais. *Missão ao Oriente Medio—Relatório*. Rio de Janeiro, 1966.
Consulado Geral do Japão (São Paulo). "Emigração japonêsa no Brasil." São Paulo, June 1968. Mimeographed.
Conto e Silva, Golbery do. *Geopolítica do Brasil*. 2d ed. Rio de Janeiro: José Olympio, 1967.
Dantas, San Tiago. *Política externa independente*. Rio de Janeiro: Editôra Civilização Brasileira, 1962.
Deutsch, Karl W. "External Influences on the Internal Behavior of States." In *Approaches to Comparative and International Politics*, edited by R. Barry Farrell. Evanston: Northwestern University Press, 1966.
Dubnic, Vladimir Reisky de. "Trends in Brazil's Foreign Policy." In *New Perspectives of Brazil*, edited by Eric N. Baklanoff. Nashville: Vanderbilt University Press, 1966.
Duffy, James. *Portuguese Africa*. Cambridge: Harvard University

Press, 1959.
Emprêsa Brasileira de Turismo. "Dados estatísticos." Rio de Janeiro, April 1968. Mimeographed.
Fenwick, Charles G. "The Ninth International Conference of American States." In *Inter-American Juridical Year Book, 1948*. Washington: Pan American Union, 1948.
Fernandes, Florestan. *A integração do negro na sociedade de classes*. 2 vols. São Paulo: Editôra da Universidade de São Paulo, 1965.
———. *The Negro in Brazilian Society*. Edited by Phyllis B. Eveleth. Translated by Jacqueline D. Skeles, A. Brunel, and Arthur Rothwell. New York: Columbia University Press, 1969.
Free, Lloyd A. *Some International Implications of the Political Psychology of Brazilians*. Princeton: Institute for International Social Research, 1961.
Freyre, Gilberto, "Acontece que são baianos." In *Problemas brasileiros de antropologia*. Rio de Janeiro: José Olympio Editôra, 1962.
———. *O Brasil em face das Áfricas negras e mestiças*. Rio de Janeiro: Federação das Associações Portuguêsas, 1962.
———. *Um Brasileiro em terras portuguêsas*. Rio de Janeiro: José Olympio Editôra, 1953.
———. *Integração portuguêsa nos trópicos—Portuguese Integration in the Tropics*. Vila Nova de Famalição: Ministério do Ultramar, 1958.
———. *The Mansions and the Shanties*. New York: Alfred A. Knopf, 1963.
———. *O mundo que o português criou*. Rio de Janeiro: José Olympio Editôra, 1940.
———. *New World in the Tropics*. New York: Alfred A. Knopf, 1959.
———. *Uma política transnacional de cultura para o Brasil de hoje*. Belo Horizonte: Faculdade de Direito da Universidade de Minas Gerais, 1960.
Galtung, Johan. "Small Group Theory and the Theory of International Relations: A Study in Isomorphism." In *New Approaches to International Relations*, edited by Morton A. Kaplan. New York: Saint Martin's Press, 1968.
Gomes, Pimentel. *O Brasil entre as cinco maiores potências no fim dêste século*. Rio de Janeiro: Leitura Editôra, 1964.
———. *Por qué não somos uma grande potência?* Rio de Janeiro: Editôra Civilização Brasileira, 1965.
Gondim, Hugo Gouthier de Oliveira. "Missão especial ao Sudeste da Asia—Relatório apresentado aos Ministros das Relações Exteriores e da Fazenda." New York, 1959. Mimeographed.
Hill, Lawrence F. *Diplomatic Relations between the United States and Brazil*. Durham: Duke University Publications, 1932.
Hilton, Ronald. *Joaquim Nabuco e a civilização anglo-americana*. Rio de Janeiro: Instituto Brasil–Estados Unidos, 1949.
Hirokawa, Ikuzo. "As indústrias japonêsas no Brasil." Paper presented at the symposium "O Japonês em São Paulo e no Brasil," São Paulo, 18–22 June, 1968.
Houston, John A. *Latin America in the United Nations*. New York: Carnegie Endowment for International Peace, 1956.
Hovet, Thomas, Jr. *Africa in the United Nations*. Evanston: Northwestern University Press, 1963.
———. *Bloc Politics in the United Nations*. Cambridge: Harvard University Press, 1960.

Iglezias, Luíz. *A verdade sôbre Angola*. Rio de Janeiro: Gráfica Nossa Senhora de Fátima, 1961.
Instituto Brasileiro de Estudos Afro-Asiáticos. *Senghor em diálogo*. Rio de Janeiro: Gráfica Editôra Livro, S.A., 1965.
"International Round-Table on the Role of Universities and Research Institutes in the Development of Oriental Studies in Latin America, September 19–24, 1966—Final Report." Mar del Plata, Argentina: Argentine National Commission for UNESCO. Mimeographed.
Jaguaribe, Hélio. *O nacionalismo na atualidade brasileira*. Rio de Janeiro: Instituto Superior de Estudos Brasileiros, 1958.
Krug, C. A., and Quartey-Papafio, E. *World Cocoa Survey*. Rome: United Nations Food and Agricultural Organization, 1964.
Lacerda, Carlos. *O Brasil e o mundo árabe*. Rio de Janeiro: Irmãos Pongetti, 1948.
Lagos, Gustavo. *International Stratification and Underdeveloped Countries*. Chapel Hill: University of North Carolina Press, 1963.
Laotan, Anthony B. *The Torch Bearers, or Old Brazilian Colony in Lagos*. Lagos: Ife-Loju Printing Works, 1943.
Laufer, Leopold. *Israel and the Developing Countries: New Approaches to Cooperation*. New York: Twentieth Century Fund, 1967.
Lima, Nestor dos Santos. *A terceira América*. Rio de Janeiro: Livraria Freitas Bastos, S.A., 1967.
Lins, Álvaro. *Missão em Portugal*. Rio de Janeiro: Editôra Civilização Brasileira, 1960.
Machado, Luíz Toledo. *Conceito de Nacionalismo*. São Paulo: Editôra Fulgor, 1960.
Magalhães, Sérgio. *Prática da emancipação nacional*. Rio de Janeiro: Edições Tempo Brasileiro, 1964.
Maranhão, Jarbas. *Brasil-Africa: Um mesmo caminho*. São Paulo: Editôra Fulgor, 1962.
Martin, Laurence W., ed. *Neutralism and Nonalignment: The New States in World Affairs*. New York: Frederick A. Praeger, 1962.
Meira Mattos, Carlos de. *Projeção mundial do Brasil*. São Paulo: Gráfica Leal, 1961.
Mendes de Almeida, Cândido. *Nacionalismo e desenvolvimento*. Rio de Janeiro: Instituto Brasileiro de Estudos Afro-Asiáticos, 1963.
Mendonça, Renato. *A influência africana no português do Brasil*. 2d ed. São Paulo: Companhia Editôra Nacional, 1935.
Modelski, George. *A Theory of Foreign Policy*. New York: Frederick A. Praeger, 1962.
Moreira, Adriano. *O Ocidente e o ultramar português*. Rio de Janeiro: Irmãos Pongetti, 1961.
———. *Portugal's Stand in Africa*. New York: University Publishers, 1962.
Moreira Alves, Márcio. *Tortura e torturados*. 2d ed. Rio de Janeiro: Idade Nova, 1967.
Nabuco, Carolina. *The Life of Joaquim Nabuco*. Translated and edited by Ronald Hilton. Stanford: Stanford University Press, 1950.
Neves, João Alves das. "O Brasil perante a África." In *Temas luso-brasileiros*. São Paulo: Conselho Estadual de Cultura, 1963.
———, ed. *Poetas e contistas africanos de expressão portuguêsa*. São Paulo: Editôra Brasiliense, 1963.
Nishimukai, Yoshiaki. "Estudos brasileiros no Japão." In *Primeiro colóquio Brasil-Japão (São Paulo, Brasil, 1966)*. Edited by Eurípedes

Simões de Paula. São Paulo: Secção Gráfica da Universidade de São Paulo, 1967.
Nogueira, Alberto Franco. *As Nações Unidas e Portugal.* Rio de Janeiro: Gráfica Olímpica, 1961.
———. *Política externa portuguêsa.* Lisbon: Ministério dos Negócios Estrangeiros, 1965.
Olinto, Antonio. *Brasileiros na África.* Rio de Janeiro: Editôra GRD, 1964.
Oliveira, Waldir Freitas. *A importância atual do Atlântico Sul.* Salvador: Universidade da Bahia, Centro de Estudos Afro-Orientais, 1961.
Paiva, Rui Miller. *A agricultura na África.* São Paulo: Diretoria de Publicidade Agrícola da Secretaria da Agricultura do Estado, 1952.
Pan American Coffee Bureau. *Annual Coffee Statistics, 1966.* New York, 1967.
Pattee, Richard. *Portugal na África contemporânea.* Coimbra: Instituto de Estudos Ultramarinos da Universidade, 1959.
Paula, Eurípedes Simões de. "Breve nota sôbre o curso de estudos orientais no faculdade de filosofia, ciências e letras da Universidade de São Paulo." In *Primeiro colóquio Brasil-Japão (São Paulo, Brasil, 1966),* edited by Eurípedes Simões de Paula. São Paulo: Seccáço Gráfica da Universidade de São Paulo, 1967.
Penna, J. O. de Meira. *Política externa: Seguranca e desenvolvimento.* Rio de Janeiro: Agir, 1967.
Pereira, J. Soares. *Terceiro Mundo: Unidade e emergência.* Rio de Janeiro: Ministro da Educação e Cultura, Instituto Brasileiro de Estudos Afro-Asiáticos, 1962.
Pincus, John. *Trade, Aid, and Development: The Rich and Poor Nations.* New York: McGraw-Hill, 1967.
Pinheiro, Alves. *Angola, Terra e sangue de Portugal.* Rio de Janeiro: J. Ozon, Editôra, 1961.
Pinto, Álvaro Vieira. *Ideologia e desenvolvimento nacional.* 4th ed. Rio de Janeiro: Instituto Superior de Estudos Brasileiros, 1960.
Portella, Eduardo. *Africa, colonos e cúmplices.* Rio de Janeiro: Editôra Prado, 1961.
Prado, J. F. de Almeida. *O Brasil e o colonialismo europeu.* São Paulo: Companhia Editôra Nacional, 1956.
"Relatório da missão do grupo técnico ao Sul e Sudeste da Ásia (13 de setembro a 17 de outubro de 1963)." Rio de Janeiro, n.d. Mimeographed.
Ribeiro, René. "Opiniões de uma 'elite' estudantil sôbre o diálogo Nova Africa-Brasil." Paper presented at the Colloquium on Relations between the Countries of Latin America and Africa, sponsored by UNESCO and the Instituto Brasileiro da Educação, Ciência, e Cultura, Rio de Janeiro, 24–30 September, 1963.
Rippy, J. Fred. *Latin America in World Politics.* New York: F. S. Crofts and Company, 1928.
Rodrigues, José Honório. *Brasil e África: Outro horizonte.* 2d ed. 2 vols. Rio de Janeiro: Editôra Civilização Brasileira, 1964.
———. *Brazil and Africa.* Translated by Richard A. Mazzara and Sam Hileman. Berkeley: University of California Press, 1965.
———. "Brazil and China: The Varying Fortunes of Independent Diplomacy." In *Policies toward China,* edited by Abraham M. Halpern. New York: McGraw-Hill, 1965.

240 BIBLIOGRAPHY

———. *Interêsse nacional e política externa.* Rio de Janeiro: Editôra Civilização Brasileira, 1966.
Rodrigues, Nina. *Os Africanos no Brasil.* 3rd ed. Rio de Janeiro: Companhia Editôra Nacional, 1945.
Rosa, Salvatore, Professor of Engineering. *Relatório da missão técnica oficial realizada de 24-9-1966 a 4-12-1966 em países das Américas, Ásia, Europa, e África.* Rio de Janeiro: Companhia de Edições Técnicas, Industriais, e Científicas do Rio de Janeiro, 1967.
Rowe, J. W. F. *The World's Coffee.* London: Her Majesty's Stationery Office, 1963.
Rummel, Rudolph J. "The Dimensionality of Nations Project." In *Comparing Nations*, edited by Richard Merritt and Stein Rokkan. New Haven: Yale University Press, 1966.
———. "Measures of International Relations." Dimensionality of Nations Project, Research Report No. 8. Prepared for Presentation before the Symposium on Political Science Research of the Institute for Defense Analysis, Washington, D.C., 26–27 June, 1967.
Russett, Bruce M. *Community and Contention: Britain and America in the Twentieth Century.* Cambridge: MIT Press, 1963.
———. *International Regions and the International System: A Study in Political Ecology.* Chicago: Rand McNally, 1967.
———. *Trends in World Politics.* New York: Macmillan, 1965.
Saito, Hiroshi. *O Japonês no Brasil.* São Paulo: Editôra Sociologia e Política, 1961.
Sampaio, Bazílio de Carvalho. "Promoção das exportações brasileiras e do frete em navios do Lóide brasileiro—Relatório pelo CEPEX, MRE, e Lóide." Rio de Janeiro: Banco do Brasil, 1967. (Mimeographed.)
Sampaio, Nelson de Sousa. "The Foreign Policy of Brazil." In *Foreign Policies in a World of Change*, edited by Joseph E. Black and Kenneth W. Thompson. New York: Harper and Row, 1963.
Schutjer, Wayne A., and Ayo, Edward Jide. *Negotiating a World Cocoa Agreement: Analysis and Prospects.* Bulletin 744. University Park: Pennsylvania State University, College of Agriculture, Agricultural Experiment Station, October 1967.
Silva, Arthur da Costa e. *Diplomacy of Prosperity.* Rio de Janeiro: Brazilian Information Service, 1967.
Silva, Pedro Ferreira da. *Assistência social dos portuguêses no Brasil.* São Paulo: Arquimedes Edições, 1966.
"Simpósio sôbre o Japonês em São Paulo e no Brasil." Held at the Círculo Militar, São Paulo, 18–22 June 1968.
Skidmore, Thomas E. *Politics in Brazil, 1930–1964: An Experiment in Democracy.* New York: Oxford University Press, 1967.
Smith, T. Lynn. *Brazil: People and Institutions.* Rev. ed. Baton Rouge: Louisiana State University Press, 1963.
Sodré, Nelson Werneck. *Raízes históricas do nacionalismo brasileiro.* Rio de Janeiro: Instituto Superior de Estudos Brasileiros, 1959.
Souza Dantas, Raymundo. *África difícil.* Rio de Janeiro: Editôra Leitura, 1965.
Souza Júnior, Antônio de. *Problemas internacionais da atualidade, Projeção política do Brasil no mundo moderno.* Rio de Janeiro: Gráfica Laemmert, 1961.
Torres, José Garrido. "Condicionamentos da communidade lusíada," Rio de Janeiro, 1968. Mimeographed.

Truman, David B. *The Governmental Process.* New York: Alfred A. Knopf, 1965.
Valente, Valdemar. *Sincretismo religioso afro-brasileiro.* São Paulo: Companhia Editôra Nacional, 1955.
Vianna, Hélio. *História diplomática do Brasil.* Rio de Janeiro: Biblioteca do Exército, 1958.
Victor, Mário. *Cinco anos que abalaram o Brasil (de Jânio Quadros ao Marechal Castelo Branco).* Rio de Janeiro: Editôra Civilização Brasileira, 1965.
Wagley, Charles. *The Latin American Tradition.* New York: Columbia University Press, 1968.
White, John. *Japanese Aid.* London: Overseas Development Institute, 1964.
Zartmann, I. William. *International Relations in the New Africa.* Englewood Cliffs, N.J.: Prentice-Hall, 1966.

Journal and Magazine Articles

"A África e os interêsses do Brasil." *Análise e perspectiva econômica* 2 (20 August 1963):10–11.
"A África portuguêsa vista por um senador brasileiro." *Boletim geral do ultramar* 490 (April 1966):210–11.
Alger, Chadwick F., and Brams, Steven J. "Patterns of Representation in National Capitals and Intergovernmental Organizations." *World Politics* 19 (July 1957):646–63.
Amado, Jorge. "Conversa com Buanga Fêlê, Também conhecido como Mário de Andrade, chefe da luta de Angola." *Tempo brasileiro* 1 (September 1962):25–30.
Andrade, Theophilo. "Visita a Marcelo Caetano." *O Cruzeiro* 40 (12 October 1968):114–15.
"Apresentação." *Política externa independente* 1 (May 1965):3–8.
Arinos de Melo Franco, Afonso. "O Brasil e a questão de Angola na ONU." *Digesto econômico* 164 (March–April 1962):58–61.
———. "As experiências nucleares e o problema do desarmamento." *Digesto econômico* 163 (January–February 1962):46–59.
———. "Geopolítica do Brasil." *Digesto econômico* 194 (March–April 1967):21–23.
———. "A ONU e a política exterior do Brasil." *Digesto econômico,* 168 (November–December 1962):129–36.
———. "A política do Brasil na ordem contemporânea." *Digesto econômico* 162 (November–December 1961):70–74.
———. "Política externa." *Digesto econômico* 180 (November–December 1964):17–29.
———. "Racismo e nacionalismo." *Digesto econômico* 177 (May–June 1964):25–30.
"Aspectos econômicos-sociais do continente africano." *Desenvolvimento e conjuntura* 6 (April 1962):67–77.
Bidwell, Richard M. "Brazil Next in Nuclear Power?" *Nuclear News* 7 (November 1965):17–22.
Binder, Leonard. "The Middle-East as a Subordinate International System." *World Politics* 10 (April 1958):408–29.
Boér, Nicolas. "A revolução e a política externa." *Cadernos brasileiros* 6 (May–June 1964):16–26.

Bowman, Larry W. "The Subordinate State System of Southern Africa." *International Studies Quarterly* 12 (September 1968):231–61.
Brams, Steven J. "A Note on the Cosmopolitanism of World Regions." *Journal of Peace Research* 5 (1968):88–95.
———. "Transaction Flows in the International System." *American Political Science Review* 60 (December 1966):880–98.
"Brasil: A escalada do negro." *Manchete* 763 (3 December 1966):63–76.
"Brazil: Side Door into Africa." *Latin America* 6 (7 July 1972):209–10.
Brecher, Michael. "International Relations and Asian Studies: The Subordinate State System of Southern Asia." *World Politics* 15 (January 1963):213–35.
Brewer, James C. "Brazil and Africa." *Africa Report* 10 (May 1965):25–28.
Burns, E. Bradford. "Tradition and Variation in Brazilian Foreign Policy." *Journal of Inter-American Studies* 9 (April 1967):195–212.
Campos, Roberto de Oliveira. "A política externa do Brasil." *Digesto econômico* 166 (July–August 1962):109–14.
———. "Sôbre o conceito de neutralismo." *Digesto econômico* 159 (May–June 1961):12–15.
———. "Variações frívolas sôbre temas graves." *Digesto econômico* 163 (January–February 1962):97–101.
Carneiro, Édison. "O problema do negro: Visita à África." *Cadernos brasileiros* 8 (September–October 1966):21–28.
Casares, C. Cerqueira. "I Congresso das comunidades portuguesas." *Boletim da sociedade de geografia de Lisboa*, series 82, nos. 7–9 and 10–12 (July–September, October–December 1964):343–403.
Castello Branco, Carlos. "Como pensa o Congresso (e como votaria se pudesse)." *Realidade* 2 (December 1967):30–42.
Castro, Josué de. "O Brasil e o mundo afro-asiático." *Revista brasiliense* 36 (July–August 1961):9–15.
———. "Le Brésil parent du monde afro-asiatique dans l'unité et le neutralisme." *Presence Africaine* 48 (1963):187–92.
———. "Contribuição da ONU e seus organismos à economia brasileira." *Revista do Conselho Nacional de Economia* 12 (November–December 1963):569–81.
Cavalcanti, Geraldo. "Missão no Togo." *Revista brasileira de política internacional* 2 (September 1959):53–60.
Cocito, Raul. "Missão comercial brasileira à Africa Ocidental." *Revista da Confederação Nacional do Comércio* 56 (January 1966):13–57.
"Cocoa Group in Geneva—New Ivory Coast Prices." *West Africa* (23 October 1965):1198.
"A Communidade Econômica Européia e o Brasil." *Revista do Conselho Nacional de Economia* 8 (March–April 1959):125–26.
"Communidade luso-brasileira." *Boletim geral do ultramar* 483 (September 1965):115–17.
Cordell, Arthur J. "The Brazilian Soluble Coffee Problem: A Review." *Quarterly Review of Economics and Business* 9 (Spring 1969):29–38.
Cornelius, William G. "The 'Latin-American Bloc' in the United Nations." *Journal of Inter-American Studies* 3 (July 1961):419–35.
Costa, Sérgio Corrêa da. "Ciência e tecnologia." *Digesto econômico* 197 (September–October 1967):17–22.
———. "A utilização dos explosivos atómicos para fins pacíficos." *Digesto econômico* 196 (July–August 1967):28–31.
"Declarações do deputado brasileiro Dr. Cunha Bueno, Ao regressar

da visita a Angola e Moçambique." *Boletim geral do ultramar* 492 (June 1966):276–78.
"Declarações do Presidente da República do Brasil." *Boletim geral do ultramar* 382 (April 1957):9–11.
Delfim Neto, Antonio. "Esperança e realidade sôbre a concorrência africana." *Revista dos mercados* 98 (October 1958):5–8.
"Deputados brasileiros visitam Angola e Moçambique." *Boletim geral do ultramar* 489 (March 1966):133.
Diégues Júnior, Manuel. "The Negro in Brazil: A Bibliographic Essay." *African Forum* 2 (Spring 1967):97–109.
Dubnic, Vladimir Reisky de. "A política externa do Brasil no govêrno Jânio Quadros." *Síntese política, econômica, social* 9 (January–March 1961):67–86.
Fischlowitz, Estanislau. "Subsídios para a doutrina africana do Brasil." *Revista brasileira de política internacional* 3 (March 1960):82–95.
Flusser, Vilém. "O problema do negro: Da negritude." *Cadernos brasileiros* 8 (September–October 1966):29–35.
Fonseca, Mário Borges da. "Substancial mercado para as exportações brasileiras na Africa." *Revista do Conselho Nacional de Economia* 14 (May–August 1965):203–12.
Frederick, Kenneth D. "Production Controls under the International Coffee Agreements: An Evaluation of Brazil's Programs." *Journal of Inter-American Studies and World Affairs* 12 (April 1970):255–70.
Galvão de Sousa, J. P. "Brasil e Portugal em face do despertar afro-asiático." *Digesto econômico* 137 (September–October 1957):43–51.
———. "O Brasil e o 'Terceiro Mundo.'" *Digesto econômico* 184 (July–August 1965):71–75.
Ganzert, Frederic W. "The Baron do Rio Branco, Joaquim Nabuco, and the Growth of Brazilian-American Friendship, 1900–1910." *Hispanic American Historical Review* 22 (August 1942):432–51.
Helfritz, Hans. "Encontro afro-brasileiro." *Humboldt, Revista para o mundo luso-brasileiro (Hamburg)* 4 (1964):29–32.
Hodgkin, Thomas. "The New West Africa State System." *University of Toronto Quarterly* 31 (October 1961):74–82.
Kaiser, Karl. "The Interaction of Regional Subsystems." *World Politics* 21 (October 1968):84–107.
Kay, David A. "The Politics of Decolonization: The New Nations and the United Nations Political Process." *International Organization* 21 (1967):786–811.
Keohane, Robert Owen. "Political Influence in the General Assembly." *International Conciliation* 557 (March 1966):1–64.
———. "Who Cares about the General Assembly?" *International Organization* 23 (Winter 1969):141–49.
Leal da Silva, José. "Por qué renunció Jânio Quadros." *Bohemia libre puertorriqueña* 53 (17 September 1961):46–50.
Leite, Cleantho de Paiva. "Constantes et variables de la politique étrangère du Brésil." *Politique étrangère* 34 (1969):33–54.
Lima, Heitor Ferreira. "Japonêses no Brasil." *O observador econômico e financeiro* 23 (October 1958):29–36.
Marques Moreira, Marcílio. "Comércio, ajuda e desenvolvimento." *Síntese política, econômica, social* 24 (October–December 1964):18–37.
Mehden, Fred R. von der. "Southeast Asian Relations with Africa." *Asian Survey* 5 (July 1965):341–49.

Mendes de Almeida, Cândido. "Política externa e nação em processo." *Tempo brasileiro* 1 (September 1962):40–64.
"Missão brasileira à África portuguêsa." *Boletim geral do ultramar* 454/455 (April–May 1963):129–31.
Modelski, George. "International Relations and Area Studies: The Case of Southeast Asia." *International Relations* 2 (April 1961):143–55.
Moreira, Adriano. "Aspectos negativos da imagem recíproca de Portugal-Brasil." *Estudos políticos e socials (Lisbon)* 5 (1967):5–23.
Neves da Fontoura, João. "Por uma política luso-brasileira." *O Globo,* 10 June 1957, 2d sec., p. 13.
"Os negros na sociedade brasileira." *Conjuntura econômica* 11 (March 1957):65–69.
Oliveira, A. Camilo de. "Linhas mestras da política exterior do Brasil." *Digesto econômico* 143 (September–October 1958):113–30.
"O país do Doutor Barnard." *Manchete* 844 (22 June 1968):116–30.
"Una oportunidad en busca de Brasil." *The Economist para América Latina* (12 June 1968):9.
Paiva, Glycon de. "Política exterior vista pelo homem da rua." *Digesto econômico* 168 (November–December 1962):61–63.
Park, Richard L. "Indian-African Relations." *Asian Survey* 5 (July 1965):350–58.
"Política externa independente: um balanço." *Revista civilização brasileira* 1 (March 1965):59–84.
Portella, Eduardo. "O dilema cultural da África e o Brasil." *Cadernos brasileiros* 4 (special ed., n.d.):32–36.
Quadros, Jânio. "Brazil's New Foreign Policy." *Foreign Affairs* 40 (October 1961):19–27.
Rangel, Ignácio M. "A África e outros novos mercados." *Tempo brasileiro* 1 (December 1962):81–102.
Reis, Artur Cézar Ferreira. "Africa e Brasil: Relações e competições econômicas." *Revista brasileira de política internacional* 6 (June 1963):209–22.
Ribeiro, René. "Estudo comparativo dos problemas de vida em duas culturas afins: Angola-Brasil." *Journal of Inter-American Studies* 11 (January 1969):2–15.
Roboredo, Armando de. "Aspectos militares da comunidade luso-brasileira." *Boletim da Sociedade de Geografia de Lisboa,* series 82, nos. 7–9, 10–12 (July–September, October–December 1964):279–88.
Rodrigues, Jayme Azevêdo. "A unidade do mundo subdesenvolvido e o conflito Norte-Sul." *Revista civilização brasileira* 1 (March 1965):89–113.
Rodrigues, José Honório. "Brasil e Extremo Oriente." *Política externa independente* 1 (August 1965):57–94.
———. "The Foundations of Brazil's Foreign Policy." *International Affairs (London)* 38 (July 1962):324–38.
———. "The Influence of Africa on Brazil and of Brazil on Africa." *Journal of African History (London)* 3 (September 1962):49–67.
———. "Nueva actitud en la política exterior del Brasil." *Foro internacional* 2 (January–March 1962):408–22.
———. "Uma política externa, própria e independente." *Política externa independente* 1 (May 1965):15–39.
———. "A política internacional brasileira e a África." *Cadernos brasileiros* 4 (spec. ed., n.d.):65–70.

———. "La política internacional del Brasil y África." *Foro internacional* 4 (January–March 1964):313–46.

Rosenbaum, H. Jon. "Brazil among the Nations." *International Journal* 24 (Summer 1969):529–44.

———. "A Critique of the Brazilian Foreign Service." *Journal of Developing Areas* 2 (April 1968):377–92.

———, and Cooper, Glenn M. "Brazil and the Nuclear Non-Proliferation Treaty." *International Affairs* 46 (January 1970):74–90.

Rotstein, Jaime. "Uma visão brasileira dos 3D." *Comentário* 7 (3d trimester 1966):234–42.

Rowe, Edward T. "The Emerging Anti-Colonial Consensus in the United Nations." *Journal of Conflict Resolution* 8 (September 1964):209–30.

Rummel, Rudolph J. "Some Empirical Findings on Nations and Their Behavior." *World Politics* 21 (January 1969):226–41.

Saenz, Paul. "A Latin American-African Partnership." *Journal of Inter-American Studies* 11 (April 1969):317–27.

Saito, Hiroshi. "Êsse imigrante trouxe 'know-how.'" *Mundo econômico* 1 (June 1968):21–22.

Sanders, William. "Summary of the Conclusions of the Ninth International Conference of American States, Bogotá, Colombia, March 30–May 2, 1948." *International Conciliation* 442 (June 1948):383–433.

Santo, Newton do Espírito. "Os movimentos nacionalistas angolanos." *Revista brasileira de política internacional* 6 (September 1963):457–78.

Segal, Aaron. "Giant Strangers: Africa and Latin America." *Africa Report* 11 (April 1966):48–53.

"Segundo congresso das comunidades de cultura portuguêsa." *Boletim geral do ultramar* 43 (July–August 1967):157–87.

Senghor, Léopold Sédar. "Latinité et négritude." *Presence africaine* 52 (4th quarter 1964):5–13.

Souza Dantas, Raymundo. "Miragem africana." *Cadernos brasileiros* 6 (January–February 1964):5–19.

———. "Sentimento africano." *Cadernos brasileiros* 9 (March–April 1967):25–33.

Theberge, James. "Brazil's Future Position in the Hemisphere and the World." *World Affairs* 132 (June 1969):39–47.

Torres, José Garrido. "Trópico e desenvolvimento." *Journal of Inter-American Studies* 11 (April 1969):223–36.

Tyler, William G. "A política norte-americana e o impasse do café solúvel." *Revista civilização brasileira* 3 (March–April 1968):87–98.

"O ultramar é bastião avançado da comunidade." *O Mundo Português*, 23 June 1968, 2d sec., p. 1.

Valladares, Clarival do Prado. "A defasagem africana, Ou crônica do I Festival Mundial de Artes Negras." *Cadernos brasileiros* 36 (July–August 1966):3–13.

Vandenbosch, Amry. "Small States in International Politics and Organization." *Journal of Politics* 26 (May 1964):293–312.

Verger, Pierre. "Nigeria, Brazil, and Cuba." *Nigeria Magazine*, spec. independence issue (October 1960):167–77.

Viana, A. Mendes. "O mundo afro-asiático—Sua significação para o Brasil." *Revista brasileira de política internacional* 2 (December 1959):5–23.

Wohlgemuth, Patricia. "The Portuguese Territories and the United Nations." *International Conciliation* 545 (November 1963): 1–68.
"World Production of Raw Cocoa." *International Chocolate Review* 23 (October 1968): 416.
Yedda Linhares, Maria. "Brazilian Foreign Policy and Africa." *The World Today* 18 (December 1962): 532–40.
Zartmann, I. William. "Africa as a Subordinate State System in International Relations." *International Organization* 21 (Summer 1967): 545–64.

Periodicals

Brazil International Report
Correio da Manhã
O Cruzeiro
O Globo
Instituto Brasileiro de Estudos Afro-Asiáticos, *Boletim informativo*
O Jornal
Jornal do Brasil
Jornal do Commércio
Manchete
O Mundo Português
Nação armada
New York Times
Política externa independente
Revista brasileira de política internacional
A Voz de Portugal
West Africa

Brazilian Government Documents

Araújo Castro, João Augusto de. *Desarmamento, desenvolvimento, descolonização.* Rio de Janeiro: Ministério das Relações Exteriores, 1963.
Banco do Brasil. *Relatório.* Distrito Federal, 1955–68.
Banco Central do Brasil. *Relatório.* Rio de Janeiro, 1955–68.
Branco, Humberto de Alencar Castello. *Mensagem ao Congresso Nacional.* Rio de Janeiro: Departamento de Imprensa Nacional, 1965, 1966.
Brasil. *Diário oficial.* Rio de Janeiro: Departamento de Imprensa Nacional, 1955–68.
———. Instituto Nacional de Imigração e Colonização. Departamento de Estudos e Planejamento. Divisão de Estatística. "Informações estatísticas—Imigração." Boletins 11 (1956), 16 (1957), 23 (1958), 26 (1959), 30 (1960), 34 (1961). Rio de Janeiro. Mimeographed.
———. Ministério da Fazenda. Serviço de Estatística Econômica e Financeira. *Comércio exterior do Brasil—Exportação.* Rio de Janeiro: Instituto Brasileiro de Geografia e Estatística, 1957–68.
———. Ministério das Relações Exteriores. *Acôrdos culturais, Atualizado até dezembro de 1965.* Rio de Janeiro, 1965.
———. Ministério das Relações Exteriores. *Gestão do Ministro Láfer na pasta das relações exteriores.* Rio de Janeiro: Departamento de Imprensa Nacional, 1961.
———. Ministério das Relações Exteriores. *Itamaraty,* 1, no. 1–2, no. 18 (January 1964–April 1965).

———. Ministério das Relações Exteriores. *Lista diplomática, julho de 1968*. Rio de Janeiro: Departamento de Imprensa Nacional, 1968.
———. Ministério das Relações Exteriores. "Lista de enderêcos." Rio de Janeiro, 1962–68. Mimeographed.
———. Ministério das Relações Exteriores. "Lista do pessoal." Rio de Janeiro, 1956–61. Mimeographed.
———. Ministério das Relações Exteriores. "Lista do pessoal no exterior." Rio de Janeiro, 1962–68. Mimeographed.
———. Ministério das Relações Exteriores. *A política exterior da revolução brasileira*. 2 vols. Rio de Janeiro: Seção de Publicações do Ministério das Relações Exteriores, 1966, 1967.
———. Ministério das Relações Exteriores. *Relatório*. Rio de Janeiro: Seção de Publicações da Divisão de Documentação do Ministério das Relações Exteriores, 1956–61, 1964, 1966.
———. Ministério das Relações Exteriores. Ceremonial. "Lista dos agraciados com a Ordem Nacional do Cruzeiro do Sul, atualizado até dezembro de 1967." Rio de Janeiro, 1968. Mimeographed.
———. Ministério das Relações Exteriores. Departmento de Administração. Divisão de Organização. *Servico exterior brasileiro*. Rio de Janeiro: Seção de Multiplicação do Ministério das Relacões Exteriores, n.d.
———. Ministério das Relações Exteriores. Departamento Consular e de Imigração, Divisão Consular. *Lista, Corpo consular estrangeiro, junho de 1968*. Rio de Janeiro: Seção de Multiplicação do Ministério das Relações Exteriores, 1968.
———. Ministério das Relações Exteriores. Departamento Cultural e de Informações. *Textos e declarações sôbre política externa (de abril de 1964 a abril de 1965)*, Rio de Janeiro: Serviço Gráfico do Instituto Brasileiro de Geografia e Estatística, 1965.
———. Ministério das Relações Exteriores. Divisão da África. "Intercâmbio comercial Brasil-África subsaárica." *Revista da Confederação Nacional do Comércio* 44/45 (January–February 1965):47–52.
———. Ministério das Relações Exteriores. Divisão de Atos Internacionais. "Relação dos acôrdos em vigor, por países." Rio de Janeiro, 1968. Mimeographed.
———. Ministério das Relações Exteriores. Divisão de Atos, Congressos, e Conferências Internacionais. *Brasil-Portugal: Tratado de amizade e consulta* (Coleção de Atos Internacionais, No. 357). Rio de Janeiro: Serviço de Publicações do Ministério das Relações Exteriores, 1955.
———. Ministério das Relações Exteriores. Divisão de Estudos Econômicos. "Intercâmbio Brasil-África." Rio de Janeiro, n.d. Mimeographed.
———. Ministério das Relações Exteriores. Divisão de Informações. *Itamaraty*, 1, no. 1–1, no. 4 (April 1968–July–August 1968).
———. Ministério das Relações Exteriores. Secretaria Geral Adjunta para o Planejamento Político. *Documentos de política externa (de 15 de março a 15 de outubro de 1967)*. Rio de Janeiro: Serviço Gráfico da Fundação do Instituto Brasileiro Geografia e Estatística, 1967.
———. Ministério das Relações Exteriores. Secretaria Geral Adjunta para o Planejamento Político. *Documentos de política externa, II (28 de outubro de 1967 a 3 de maio de 1968)*. Rio de Janeiro: Serviço Gráfico da Fundação do Instituto Brasileiro Geografia e Estatística, 1968.

---. Ministério das Relações Exteriores. Secretário Geral Adjunto para a África e Oriente Próximo. "Promoção comercial brasileira no Oriente Próximo." Rio de Janeiro, 6 February 1968. Mimeographed.
---. Presidência da República. *Visita do Presidente João Café Filho a Portugal.* Rio de Janeiro: Departamento Administrativo do Serviço Público, 1955.
---. Presidência da Republica. Serviço de Documentação. *Resenha do govêrno do Presidente Juscelino Kubitschek (1956–1961).* Vol. 1. Rio de Janeiro: Departamento de Imprensa Nacional, 1960.
Brazil. Ministry of Foreign Relations. *The African Contribution to Brazil.* Rio de Janeiro: Edigraf, 1966.
Emprêsa Brasileira de Turismo. "Dados estatísticos." Rio de Janeiro, April 1968. Mimeographed.
Goulart, João. *Mensagem ao Congresso Nacional.* Rio de Janeiro: Departamento de Imprensa Nacional, 1963–64.
---. *Mensagem ao Congresso Nacional.* Rio de Janeiro: Serviço Grafico do Instituto Brasileiro Geografia e Estatística, 1962.
Instituto Brasileiro de Geografia e Estatística. *Anuário estatístico do Brasil.* Rio de Janeiro, 1956–1967.
Konder Reis, Antônio Carlos. *Missão na ONU: Relatório apresentado pela delegação de observadores parlamentares do Senado à XVIII[a] Assembléia Geral da Organização das Nações Unidas.* Brasília: Departamento de Imprensa Nacional, 1964.
Kubitschek de Oliveira, Juscelino. *Mensagem ao Congresso nacional.* Rio de Janeiro: Departamento de Imprensa Nacional, 1956–60.
Magalhães, Américo Laeth de. *Brasil-Portugal: Documentário da visita oficial ao Brasil do General Francisco Higino Craveiro Lopes, presidente da República Portuguêsa (5–25 de junho de 1957).* Rio de Janeiro: Departamento de Imprensa Nacional, 1960.
Melo Franco, Afonso Arinos de. *Discursos.* Rio de Janeiro: Ministério das Relações Exteriores, 1961.
Napoleão, Aluízio. *Rio Branco e as relações entre o Brasil e os Estados Unidos.* Rio de Janeiro: Ministério das Relações Exteriores, 1947.
Quadros, Jânio. *Mensagem ao Congresso Nacional.* Rio de Janeiro: Departamento de Imprensa Nacional, 1961.
O Senador Cunha Mello na ONU. Rio de Janeiro: Departamento de Imprensa Nacional, 1959.
Tratados e actos internacionais, Brasil-Portugal. Lisbon: Serviço de Propaganda e Expansão Comercial do Brasil, 1962.

United Nations Documents

Department of Economic and Social Affairs. Statistical Office. *Monthly Bulletin of Statistics* 22 (June 1968):xii–xiv.
Department of Economic and Social Affairs. Statistical Office. *Yearbook of International Trade Statistics, 1966.* New York, 1968.
Economic and Social Council. *United Nations Coffee Conference, 1962: Summary of Proceedings* (E/CONF.42/8), 1963.
Economic and Social Council. *United Nations Human Rights Seminar on Apartheid, Brasília, Brazil, 23 August–5 September, 1966* (SO216/3(11)LA1966), 1966.
Economic and Social Council. United Nations Conference on Trade and Development. *Proceedings of the United Nations Conference*

on *Trade and Development (Geneva, 23 March–16 June, 1964).* 8 vols. (E/CONF.46/141, vols. 1–8), 1964.
General Assembly. *International Conference on Human Rights, Tehran, April 22–May 13, 1968* (A/CONF.32/TEH.68), 1968.
General Assembly, Eleventh Session, Fourth Committee. *Statement Made by the Representative of Brazil at the 617th Meeting of the Fourth Committee on 30 January 1957* (A/C.4/349).
General Assembly, Twenty-Second Session. *Provisional Verbatim Record of the Fifteen Hundred and Sixty-Second Plenary Meeting, Thursday, 21 September 1967* (A/PV.1562), 21 September 1967.
Office of Public Information. *U.N. Monthly Chronicle* 1, nos. 1–9, no. 3 (May 1964–March 1972).
Office of Public Information. *Yearbook of the United Nations.* New York, 1956–1971.
Security Council, Eighteenth Year, 1043d Meeting, 24 July 1963. *Official Records* (S/PV.1,043).
United Nations Conference on Trade and Development. *Proceedings of the United Nations Conference on Trade and Development, Second Session (New Delhi, 1 February–29 March, 1968).* Vol. 9. (TD/97, vol. 1), 1968.
United Nations Conference on Trade and Development. United Nations Cocoa Conference, 1967. Economic Committee. *Summary Records of the First to Sixteenth Meetings Held at the Palais des Nations, Geneva, from 29 November to 11 December, 1967* (TD/COCOA.2/Ex/C.1/SR.1–16), May 1968.
United Nations Conference on Trade and Development. United Nations Cocoa Conference, 1967. Executive Committee. *Summary Records of the First to Thirteenth Meetings Held at the Palais des Nations, Geneva, from 29 November to 19 December, 1967* (TD/COCOA.2/Ex/SR.1–13), 1 May 1968.

Personal Interviews

Amílcar Alencastre, author and former professor of the Instituto Brasileiro de Estudos Afro-Asiáticos, Rio de Janeiro, 7 October 1968.
Cândido Mendes de Almeida, executive director of the Instituto Brasileiro de Estudos Afro-Asiáticos, former Chefe do Departamento de Política do Instituto Superior de Estudos Brasileiros, Rio de Janeiro, 15 March, 14 May, and 17 June 1968.
Afonso Arinos, former foreign minister and ambassador to the United Nations, Rio de Janeiro, 22 May 1968.
Adalberto Camargo, federal deputy from the state of São Paulo, São Paulo, 23 June 1968.
Casério B. Ceschin, regional director of Ultragaz for Rio de Janeiro and former general manager of Nigerian operations for Ultragaz, Rio de Janeiro, 16 September 1968.
Raymundo Souza Dantas, former ambassador to Ghana, Rio de Janeiro, 14 September 1968.
Manoel Orlando Ferreira, former director of the Conselho Nacional de Economia and director of the Centro Nacional de Produtividade na Indústria, Rio de Janeiro, 21 May 1968.
Ikuzo Hirokawa, president of Kanematsu do Brasil and of the Câmara de Comércio e Indústria Japonêsa do Brasil, São Paulo, 20 June 1968.

Antonio Houaiss, former representative on the Fourth Committee of the United Nations General Assembly, Rio de Janeiro, 29 October and 7 November 1968.
Gilberto Machado, head of the Departmento do Comércio Exterior da Federação do Comércio do Estado de São Paulo, São Paulo, 6 August 1968.
Renato Mendonça, ambassador to India, Rio de Janeiro, 11 November 1968.
Adolpho Justo Bezerra de Menezes, ambassador to Pakistan and subsequently Secretary-General for Commercial Promotion of the Foreign Ministry, Rio de Janeiro, 25 January and 30 October 1968.
Paulo dos Santos Matoso Neto, former leader of the Movimento Afro-Brasileira Pro-Libertação de Angola, São Paulo, 20 June 1968.
Yoshinori Nuimura, Vice-Consul for Cultural Affairs, Japanese consulate-general in São Paulo, São Paulo, 21 June 1968.
Antonio Olinto, former cultural attaché in Nigeria, Rio de Janeiro, 18 March 1968.
Eduardo Portella, former executive-director of the Instituto Brasileiro de Estudos Afro-Asiáticos, Rio de Janeiro, 1 November 1968.
Fernando Quiroga, director of newspaper *Duas Bandeiras* and Portuguese opposition leader in exile, Rio de Janeiro, 17 October 1968.
Antonio Carlos Konder dos Reis, federal senator (ARENA) from Santa Catarina, a member of the Senate Foreign Relations Committee, and a delegate to the second UNCTAD, Rio de Janeiro, 20 September 1968.
Jayme Azevêdo Rodrigues, former Secretary-General for Economic Affairs of the Foreign Ministry, Rio de Janeiro, 17 September 1968.
José Honório Rodrigues, historian and former director of the Instituto Brasileiro de Relações Internacionais, Rio de Janeiro, 17 September 1968.
Hiroshi Saito, professor at the Escola de Sociologia e Política de São Paulo, and technical director of the Centro de Estudos Nipo-Brasileiros, São Paulo, 20 June 1968.
Bazílio de Carvalho Sampaio, secretário de gabinete da Gerência de Exportação do Centro de Promoção da Exportação, CACEX, Banco do Brasil, Rio de Janeiro, 3 October 1968.
J. N. van Schalkwyk, commercial secretary of the South African Legation, Rio de Janeiro, 29 August 1968.
Henri Senghor, Senegalese ambassador to Brazil, Rio de Janeiro, 24 September 1968.
Khalid Halim Siddiqi, cultural attaché of the Indian embassy, Rio de Janeiro, 29 August 1968.
José Garrido Torres, former president of the Banco Nacional de Desenvolvimento Econômico and president of the Lowndes Bank, Rio de Janeiro, 14 October 1968.
Yaw Bamful Turkson, Ghanaian ambassador to Brazil, Rio de Janeiro, 22 July 1968.
Akio Yanaguishawa, chief of the Immigration Section of the Japanese Consulate-General in São Paulo, São Paulo, 21 June 1968.

Recent Publications

Araújo Castro, João Augusto de. "O congelamento do poder mundial," Brazilian Embassy, Washington, D.C., 11 June 1971. (Mimeographed.)

———. "O congelamento do poder mundial." *Revista brasileira de estudos políticos* 33 (January 1972):7–30.
———. "Environment and Development: The Case of the Developing Countries." *International Organization* 26 (Spring 1972):401–16.
———. "The United Nations and the Freezing of the International Power Structure." *International Organization* 26 (Winter 1972): 158–66.
Bergsman, Joel. *Brazil: Industrialization and Trade Policies.* New York: Oxford University Press, 1970.
Brasil. Ministério das Relações Exteriores. *Gestão Magalhães Pinto no Ministério.* Rio de Janeiro: Secção de Multiplicação do Ministério das Relações Exteriores, 1969.
Carvalho e Silva, Jorge de. "O Brasil em frente aos grandes problemas políticos internacionais contemporâneos," *Revista brasileira de estudos políticos*, No. 32 (July 1971):9–24.
Castro Lobo, Oswaldo. "O Brasil na presente conjuntura do comércio internacional," *Revista brasileira de estudos políticos*, No. 32 (July 1971):57–82.
Chilcote, Ronald H. "Brazil and Portuguese Africa in Comparative Perspective: University of California Colloquium (January–March, 1968)," *Latin American Research Review*, 6, No. 1 (Spring 1969):125–36.
Damacho de Vicenzi, Marcos. "Café," *Revista brasileira de política internacional*, 13, No. 51–52 (September–December 1970):77–86.
"Discurso do Presidente da República," *Boletim especial* (Brazilian Embassy, Washington, D.C.), No. 69/70 (20 April 1970).
Dulles, John W. F. *Unrest in Brazil: Political-Military Crises, 1955–1964.* Austin: University of Texas Press, 1970.
Fontaine, Roger. "The Foreign Policy-Making Process in Brazil." Ph.D. dissertation, The Johns Hopkins School of Advanced International Studies, 1970.
Gibson Barbosa, Mário. "Política brasileira de comércio exterior," *Revista brasileira de política international*, 13, No. 49–50 (March–June 1971):63–70.
"Goldenes Zeitalter," *Der Spiegel*, No. 23 (29 May 1972), pp. 106, 109.
Macedo Soares, José Antonio C. B. de. "Cacau," *Revista brasileira de política internacional*, 13, No. 51–52 (September–December 1970):73–76.
Minter, Bill. "Brazil: A New Afro-Asian Policy and Its Reversal," *NACLA Newsletter* (September 1970):14, 17.
Mizuno, Hajime. "Os investimentos japonêses no Brasil e suas perspectivas." In *III colóquio de estudos luso-brasileiros: Anais.* Tokyo: Sophia University, 1969.
Nevins, Lawrence. "Brazil and Africa," *Journal of Inter-American Studies*, 6, No. 1 (January 1964):121–23.
Rosenbaum, H. Jon. "Brazil's Foreign Policy: Developmentalism and Beyond," *Orbis*, 16, No. 1 (Spring 1972):64–77.
Rosenbaum, H. Jon, and Tyler, William C., eds. *Contemporary Brazil: Issues in Economic and Political Development.* New York: Frederick A. Praeger, 1972.
Schneider, Ronald M. *The Political System of Brazil: Emergence of a "Modernizing" Authoritarian Regime, 1964–1970.* New York: Columbia University Press, 1971.

Selcher, Wayne. "Brazil and the Independence of Sub-Saharan Africa: A Bibliographical Survey." *Current Themes in African Historical Studies.* Edited by Daniel G. Matthews. Westport, Conn.: Negro Universities Press, 1970.

"South Africa's Policy towards Latin America." *Background to South African and World News* (December 1968).

Stepan, Alfred. *The Military in Politics: Changing Patterns in Brazil.* Princeton: Princeton University Press, 1971.

LATIN AMERICAN MONOGRAPHS—SECOND SERIES

NUMBER 1 (1965): *Fidel Castro's Political Programs from Reformism to "Marxism-Leninism"*
by Loree Wilkinson

NUMBER 2 (1966): *Highways into the Upper Amazon Basin*
by Edmund Eduard Hegen

NUMBER 3 (1967): *The Government Executive of Modern Peru*
by Jack W. Hopkins

NUMBER 4 (1967): *Eduardo Santos and the Good Neighbor, 1938–1942*
by David Bushnell

NUMBER 5 (1968): *Dictatorship and Development: The Methods of Control in Trujillo's Dominican Republic*
by Howard J. Wiarda

NUMBER 6 (1969): *New Lands and Old Traditions: Kekchi Cultivators in the Guatemalan Lowlands*
by William E. Carter

NUMBER 7 (1969): *The Mechanization of Agriculture in Brazil: A Sociological Study of Minas Gerais*
by Harold M. Clements, Sr.

NUMBER 8 (1971): *Liberación Nacional of Costa Rica: The Development of a Political Party in a Transitional Society*
by Burt H. English

NUMBER 9 (1971): *Colombia's Foreign Trade and Economic Integration in Latin America*
by J. Kamal Dow

NUMBER 10 (1972): *The Feitosas and the Sertão dos Inhamuns: The History of a Family and a Community in Northeast Brazil, 1700–1930*
by Billy Jaynes Chandler

NUMBER 11 (1973): *The Moving Frontier: Social and Economic Change in a Southern Brazilian Community*
by Maxine L. Margolis

NUMBER 12 (1973): *San Rafael—Camba Town*
by Allyn MacLean Stearman

NUMBER 13 (1974): *The Afro-Asian Dimension of Brazilian Foreign Policy, 1956–1972*
by Wayne A. Selcher